Geet Gawai

"If the Indians were to survive, as human beings, their survival depended largely on their own power of resilience. They devised their own pastimes, recreated some semblance of the lost India in festivals and feasts...

"When goaded beyond their apparently infinite endurance and patience, they would try to rebel; but the protest most always ended in repression.

"For many, the plantation brought sickness and premature death... For most the plantation remained the boundary of existence.

"Although the indentured coolie could be held in legal bondage only for a period of years, the plantation held most of them for life.

"The plantation imposed a total way of existence for almost a century upon generations of bonded Indians."

—Hugh Tinker

A New System of Slavery

Inscribed as Intangible Cultural Heritage of Humanity at UNESCO

Geet Gawai

Bhojpuri folk songs in Mauritius

An Ode To *Geetharines* of Mauritius

Dr. Sarita Boodhoo

PRABHAT PRAKASHAN
prabhatbooks@gmail.com

DIASPORA RESEARCH & RESOURCE CENTRE
Antar Rashtriya Sahayog Parishad
arspindia@gmail.com

Published by
PRABHAT PRAKASHAN PVT. LTD.
4/19 Asaf Ali Road,
New Delhi-110 002 (INDIA)
e-mail: prabhatbooks@gmail.com

ISBN 978-93-95386-74-6
GEET GAWAI
by Dr. Sarita Boodhoo

Edition
2025

Price
₹ 750.00 (Rupees Seven Hundred Fifty only)

Printed at
R-Tech Offset Printers, Delhi

To
Mrs. Bhayawati Devi
Makhansingh Gayasingh
My great grand paternal aunt
My father's *Phouphou*
who wrote the first book on *Geet Gawai,*
The Vivah Mangal in 1910

Dedication

..."and they came 188 years ago, from the banks of the Ganges, Karnataka, Madras, Andhra Pradesh and the ghats of Maharashtra and carried in their veins the capacity for untold sacrifices..."

..."With their sweat, tears and blood they nurtured and raised the lush sugarcane..."

..."and their souls, muscles and sinews joined in one great propelling force to resist humiliation, exploitation, injustice and insolent might and poverty..."

..."and they managed to survive not only physically and intellectually, but culturally also as a people with their own values and attitudes that today form the very basis of MAURITIANISM..."

—Dr. Sarita Boodhoo

Safeguarding Measures

UNESCO:

"What measures are proposed to help to ensure that the element's viability is not jeopardised in the future especially as an unintended result of inscription and the resulting visibility and public attention?"

The onus lies on the State Party.

—Dr. Sarita Boodhoo

Geet Gawai: An Overview

I have great pleasure to be associated with the publication of the book entitled *Geet Gawai–An Ode to Geetharines of Mauritius* written by Dr. Sarita Boodhoo. The *Geet Gawai* is a musical ensemble that encapsulates the cultural legacy brought to Mauritius by Indian indentured immigrants. Its importance has been recognised by UNESCO and in 2016 it was listed as the Intangible Cultural Heritage of Humanity.

I have read the manuscript and I find it to be a valuable work of research on the rich heritage of Bhojpuri folk songs known as *Geet Gawai* which the Girmitiyas took with them to Mauritius about two centuries ago from the Bhojpuri speaking regions of India. My affection for Bhojpuri language and its rich traditions goes back to my childhood. I have been closely associated with the Bhojpuri language and culture since my university days. I have studied the fascinating works of Udai Narain Tiwari on Bhojpuri. I have also witnessed many plays of Bhikhari Thakur popularly known as 'Shakespeare of Bhojpuri'.

I met Dr. Sarita Boodhoo during the 3rd World Hindi Conference held in New Delhi in October 1983, organized by the *Rashtra Bhasha Prachar Samiti* of Wardha. I was Member of the Foreign Delegates Committee of the conference. It was my privilege to meet Mrs. Sarita Boodhoo, who was Secretary to the Mauritian delegation headed by her husband Shri Harish Boodhoo, the then Chief Whip and fomer Deputy Prime Minister of the Government of Mauritius. Dr. Sarita Boodhoo's love and devotion to the promotion and preservation of Hindi and Bhojpuri and the Indian culture in general is well known. She has been a living ambassador of Indian civilisational ethos and maintained a deep bond between India and Mauritius for several decades. Her association with the Antar Rashtriya Sahayog Parishad dates back to the early days of its foundation when she met Shri Baleshwar Agrawal, Secretary General of ARSP, way back in 1975 in Mauritius. She is a life member of the ARSP and supportive of its activities in the Indian diaspora. In April 2019, she headed a team of 25 *Geet Gawai* performers and custodians on a cultural tour of India where they performed in various cities. They were invited to perform at the ARSP which was very much appreciated and given a wide coverage by various printing and broadcasting media including Doordarshan.

I am sure this work will be greatly beneficial to researchers, scholars and writers in the discovery of varied facets of Indian culture, so well preserved and promoted by the Indian diaspora. I also wish that these kinds of traditional folk songs should be digitized so that it will be preserved for the many more generations to come. I commend Dr. Sarita Boodhoo for such a scholarly and thoroughly researched work which will prove to be a milestone to research scholars and Indologists.

I would like to thank Amb. Virendra Gupta, President, ARSP, Shri Shyam Parande, Secretary General, ARSP for their constant guidance and support in all our endeavours. I am grateful to Amb. Anup Mudgal, Former Chairperson, DRRC and Prof. Gopal Arora, Secretary, ARSP for the initiation and completion of this important work. I also greatly acknowledge the support of Dr. Ruchi Verma, Research Fellow, DRRC for the coordination for bringing out this valuable edition.

—Narayan Kumar
Honorary Director
DRRC-ARSP
New Delhi

Foreword

There are over thirty million members of Indian diaspora spread across the world. Large numbers of them were taken by the colonial powers under the Indentureship system to work in plantations in far off countries including Mauritius after abolition of slavery. They endured severe hardship and deprivation for several generations. However, despite the oppressive conditions and unending challenges, they managed to preserve their Indian cultural values and maintained active contacts with their roots.

Language is the most important aspect of any tradition and culture. As such, preserving and propagating the language is very important. People of Indian Origin in Mauritius have maintained close link with their native languages. This cultural connect is vividly represented in '*Geet Gawai*' a traditional folklore which originated in the Bhojpuri belts of India and well preserved in Mauritius. This tradition has unifying effect on Indians from different regions of India in Mauritius and other parts of the world.

The *Geet Gawai* is a musical ensemble that encapsulates the intangible cultural heritage brought to Mauritius by Indian indentured immigrants. It is a combination of rituals, prayers, songs, music and dance which is also a living means of expression of the oral traditions prevalent in the Bhojpuri region in India. The significance and importance of *Geet Gawai* has been recognised by UNESCO and in 2016 it was listed as an Intangible Cultural Heritage of Humanity.

Dr. Sarita Boodhoo was one of the pioneering forces in steering the nomination of *Geet Gawai* for inscription on the UNESCO Representative List of the Intangible Cultural Heritage of Humanity. She has had close contacts with India as she has completed her tertiary studies from India and carried out several projects for promoting India and Mauritius relations. Her effort to promote the language among the youth in particular is also noteworthy.

Antar Rashtriya Sahayog Parishad considers it a privilege to have been associated with the compilation and publication of *Geet Gawai*, an important part of Indian heritage, in a book form. We are grateful that Mrs Sarita Boodhoo agreed to undertake the requisite research leading to the compilation of a whole book at our request. This is not her first book. She has written a massive book named- *'Kanya Dan: The Whys of Hindu Marriage Rituals'* (including a compilation of over hundred Bhojpuri songs) which the former Prime Minister of India, Shri Atal Bihari Vajpayee had described as a "magnum opus" and which was launched in January 1995 at the Rashtrapati Bhawan, New Delhi by the President of India H.E Dr. Shankar Dayal Sharma.

Antar Rashtriya Sahayog Parishad is happy to be associated with this important publication as part of our mission for expanded outreach with Indian diaspora. We hope this publication would be a useful resource for practitioners of *Geet Gawai*, scholars and researchers.

—Amb. Virendra Gupta

President, ARSP

New Delhi

Preface

The Idea of writing *Geet Gawai-An Ode to Geetharines* of Mauritius came to me a long time back. I had made several attempts at assembling the *Sanskar Geet.* Over several decades I have met and interviewed a good number of *Geetharines,* the Bhojpuri folk songs tradition bearers and singers. They have always fascinated me. In the early phase of the setting up of the Bhojpuri Speaking Union and the first Bhojpuri Speaking Union *Geet Gawai* School at Petit Raffray, I had interviewed quite a few more of the *Geetharines-Guruwaines* the Guru Matas, those who taught the *Geet Gawai* Bhojpuri songs to the avid learners.

I wanted to honour these tradition bearers who held the *Geet,* the *canto hondo*- the deep song within their bosoms and throats. Unknowingly and without appropriation, they have been singing from generation to generation the *Geet Gawai.* Thus, keeping alive an ancient intangible cultural heritage brought by the *Girmitiyas*- the Indian Indentured workers from the Bhojpuri belt of India.

Way back, I set up the Mauritius Bhojpuri Institute in May 1982 as an NGO, to give a voice to these tradition bearers and to Bhojpuri language, literature and heritage culture. That was the first bold step towards giving an institutionalised recognition to a language and its rich repository of cultural heritage left to languish in the backwaters of Mauritian cultural life.

For a first multimedia ballet-*Parbatia* Saga of Indian Immigrants, I had presented on 19 September, 1982 to encase the Bhojpuri linguistic and cultural heritage of five generations of *Girmitiyas* and their descendants in Mauritius, I needed to choreograph the thematic interpretation of the concept. I was supported by a dedicated team of young promising artists including the late Meera Mohun and family members. Looking for *Geetharines* nearby, I was directed to a nearby village Richelieu- two kilometres on the western outskirts of the city of Port- Louis. I was astounded to find women singing such rich Bhojpuri songs some with historical background. Many of these songs eventually formed the basis of the ballet, an instant success that brought the richness of the Bhojpuri language and culture to the forefront of Mauritian cultural life.

The ballet brought out the beauty and depth of Bhojpuri language and associated cultural oral traditions.

When I was writing and researching for my anthropological work *Kanya Dan The Whys of Hindu Marriage Rituals* in the late 1980s and early 1990s, I gained access to a further array of tradition bearers from all over the country. I collected some hundred oral Bhojpuri songs, many of which were immortalised within the pages of the Kanya Dan, which the former Prime Minister of India, Shri Atal Behari Vajpayee had qualified as a *"magnum opus"*.

I was indeed enamoured with the lyrics and hauntingly lilting and attaching tunes, melodies and words of the Bhojpuri *Sanskar Geet* sung at weddings, birth rites and other ceremonies: the *Sohar* and *Lalnas;* the festive songs of Holi which I had collected from Dadi Jasmuth of Cassis, my own mother Chandrawtee, my mother-in-law Fooldie, my *chachiya saas*, Mrs Raghunundan, then 92 years old in 1989.

When I embarked upon the project of the commemoration of the 150th anniversary of the arrival of the first Indian Indentured Immigrants in 1983-1985, I came across many more *Geetharines*...I took down the songs and kept on making notes. During the 1983 General Elections, Lady Sarojini Jugnauth and I went to address a number of women in many parts of Mauritius. It was at one such meeting at Vacoas that women sang the Godna and Harparawri songs which I heard for the first time. At Giquel Street, Port-Louis from Mrs Sati Bhagwantee Purang-Padaruth Tiwari I came across Janeo songs.

At my own wedding in December 1973, Shanti Bundhoo, Geetharine of Cassis Road and her *Geet Gawai* group came to sing over several evenings. Though I was a career woman, still I wanted it that way! In fact, *Geetharines* have sung at the marriage ceremonies of my brothers and sisters too.

On all these occasions I was captured by the auspicious vibrations of these age-old songs. They produced and cast a benign magic spell on me. They lingered nostalgically within my consciousness for days.

Somehow, I was always taken up with pressing socio cultural and political engagements for several years these being the priorities of the time. There was never enough time to make a deep and serious study of these rich treasures. Yet, I always felt they needed to be done urgently. The songs remained unwritten, at the back of my mind. When I was appointed Chairperson of the Bhojpuri Speaking Union, by Cabinet Decision on 3 August, 2012, I felt a surge of energy welling within me. Here came an opportunity for me to give Bhojpuri language and its *cantadoras* and *Geetharines* their right and merited place in history.

Many wild yet realisable ambitions crept into my mind, regarding Bhojpuri language and its rich cultural heritage. I felt the urgent need of the moment was to inventorize these *Geetharines* and singers of other genres. I wanted to document their works. They needed to be on audio archives and in print. Fund was lacking, equipment for such sophisticated scientific work was unavailable.

I felt like the dancing peacock, who danced madly and displayed its beautiful magical plumes. But when it looked at its feet it was saddened and downcast to see the grim reality. I was saddened to see many of these old *Geetharines* I had encountered for several decades dying and with them disappeared forever the rich rare treasures of songs.

In the meantime, Mauritius Government had sent the Nomination Dossier of Bhojpuri folk songs-*Geet Gawai* to UNESCO as an Intangible Cultural Heritage of Mauritius. I worked as a consultant at the University of Mauritius and collaborated with the National Heritage Fund for four years on the dossier. I was delighted to form part of the Government official delegation to Addis Ababa, Ethiopia in November-December 2016 to the UNESCO Inter-Governmental Meeting. The listing of *Geet Gawai* as an Intangible Cultural Heritage of Humanity by UNESCO gave *Geet Gawai* an International aura.

On my numerous visits of research to the Bhojpuri belt in Bihar and UP, I was amazed to see the connectivity of the Bhojpuri folk songs. Indeed, many of them were retained intact in both India and Mauritius. This incited me to further continue my research along this line. I also saw the same connectedness with the countries of the Indian diaspora such as the South Africa, Fiji, Suriname, Guyana, and Trinidad. Unfortunately in many of these countries, the songs have almost disappeared. Very few are still retained by some elderly ladies...In Mauritius we are still lucky. We have the endorsement and back up of the Government in its cultural policy. In fact, since November 2019, the Ministry of Arts and Culture has been given a new appellation as the Ministry of Arts and Cultural Heritage to widen its scope of operation and give further credence to the rich cultural heritage preserved in Mauritius.

I came across many cultural anthropologists and scholars who visited Mauritius for their research and books such as Professor Catherine Servan Schreiber from Sorbonne, France and Mrs Bhanu Dwarka from New York, Professor Seiko Sugimoto from the University of Kyoto, Japan and Professor Helen Myers musicologist and specialist in Bhojpuri folk songs from Pennsylvania, USA, Professor Kuber Mishra, noted linguist and Professor Krishna Deo Upadhyaya, eminent internationally renowned folklorist from India and Professor Alexandra Pavor from Russia. Many of these Professors had university grants and Academic financial support for their works and publications, I had none. Many local researchers and undergraduates too have approached me in the preparation of their dissertations.

However, when the Antar Rashtriya Sahayog Parishad (ARSP) approached me to write a book on *Geet Gawai* it was a tremendous challenge. I was delighted but apprehensive too. The ARSP had been persuading me to come up with a research paper for their academic journal of the Diaspora Research and Resource Centre (DRRC) in April 2019. The Director of the DRRC, Ambassador Anup Kumar Mudgal impressed upon me to come forward with the research material in a book form. In the same year I had taken the bold decision of taking twenty five of the *Geetharines* on a Cultural Heritage Tour of India from 7th April to 25th April 2019, all at their own costs. Brave ladies. They performed at several localities including the Antar Rastriya Sahayog Parishad in Delhi. The ARSP Directors, Executive members and guests were mesmerised by the richness, depth and originality of the Bhojpuri *Geet Gawai* songs and the simplicity and yet professional performance of the *Geetharines*. I was therefore, emboldened to embark on my writing mission. Then came the Pandemic Covid 19 as from March 2020 to Mauritius, which did not allow me to make further trips to India.

Facing a deadline is exacting and demanding. But it has the merit of getting the writer focused. A large part of this Preface was written and mulled over during the April 2019 trip to India. I started writing it in Srinagar, Kashmir on 20 April 2019 at Asian Park Hotel and continued it on our return journey to Mauritius on Air Mauritius MK745 on 25 April, 2019.

It is amazing to note a parallel experience in the discovery of Bhojpuri folk songs by Dr Chadramani Singh, author and Tagore National Scholar, who eventually brought out a book "Marriage Songs of Bhojpuri Region" in 1979. I was given a copy of this book by the High Commissioner of India Shri Prem Singh in 1984 when I was working over the 150th anniversary of the Indian Indentured Immigration to Mauritius. The book has been an eye opener to me revealing the close similarities between the practices in the Bhojpuri belt in India and in Mauritius and showing the many types of songs we share. I am further astounded by the preservation of these songs and practices by Mauritian practitioners associated therewith even after a long lapse of almost 200 years!

I am including here some excerpts from Chandramani Singh's book to make the analogy more specific.

I give this excerpt from Dr Chandramani Singh's book *"Marriage Songs from Bhojpuri Regions"* as a parallel on my own work. "Bhojpuri songs have impressed me from my early childhood. Later, I got interested in folk lore in general but Bhojpuri songs were the first to attract my attention, because many of my family members spoke that language and I was growing up in a Bhojpuri-speaking area. About thirty years back- I do not remember the exact year- a marriage took place in my village, in a family closely related to ours. My grand-mother was invited to attend this marriage and being the eldest female member of the clan in that village, was supposed to sing morning and evening songs, as invitation to the gods. I was then six or seven years old and very lively, as all children are at that age; clinging to my grand- mother, I used to go and listen to these songs. The women sang five songs in the morning and five in the evening, many composed in praise of natural powers and of ancestors, and then a number dedicated to Lord Shiva and to the Goddess Kali. After this a group of young girls sang marriage songs and in the end there was Jhumar- a circle dance.

"At that time, I was struck simply by the songs' melodious character, not then understanding the deeper meaning imbedded in the words. As a young child, I remembered the songs without any effort, just by hearing them every day. Later, I was sent to school for a modern education.

"Though I did not forget Bhojpuri and used to speak it with some members of my family, I did not get much chance to hear new songs. I could, however, not forget the ones I had heard in my childhood.

"In B.A., I offered Hindi Literature as one of my optional subjects and studied G.A. Grierson's work on linguistics. I must confess that I could not get much out of it; but it encouraged me to work further on the Bhojpuri Dialect. In summer vacation, I went through all available material on it- works done by G.A. Grierson, Udai Narain Tiwari, Devendra Satyarthi, Krishna Dev Upadhyaya and W.G Archer. But soon I had to stop this self-induced study of mine, as I wanted to do an M.A. in Indian Art History and later the Ph.D. in Pahari painting. At this stage, my love for Bhojpuri folk songs found further encouragement. W.G. Archer, the well-known scholar of Pahari painting, had collected a good number of these songs in his early years in India, and had them published. Though we had met several times earlier, I discussed folk songs with him only in 1968, when I met the Archers in London. I am sure he must have forgotten this talk, but I could not, because it had inspired my long-cherished desire to work further on the Bhojpuri of my youth". (Dr Chandramani Singh has written on Protected Monuments of Rajasthan, Centres of Pahari Painting and was involved at the Bharat Kala Bhavan, at Banaras Hindu University Museum).

The *Geetharines* have gone through tremendous ups and downs in their personal as well as in their social and economic lives. What could have been life for the first *Geetharines* who despite all the humiliations, poverty, sufferings, poor habitations and injustice faced, still they managed to secure in their throats and memories these gems of humanity, the *Geet Gawai*? The *geets* crossed the *Kala Pani* with them and are the pride of Mauritius. They are so well preserved thanks to their continuous singing and passing on of the torch to us of this "Cultural Heritage of Humanity!"

For this reason, I have felt it relevant and proper to give at the beginning of the book a gist of the immigration history, the conditions of recruitment, the dangerous voyage across the threatening oceans, the painful and slow adjustment into an alien society and environment. Despite all these hazards and obstacles, they were able to rise up the ladder and make a respectable place in the society for themselves and for the songs they preserved in their bosom and memories.

They faced stoically their painful tearing away from kith and kin back home. They faced the agonizing upheavals of the oceans. They faced as well on arrival, the gruesome sugar estate conditions of work and deplorable maltreatment and yet were able to survive and surmount it and continued singing.

I firmly believe that these precious songs that have been preserved by the *Geetharines* against all odds establish a strong, permanent and dynamic bond between India and Mauritius as well as the Indian Diaspora and will forever consolidate further the Indo-Mauritian and diasporic ties.

Geet Gawai An Ode to Geetharines of Mauritius will be a useful instrument to not only the public in general in understanding the whys of the oral songs. I have also given their usefulness in rites, rituals and customs but also why they are sung on particular occasions. I have taken the pains of giving not only where possible the songs in Devanagri as given to me by the tradition bearers. Many of these songs have become rare and are known in their original forms by only one or two tradition bearers. Many who gave me these songs died with their rich collections. These songs have a very rich Bhojpuri vocabulary replete with Sanskrit words.

Quite a good number of these songs tell stories, stories of romance, Puranic tales or stories of Ram and Sita. It is amazing how the tradition bearers, the *Geetharines* sing these songs at a stretch. Some of them are very lengthy.

The research I undertook will help generations to come. I went into the etymology of the rich Bhojpuri words and vocabulary. In some cases I obtained help from the *Geetharines*. In other cases I undertook my own personal research. I have gone at great pains to do the transliteration in Roman Script with a fair English translation to the best of my ability, with further interpretations and explanations for the benefit of those non-familiar with the Bhojpuri language.

UNESCO Criteria (4) at the 11 Session of the UNESCO Intergovernmental Committee for the Safeguarding of the Intangible Cultural Heritage in Addis Ababa, Ethiopia in November-December 2016, stipulated that the Committee "Encourages the submitting State when promoting the element at the international level, to provide a translation of lyrics of the songs...... into widely spoken languages".

Keeping the above in mind and having worked as a Consultant on the Nomination Dossier of Bhojpuri folk songs in Mauritius-*Geet Gawai* with the University Of Mauritius, National Heritage Fund and the Ministry of Arts and Culture from 2011 to 2015, I cannot but agree fully with the above mentioned UNESCO's Recommendation. This book, I hope will partially meet that requirement. I have made an attempt to do as much translation and transliteration of *Geet Gawai* Songs. In a near future more will come to meet that Obligation as a firm commitment on our behalf.

I am sure the book will be useful also to students of Cultural Anthropology and to Musicologists. It has a vast spread of information and material that will prove to be of practical use in ethno cultural studies and may prove to be handy to students of History and Cultural Heritage and Bhojpuri linguistics in their academic pursuit.

I am of opinion that these studies of a historic-cultural heritage dimension will also act as a fillip to researchers and scholars on the Indian front as well as worldwide. It may incite researchers and Indologists to give a fresh look to their own rich cultural heritage such as folk songs and folk tales which are being rapidly swallowed by modernity and commercialisation and help themselves dig into other aspects of linguistic heritage comprising of proverbs, puzzles, folk beliefs and practices.

I pay tribute hereby to the ancestor-*Geetharines*, the generations after them, the present day *Geetharines* and the future generations of *Geetharines* to come. This book is an Ode to the *Geetharines* of Mauritius.

2 January, 2023

—Dr. Sarita Boodhoo
Founder-Director
Mauritius Bhojpuri Institute
Chairperson
Bhojpuri Speaking Union
Mauritius

Contents

1

Introduction: Kalkutta Se Chuttal Jahaj

Kalkutta se chuttal jahaj,
Panwariya dhire chalo
Dhire chalo, oh dhire chalo.

Oo mein aa gail ba dada hamaar
Oo mein aa gail ba dadi hamaar
Oo mein aa gail ba nana hamaar
Oo mein aa gail ba nani hamaar
Panwariya dhire chalo
Kalkutta se chuttal jahaj,
Panwariya dhire chalo.

Oo mein aa gail ba eireen hamaar
Oo mein aa gail ba phuli hamaar
Oo mein aa gail ba harwa hamaar
Panwariya dhire chalo
Kalkutta se chuttal jahaj,
Panwariya dhire chalo.

Oumein aa gail ba peinjan hamaar,
Oumein aa gail ba chan wa hamaar,
Panwariya dhire chalo
Kalkutta se chuttal jahaj
Panwariya dhire chalo.

Oumein aa gail ba sari hamaar,
Oumein aa gail ba dhoti hamaar,
Oumein aa gail ba pughree hamaar,
Panwariya dhire chalo
Kalkutta se chuttal jahaj
Panwariya dhire chalo.

Oumein aa gail ba Ramayana hamaar,
Oumein aa gail ba Gita hamaar,
Oumein aa gail ba Koran hamaar
Oumein aa gail ba Purana hamaar,
Panwariya dhire chalo
Kalkutta se chuttal jahaj
Panwariya dhire chalo.

English translation of Kalkutta se Chuttal Jahaj,
a popular Bhojpuri song from Mauritius,
adapted by Sarita Boodhoo

Our sailing ship is leaving Kalkutta
O boatman steer the (sailing) ship gently,
O wind steer the (sailing) ship smoothly.
Our *dada* (paternal grandfather) has come on that ship,
Our *dadi* (paternal grandmother) has come on that ship,
Our *nana* (paternal grandfather) has come on that ship,
Our *nani (maternal grandmother) has come on that ship.*
O boatman steer the sailing ship gently,
O wind steer the ship smoothly,
Our sailing ship is leaving Kalkutta.

Our earrings have come on that ship,
Our nose-rings have come on that ship,
Our necklace has come on that ship,
O boatman steer the sailing ship gently
Our sailing ship is leaving Kalkutta,
O wind steer the ship smoothly.

Our anklets have come on that ship,
Our bracelets have come on that ship,
O boatman steer the sailing ship gently
O wind steer the ship smoothly,
Our sailing ship is leaving Kalkutta.

Our sari has come on that ship,
Our *dhoti* has come on that ship,
Our *pughree* has come on that ship,
O boatman steer the sailing ship gently,
Our sailing ship is leaving Kalkutta.

Our *Ramayana* has come on that sailing ship
Our *Gita* has come on that sailing ship
Our *Koran* has come on that sailing ship
Our *Purana* has come on that sailing ship.

O boatman steer the sailing ship gently,
O wind steer the ship smoothly,
Our sailing ship is leaving Kalkutta.

This Bhojpuri song sets the tone of the *Geet Gawai* process in Mauritius. It is a popular traditional song from Mauritius based on original Bhojpuri tune, style and ethos. It speaks of the history and emotions of Indian indentures who came from the port of Calcutta to work on the sugar plantations from 2nd November, 1834 onwards, after the abolition of slavery. They brought along their civilisational ethos in the form of jewellery, dress and scriptural literature which sustained their identity and nurtured their souls.

"The ship (of immigrants, Girmitiyas) has left the port of Calcutta (British capital) and on this ship has come (to Mauritius) my dada (grandfather), dadi (grandmother), my sari. It reflects that emigration of labour also meant the transportation of values, lores, traditions, dress, food habits, (parampara) and art-forms."

This song sung during *Geet Gawai* events has a historical significance: It speaks of the port from which the *'coolie ship'* left, that is, Calcutta. This author recreated the song at the Mauritius Bhojpuri Institute (MBI) in 1982 for a Bhojpuri ballet, based on an original traditional song sung by *Geet Gawai* women in the village of Richelieu, Petite Rivière, west of Mauritius in 1982. She attended the *Geet Gawai* session and recorded the song used with improvised music in thc MBI ballet in 1982.

□

2

The *Girmitiya* Movement

The Term *Girmitiya*

Girmitiya is a Bhojpuria form of the term 'Agreement'. Most of the recruits for the indentured labour system were from the hinterland of Calcutta, especially from the basins of the Bhojpuri-speaking belt along the Ganges plains. These regions included districts such as Shahabad, Ara, Balia, Gorakhpur, Jaunpur, Chapra. When the *arkatiyas* went round looking for potential workers, they talked of an agreement or contract of five years which the workers would have to sign. They made very luring proposals to the prospective recruits. The 'First Great Experiment' as the British called it, started mostly in the Bhojpuri-speaking belt of Bihar, the sugarcane producing area, and the eastern United Provinces. A depot was set up in the Calcutta Maidan at Bhowanipore. The first post for recruitment of indenture Iabour was Mauritius as from 2 November, 1834. As word got around among the population, the term 'Agreement' couldn't be pronounced properly by the Bhojpuri-speaking people. *Girmitiya* is a strong, symbolically loaded term that marks in Bhojpuri the whole process of the indentured system. It originates from agreement, the contract that was signed on the one hand by the recruiting agent or the recruiting officer and on the other hand, the thumb marks of the recruited, the *Girmitiyas,* to whom the contract was read out. The contract was made in Bengali language.

Therefore it came to be known as *Girmit*. Agreement became simply *girmit* for them. And from *girmit* developed the word *Girmitiya*. *Girmitiya* defined the *girmit* who accepted the terms and conditions of the five year contract *'to work from sunrise to sunset'*. So throughout the plantation colonies, the words *Girmit* and *Girmitiya* became very strong symbolical terms for the indentured labourers and the indenture labour system. In Mauritius, the Biharis and other recruits coming from Calcutta came to be defined as *Calcuttia* and the language they spoke as *Calcuttia boli* too. In Mauritian kreol the term *Girmitiya* was translated as *'Engagé'*, used also in Mauritian Bhojpuri and used as such in some local Bhojpuri songs and poems by noted Mauritian poets.

Today *Girmit* and *Girmitiya* are iconic terms in the Indian diaspora and have assumed the whole saga and trauma associated with the despicable indentured labour system.

The embarkation was at the port of Calcutta, the capital of the British Imperial Government. As the indentured were not lettered in the English language, they could not pronounce it properly.

Gandhiji had first used the term *Girmit* in his book *'The Story of My Experiments with Truth'* (An Autobiography of Gandhi) (26 November 1925):

"The indentured labourers were those who went to Natal (South Africa) on an agreement to serve for five years, and came to be known there as Girmitiyas from Girmit, which was the corrupt form of the English word 'agreement'."

The other term used for the indentured labourers was *Coolie* in South Africa and in Mauritius. In South Africa, the Tamil indentures and merchants too were referred to as *'sami'*. So in South Africa, Gandhiji was referred to by the Englishmen as *'coolie barrister'* despite his legal professional status, and Indian merchants were known as *'coolie merchants'*.

Basins of Recruitment

Two-thirds of the indentured labourers recruited for Mauritius came from the North-Western Provinces and Oudh; one-sixth came from Bihar. A tiny fraction also came from the Punjab, and also from Madras and Bombay Presidencies. This pattern of recruitment prevailed throughout the indenture period. In fact towards the last years of emigration, more indentures came from

UP as people in eastern UP and western Bihar came to be more aware of the abuse and oppression prevailing. In the beginning, with the Arbuthnot (private) contract in September October, 1834, 36 Hill Coolies known as *Dhangars* had been recruited from the Chhota Nagpur Plateau of Bihar.

According to *Ship Arrival Registers* (*Courtesy,* Satyendra Peerthum, historian, AGTF) from 1826 to 1910, there were 63,289 tribals, largely Dhangars, Oraon, Mundas, Ho, Santal and others who arrived in Mauritius. The larger part comprised of Dhangars, who were considered docile and hardworking and were attached to the soil. These formed part of 14 per cent of *Ship Arrival Registers.* There were 67,810 Muslims constituting 15 per cent arrivals as per *Ship Arrival Registers*; 3,16,451 immigrants were registered as Hindus and formed the bulk of the arrivals amounting to 70 per cent of *Ship Arrival Registers.*

There was a consequent percentage from Andhra (through Visakhapatnam port), Telangana, Karnataka and Orissa and neighbouring regions comprising of 31,644 recruits and forming 7 per cent of *Ship Arrival Registers.* 113,017 Indentured labourers arrived from Madras Presidency and Kerala from 1834 to 1910, forming 20 per cent of the total number of imported labour. It is interesting to note that thousands of recruits from Pondicherry, Cochin, Karikal, Cuddalore, Tranquebar and Coromandel from the Malabar coast were also shipped through the Madras port to Mauritius as indentured labourers.

The largest number of *Girmitiyas* came from Bihar and part of it from Jharkhand now, amounting to 181,064 persons and giving the largest percentage of indentured immigration of 40 per cent during the 90 years of 1834 to 1924.

Some 81,138 indentured labourers also came from Uttar Pradesh, forming some 18 per cent of the total importation.

As for the Bombay Presidency, Rajasthan, Gujarat and Punjab, the figures given on the *Ship Arrival Registers* amounted to 45,207 labourers giving 10 per cent of total importation figures. A few migrants came from Nepal borders with India, especially the Terai, and what is today Pakistan and Bangladesh but which were during British India, part of the Indian sub-continent.

It should also be recalled that prior to Indian indentured movement, there was a sizeable population of thousands of people of Indian origin, largely of Bengali and Pondicherrian and (Malabar coast) roots and who were already settled on the island during the French period. Some are traced back to even the Dutch period.

Another settlement that occurred during the Indian indentured labour movement was that of traders, merchants and businessmen. They comprised a very tiny percentage of the Indian population of Sindhi and Gujarati origin and mostly Muslims, known in Mauritius as the 'White Muslims', hailing from Kutch and Surat in Gujarat. They traded in *dal*, rice and other essential food and dress items that were the needs of the indentured labourers. There were also a few jewellers among the Gujarati community, known as *sonars* to the *Girmitiyas*.

It is a well-established fact throughout the plantation Indian diaspora that as soon as the indentured labourer saved some money, he would buy jewellery for his wife. The female indentured immigrant would adorn herself with jewellery. This remark is even found in the official Governor's dispatches.

These Sindhi and Gujarati traders, merchants and jewellers operated from Central Port Louis along the main thoroughfare, such as the Royal Road and Desforges Street, now known as Sir Seewoosagur Ramgoolam Street and even the Chaussée Street.

As a result, with its already diverse European population of French, British, Portuguese origin, and the descendants of Malagasy, Mozambique, East African and Senegalese origin slaves, the large influx of Indian indentured population came to give Mauritius a very diverse demographic profile. Needless to say, the massive flow of Indian indentured labourers from 1834 to 1924 has contributed to the emergence of a huge diverse mass of people of Indian origin in Mauritius. The highest percentage reached 70 per cent around 1860. This figure has been maintained till date, bringing a new demographic dynamic into play, affecting the socio-economic, cultural and political life of the island.

This reversal in geo-politics was noticed with the historical change of the 1885 Constitution in 1948. The huge Indian population, as from 1860, appeared as a sure menace to the oligarchy. That is why they did not want any constitutional change.

Areas of Recruitment

I give details herewith as follows of the principal areas of recruitment from the north and north-east regions, most of which I have visited during my research periods (1983—till January 2020)

1. The *Hill Coolie* districts comprised principally of
    - Santhal Parganas (West Bengal)
    - Hazaribagh (formerly in Bihar, now a part of Jharkhand)
    - Ranchi (formerly in Bihar, now the capital of Jharkhand)
    - Manbhum (formerly in Bihar, now forms part of Jharkhand)
    - Singhbhum (formerly in Bihar, now forms part of Jharkhand)
    - Palamau (formerly in Bihar, now forms part of Jharkhand)
    - Birbhum (West Bengal)

Immigrants from Jharkhand (formerly Bihar) also came from as far as Jamshedpur, Ramgarh, Purulia, Deoghar, Sahibganj, Chhota Nagpur, Dumka and even Jamshedpur (*Ship Register Information*)

Bihar

The State of Bihar, which fell under the Presidency of Bihar, Oudh, Orissa and Bengal but became a proper State by itself, as from 1912, sent us the highest number of Indian indentured (*Girmitiya*) immigrants. I have followed the trail of some areas, such as along the Ganges river in Patna, along the Ganges in Chhapra, Ballia to see the *Ghats* at which they were shipped, such as at Balu Ghat in Ballia. The former large Shahabad district, which was the largest basin of recruitment, came to be subdivided in the last few decades into more administratively manageable districts, such as Arrah, Chhapra, Buxar, Sasaram and Bhojpur, which now comprises two Bhojpurs.

I have followed the trail of Indian indentured immigration up to Champaram (both east and west, where Gandhiji had begun his first Indian *satyagraha* movement (1917) against the indigo plantation white farmers. I went up to Siwan, Gopalganj and Saran. In East Bihar, I went to Araria and Supaul, to Bhagalpur, Purnea, Munger and Kisanganj. I also visited down south into Gaya. I made it a point to visit Muzaffarpur, Katihar, the Darbhanga region of east Bihar, known as the Maithili belt. There were also immigrants who came from Jahanabad and Aurangabad as per *Ship Register Records*.

Uttar Pradesh known as Oudh and the United Provinces during British period

There was a consequent number of indentures recruited from Ballia which was then within the state of Bihar. Indentures came from Ghazipur, Azamgarh, Fyzabad (now Ayodhya), Hardoi. They came from Basti on the India-Nepal border, Gonda, Gorakhpur, Benaras, Sarnath, Allahabad now Prayagraj, Mirzapur, Jaunpur, Mau and Sasaram, Agra and Sitapur. I have been able to visit all these districts in Uttar Pradesh and interacted with local people, scholars and other personalities in the course of my research work.

In fact, I have traced my own paternal ancestor's roots from Daurapur Gaon, also known as Darampur (written Dorapore then) in Ballia *Zila*: Ghazeepore. I visited the village and met my Indian relatives in 2017. The ladies sang Bhojpuri songs for me! Immigrant Makhan Immigrant No. 359832 came from Dorapore and went to Calcutta where he boarded the ship, *'Hindostan Ship No. 1218'* at age 18. Date of arrival in Mauritius: 18 September, 1872.

From Calcutta to Mauritius!

I have met the family in Ballia and reconnected.

It is worthwhile noting that from *Ship Register Records*, immigrants have come from as far west as Lucknow, Aligarh, Kanpur and Agra as well as from Chitrakut, Fatepur, Ghaziabad, Etawah, Mathura, Hardoi, Meerut, Pratapgarh, Bareilly, Moradabad, Firozabad and Sultanpur. Indeed, a very large sprawling network!

In the latter phase of the indentureship, Benaras had become an important centre of recruitment. Protest voices began thereafter to be raised and the agitations against Indian Indenture system had begun to gather ground. In fact, the emigration agents had even opened a temporary depot at Benaras! But with the mounting clamour against using a pilgrimage centre to lure innocent people, the depot at Benaras was soon closed down.

West Bengal

Besides throwing their nets in and around Calcutta port on people who were milling around in search of work, having come from the interior land of the hinterland of Calcutta and the Gangetic Plain, the *arkatias* got into their nets the docile Dhangars ousted from their land and who had come down to the plains, looking for jobs in the mushrooming British mills, such as indigo and so on. People were moving eastwards in search of jobs. Hence the many Bhojpuri songs that developed are known as *'Purvis'*.

Besides the immediate vicinity of the port of Calcutta, other areas from which indentures have been recruited are: Raniguni, Bancoorah, Purolia, Midnapore, 24 Parganas, Bhirbhum and Dhubri.

Madhya Pradesh

Recruits have come from as far as Madhya Pradesh's Gwalior, Bundel Khand, Ujjain, Jabalpur, Sheopur, Rewa, Indore, Gouraha and Rajgarh. It may be that these people had come to Calcutta metropolitan area to look for work and were easily a victim to the lures of the emigrating agents and *arkatias*.

Some recruits were registered as coming from Bikaner, Ajmer, Chittor, Udaipur, Sirohi and Hanumangarh.

I have an ancestor coming from Ajmer and who boarded the ship for Mauritius in Bombay. His name was Immigrant Jairam No. 305038, who came from Ajmer, Rajasthan. After indentureship, immigrant Jairam was registered as an Old Immigrant. He bought land and properties and became a Sirdar/job contractor. He married his daughter Rookmin Jairam to another Sirdar, *Old Immigrant*, Immigrant Makhun (Makhan) and my paternal ancestor.

Chhattisgarh

The Bhojpuri regions of Bilaspur, Raigarh and Raipur have

also been registered on ship records as sending recruits to Mauritius. At that time, Chhattisgarh was not yet formed as a State.

These recruitment areas were then part of Bihar.

In fact, towards the last years of emigration, more *Girmitiyas* came from United Provinces, as the people in eastern UP and western Bihar became more aware of the abuses and oppression in *Mirich Des* or *Tapu* as Mauritius and other plantation colonies were generally known.

The first contractors were from a private company by the name of Arbuthnot. The first recruits were largely from the Dhangars community of Chhota Nagpur Plateau of Bihar. There were also Oraons, Mundas, Ho, Santhal and so on.

The Arbuthnot experiment of recruiting 36 Dhangars was a ray of hope for despairing sugar planters after the Abolition of Slavery Act on 1 February, 1835. It set the tone for the 'great experiment' in importing Indian labour on contract. Mauritius was the *'first post'* in this experiment.

After the arrival of the Dhangars, *arkatias* and *duffadars* recruited further inland in the hinterland of Calcutta and the Gangetic Plains.

Immigration and Bhojpuri Belt

The Bhojpuri belt encompasses a wide geographical region that is found in West Bihar, Eastern Uttar Pradesh, eastern part of Chhattisgarh as well as in Jharkhand. They include different forms and variations of Bhojpuri ranging from a pure Bhojpuri form from Ballia, Ghazipur, Bhojpur, Rohtas to a western Bhojpuri spoken in Jaunpur, Azamgarh, Varanasi and Mirzapur. Nagpuria is spoken in Chhota Nagpur, now in Jharkhand, from where the earliest *Girmitiyas* hailed. Madhesia is yet another form of Bhojpuri spoken between the Maithili regions in north Bihar and the Bhojpuri regions of Gorakhpur (middle land of Bhojpuri). Another form of Bhojpuri is known as *Tharu* which is spoken in the Terai region of the Himalayas stretching from northern Uttar Pradesh right up to Champaran in north-west Bihar and covering the hill slopes of Nepal.

As of 1834, 75 Indian immigrants were introduced into Mauritius. The figure rose to 5,000 in 1837. By 1858, the figure rose to 28,000. If in 1865, one-third of the population of Mauritius was Indian, in 1871, two-thirds were Indians—a proportion that has been maintained to this day more or less. The majority of indentured workers were from Bihar and eastern Uttar Pradesh.*

The Voyage

In the days of the sailing ships, the rigours of the long sea voyage were quite difficult to undergo. The passage from Hoogly river, a tributary of the Ganges, to Bay of Bengal and the open Indian Ocean, the *'sat samundar par'*, the *'kalapani'* was a most testing movement for the inland-dwelling indentured, who had never before made such an experiment.

A new trial, a new vicissitude was awaiting the *Girmitiyas*—the long tempestuous sea voyage which few, if any, had ever experienced ever before.

A majority of these *Girmitiyas* had been lured and made to leave their villages and families. They were told, *"Tapu mein pathar ulat ba, ta sona mili"*. Now duped and falling in the trap, they were to undergo a completely different tribulation—the hazardous and rough sea voyage of one-to-two months. Some would fall sick and die and their bodies thrown overboard.

As the ship progressed towards Mauritius, the emigrant would become languid and nostalgic, thinking of his native village, the family left behind. He or she would share and reminisce to new acquaintances met on board about all those left behind.

Kissas, kahanis, jokes, *pahelis,* anecdotes would be exchanged and shared on board. Surely, there would be moments when songs would be shared.

The vast Gangetic belt has nurtured in its bosom thousands of folk songs related to different seasons—the *bara masas,* to life cycles, to moods and moments, to the weather, to Nature, to village gods and goddesses, the *parvas* and the *tyohars*. The *birhas* would be remembered. These songs must have echoed from the bosom of the travelling immigrants as they faced nothing but

---

* Bhojpuri Traditions in Mauritius, Mauritius Bhojpuri Institute, Dr. (Mrs.) Sarita Boodhoo, 1999, 2000.

heaving waves and wide ocean for days and days.

Men and women would recall those thousand-year old songs, each from a different village or a linguistic district. Some were from the Bhojpuri villages, some from the Magahi belt, some from the Maithili linguistic area or the Kashiki area of Benaras and others from the Awadhi belt and yet there was a common thread linking them all. There was an unspoken commonality, for the districts of recruitment covered a vast network of thousands of kilometres radius. Bonding and sharing misfortunes, happy moments, sad moments the journey would be somehow endured and the *'sat samundar'* crossed.

The Landing at Immigration Depot at Port Louis

And so after a long and tiresome sea voyage, the *Girmitiyas* landed at the Immigration Depot in Port Louis, known as Aapravasi Ghat since 1986 and before that as Coolie Ghat. Formalities and registration terminated, the waiting plantation owner or his manager or *sirdar* would lead the already tired *Girmitiyas*, men, women and children for long distances on foot to the respective sugar estate camps. When the railways came in 1865, they were put on board the trains. Some were even taken by small boats, again along the coast to coastal sugar estates, such as at Medine, Bambous and south-west coastal sugar estates, such as at Ferney, Bel Ombre. The railings are still visible to tell the story of a by gone era.

Kunwar Singh Report

Though the Indian indentured system in Mauritius was on the wane as from 1900 and by 1910, it had reached a trickle, some greedy planters were still hoping against hope to have more Indians to work on their sugar fields. Shri Madan Mohan Malviyaji, founder of the Benaras Hindu University and member of the Imperial Council of Legislation had raised the issue. He was prodded by Mahatma Gandhi, who was fighting against this issue since his South African experience, as from 1895 till 1915, when he had completely got rid of the infamous £3 tax imposed on indentured Indians. Shri Gopal Krishna Gokhale too had raised his voice against the system.

Shri Malviyaji had brought his motion towards the abolition of

Indian indenture twice, once on 15 March, 1916 and secondly on 20 March, 1917. The pressure was mounting among even the civil society throughout India to put a term to the infamous exploitation of man by man.

Finally, the British India government under Lord Hardinge, the Viceroy and Governor General, did finally agree to put a definite end to the export of indentured labour to the plantation colonies. A law was passed in 1922. The Mauritius government had even sent a delegation of planters in 1922 to plead with the Indian Imperial government to review the abolition of indentureship.

With the pleading of the Mauritian planters, a temporary movement was allowed for a year when in 1922-1923 around 1,500 indentured labour was shipped to Mauritius. The indentured labourers were not happy with the conditions of work and severe penal law and the wages dished out to them. They protested vehemently. In December 1924, the Government of India sent Kunwar Maharaj Singh to conduct an investigation.

Kunwar Singh's Visit to Mauritius

Kunwar Maharaj Singh arrived in Mauritius by the '*Humayun*' on 19 December, 1924.

Kunwar Singh was quite agreeably surprised at the socio-cultural and economic progress of the Indians in Mauritius. He attended several functions and saw personally the manifestation of their tradition and culture.

He visited about 40 sugar estates. These were often surprise visits. He had meetings with the sugar estate managers, overseers and also met the workers. Judging by his outstanding royal personality and status, the estate managers went out of their way to please him and the local press gave him a magnificent welcome.

He was given about a dozen great receptions by the socio-religious-cultural associations throughout the island. At the end of his exhaustive visit, he presented his 50 page report to the Government of India, from what he had seen: *"There is no need to restart immigration of unskilled workers from India to Mauritius."*

In his recommendations, he urged measures to be taken for estate owners to make better provision of living quarters for their workers. More medical staff and doctors should be provided on estate hospitals. He was strictly opposed to child employment in the sugar factories. He proposed the introduction of compensation for all agricultural workers. He had seen the ravages that the consumption of rum had done to the community. He urged that "a substantial restriction on the sale of liquor" be enforced. He was also in favour of the grant of lands to the workers, as in Trinidad. After meeting indentures all over the country and visiting some 40 sugar estates and notables of the Indian community, he came to the definite conclusion that the system must be stopped. So on 31 May, 1924, it was declared abolished definitely in Mauritius.

Indians: Life Blood of Mauritius

In 1844, thanks to the Indians, Mauritius was in a position to compete with the other sugar-producing countries of the world. The Indians helped to change the face of Mauritius as well as its economy.

In a despatch to the Secretary of State for Colonies, the then Governor J.M. Higginson had written on 16 June, 1851:

"... Immigrant labour forms, as Your Lordship is aware, the very life blood of this important possession of the Crown." He also *warned the Crown: "The decadence of Mauritius is inevitable when India ceases to supply her with the means of carrying on the cultivation of the soil..."*

By 1850s, there were thus Indians all over in Mauritius. They were enticed to come with their families and it was even envisaged to bring and implant whole villages from India to stabilise the labour community. At one time, the authorities had even proposed the setting up of an Indian colony in Mauritius!

"The arrival of these brave Aapravasis from India was much more than the mere transportation of a group of labourers to an unknown land. It was a profound transfusion of the very pluralistic soul of India and her cultural heritage", which is alive in Mauritius in all its colours to this very day."*

---

* Ambassador Anup Kumar Mudgal High Commissioner of India in Mauritius September 2014 in Preface to "A Unique Place in Time and Space A Pictorial Presentation of the Aapravasi Ghat World Heritage Site and the Indenture Experience in Mauritius (1834-2014) – AGTF 2014

The Indenture Labour Route

"This route represents therefore not just the development of a new system of a contractual labour, but also the conservation of the civilisational heritage, traditions and values that these people carried with them to far off destinations, including Mauritius."*

Work Assigned to Women on Sugar Estates

"At 4 o'clock in the morning, the Sirdar sounded the first call to awake the women of the camp." *Field workers would be organised into groups: the grande bande* and the *petite bande.* The *grande bande* would be given arduous work and the *petite bande* was allocated light work. Mostly women labourers joined the '*petite bande*'. With their tools on their shoulders, they would leave for the sugarcane fields for the day's work.

"Men and women performed almost the same tasks except cane-cutting, which was a man's job." The women workers were not necessarily indentured. They were day workers employed on a verbal contract. "They had to work the same number of hours on the plantation. They were allocated other tasks, like cleaning up of the fields and *depaillage* (removal of dry leaves from the sugarcanes). The hours of work varied from 4 a.m. to 8 p.m. (for work assigned in sugar houses) and from 4.30 a.m. to 5 p.m. in the cane fields. For most labourers, the hard day's work ended at 6 p.m. after which they were given additional hours if the tasks were not completed. Even on Sundays they had other works, such as cutting wood or grass or maintaining the *Sahebs*' houses and yards. This was known as *corvée*.

"Most sugar camps lacked basic amenities, such as water. Every day, women had to make at least five trips to fetch water from the river or the well in order to meet the needs of the family."

Female Arrival Figures

Women were marginalised in the indenture system. Between 1834 and 1924, around 451,786 Indians had landed in Mauritius.

---

* Mahen Utchanah, former Chairman of AGTF. In a Foreword to "A Unique Place in Time and Space—A Pictorial Presentation of the Aapravasi Ghat World Heritage Site and the Indenture Experience in Mauritius (1834-2014) published (in the context of the 180th Anniversary of Indentured Labour in Mauritius) in 2014."

But fewer women were part of this movement. It is estimated that around 1829 to 1910, some more than 100,760 Indian women immigrants came to Mauritius, amounting to some 22 per cent of total number of immigrants. They were mostly young women and girls ranging between 10 and 50 years of age. The British authorities then had to impose a quota system for each arriving ship from India for an adequate proportion of women.

Some Profiles of Women *Girmitiyas*

Mawracheea came at age 20 in 1838 from Bihar, i.e. four years after the system of indentureship was put into place. She worked as labourer at Belle Mare Sugar Estate in the district of Flacq. Later, after her contract expired, she worked as a domestic servant. She passed away in 1909 at the age of 91.

Between 1834 and 1874 around 89,812 women indentures landed in Mauritius, mostly from Bihar. As from 1850s, with the change in laws and regulations, a large number of female immigrants arrived with their husbands. The Protector of Immigrants, who was appointed to regulate and look after the welfare of the *Girmitiyas* had the added "responsibility of confirming marriage of young Indian immigrant couples. In 1850, nearly 640 marriages of Indian immigrant couples were contracted, as confirmed by the Immigration Office in Port Louis.

In 1959, this figure rose to 6,098 marriages of Indian indentures. In 1860, some 199 marriages were celebrated by Indian immigrant couples which was recorded by the Civil Status Office and at the Immigration Office.

"Marriage certificates were issued to married Indian couples" when they landed at the Immigration Depot "in the presence of the Protector of Immigrants and two witnesses." *"We, the above described Indians hereby declare that we have been married to each other according to the forms and Ceremonies of our creeds and that the children above named are the lawful issue of such marriages."* They apposed their thumb marks above the paragraph.

There was decidedly a net increase of females which amounted to 46.4 per cent in 1858 and reached the higher number of 48.8 per cent by 1859 (*Protector of Indian Immigrants Report 1859*). There was therefore a stabilisation of the Indian society as early as 1850s, i.e. hardly 16 years after indentureship from India was introduced and after it being stopped for some years, from 1838 to 1842. It resumed in 1843 again after promises of better treatment of *Girmitiyas* by the sugar barons.

Profile of a Woman Indenture

From Bihar, immigrant Lolytah came to Mauritius at the age of 18, with her husband Ramdhun, in 1851. This was when laws were passed to encourage immigrants to come along with their wives and families. She lived with her husband on La Louise Sugar Estate in the district of Flacq. In 1866, after the death of her husband, she engaged herself in the '*petite bande*' on the same sugar estate where her husband worked. She slowly economised her meagre salary and bought a small plot of land in Bel Air Rivière Sèche village, where she lived till her death in 1907 (MGI Indian Immigration Archives).

The women indentures made a significant and long standing contribution to the making of Mauritius. They also consolidated the stabilisation of its society in general, providing a well–nurtured matrix for its societal development through the fabric of human values, customs, traditions, folk lore and religious observations and beliefs. Thus arose the networking of the *Geet Gawai* groups.

Profiles of Immigrant Mootree

Immigrant Mootree came to Mauritius at the age of three in 1844, with her father Kheeroodhur. She was married in 1854 as a child to the immigrant Teerbhoohan. After her husband's death, she received a non–marriage certificate from the Immigration Depot. She worked first as a labourer and later made rapid social mobility to become "a small property owner". (MGI Indian Immigration Archives).*

Conditions Were Harsh

The sugar industry began to develop as from 1825, when customs tariff was abolished. The surface under sugarcane

* Also from A Unique Place in Time and Space—A Pictorial Presentation of the Aapravasi Ghat World Heritage Site and the Indenture Experience in Mauritius (1834–2014) AGTF 2014.

doubled within five years. In 1850, Mauritius became the most productive sugar colony in the British Empire. It was the backbone of the economy. With the need for labour, women *Girmitiyas* were encouraged. Thus landed in Mauritius together with them the Bhojpuri folk songs—*Geet Gawai.*

Working and living conditions of indentured workers were harsh. They were maltreated. Together with this hard work was added other hurdles, such as irregularity in payment of wages, inadequate rations, poor housing conditions, lack of proper medical facilities and treatment. On top of that, if they missed work due to illness or other reasons, they were severely punished or if they left the sugar estates without permission, they were huddled like cattle and sent to the Vagrant Depot.

There was high mortality rate. As a result, hardly five years after the *Girmitiya* system had started, the British Government in India put a ban on it. The planters in Mauritius were very disturbed at the fact that they would be ruined. With the assurance of a more humane treatment to Indian workers, indenture from India resumed with the appointment of a Protector of Immigrants in 1842.

□

3

The Different Forms of Bhojpuri Language

Language spoken by the indentured immigrants included a large variety of dialects. "The language of the great majority of Indian immigrants arriving since 1834 was Bhojpuri," says L.P. Ramyead in his book, *The Establishment and Cultivation of Modern Standard Hindi in Mauritius, 1985*. He continues, "There must have been small dialectal differences in the Bhojpuri spoken by Biharis hailing from different parts of the vast province of Bihar and somewhat wider differences in the Bhojpuri of the Biharis and that of the immigrants originating from the north-western provinces." These included Maithili, Awadhi, Madhesi, Magahi, Bengali, Santali and Hindustani (Hindi and Urdu).

A common Bhojpuri emerged out of all these variations as early as 1900 and it went on integrating Bhojpuriased versions of Creole words as new immigrants came and were absorbed in the society while descendants of older immigrants lost touch with the original dialect back home. Now these are reflected, in the new songs created based on the old patterns. But quite a good number of traditional marriage songs are kept intact as found in different parts of Bihar and eastern Uttar Pradesh, such as *Gai ke Gobar, Nimiya ke Daar, Kehi Jala Hazipur*.

As mentioned earlier, the main centres of recruitments were from the Calcutta hinterland and Benaras city. Some were from western Uttar Pradesh also as far up the Gangetic Plains in Lucknow and even Allahabad. Some even came as far up the Ganges plains as Meerut . Most were coming from the districts found to the east of Benaras, e.g. Arrah, Midnapur, Burdwan, Cuttack, now in Orissa. Other regions of recruitment were Azamgarh, Gorakhpur, Jaunpur, Ghazipur, Muzaffarpur, Shahabad, including Chhapra, Bhojpur, Patna, Gaya, along with Hazaribagh, now in Jharkhand.

Therefore the *Geet Gawai* singers who are settled in Mauritius, came from a broad geographical background with many components of dialects particular to those regions.

It is amazing then how being thrown in each other's company, a single Bhojpuri was forged with a single system of Bhojpuri folk singing, known as *Geet Gawai.* For no matter where one goes in Mauritius, *Geet Gawai* is deeply embedded. There is bound to be *tolis* of Bhojpuri folk songs.

Some districts of Uttar Pradesh and Bihar are classified as pure Bhojpuri regions:

(1) Ballia, Ghazipur, Bhojpur, Rohtas fall into this category.

(2) Western Bhojpuri is spoken in Jaunpur, Azamgarh, Varanasi (Benares) and Mirzapur.

(3) Nagpuria, another form of Bhojpuri spoken in Chhota Nagpur province of Bihar, from where the earliest *Girmitiyas* (indentured) hailed.

(4) Madhesia is a form of Bhojpuri spoken between the Maithili regions and the Bhojpuri region of Gorakhpur (middle-land Bhojpuri).

(5) Tharu is a form of Bhojpuri spoken in the Terai region of the Himalayas, stretching from northern U.P. to Champaran and covering the hill slopes of Nepal.

The Dhangars or Oraons, the tribal people of Ramnagar and Bagaha in Champaran, use the Nagpuria dialect of Bhojpuri in the course of their conversation with non-Dhangar people. The Ganges which is so indelibly ingrained in the souls and veins of the *Girmitiyas* forms the northern boundary of the district separating it from Ghazipur, Ballia and Saran. The Sone river, which cuts across the heartland of the Bhojpuri belt, is well known for its *mela* and *Ekadashi* or *Kartik melas.*

Dr. G.A. Grierson writes in the *Linguistic Survey of India,* volume 5, Part 2: "Bhojpuri is the practical language of an energetic race, which is ever ready to accommodate itself to circumstances and which has made its influence felt all over India (and we should add all over the Indian diaspora in the plantation colonies). The Bengali and the Bhojpuri are two of the great civilisers of Hindustan, the former with his pen and the latter with the cudgel."

The *Girmitiyas* came from a vast area of the Gangetic Plain which encompasses several linguistic groups, such as Bhojpuri, Magahi, Maithili, Kashiki (from Benaras region), Tharu and others. At one time, even Bengali was spoken in Mauritius and also Oriya. There was an attempt even to set up the teaching of Bengali in the 1970s. There are some 25,000 Bengali-origin Mauritians, but all these have merged gradually with the dominant language, Bhojpuri, and over the years have come to form a Mauritian Bhojpuri language absorbing all the above-mentioned as well as the different types mentioned herewith.

School Cursus

The introduction of Bhojpuri Language as a teaching/ learning subject in the school curriculum by the Ministry of Education, Tertiary Education, Science & Technology will assure a permanency and rootedness not only to the vehicl e of *Geet Gawai* but also as an important lingua franca and m edium of communication, entertainment and mode of a rich li terature of the island.

□

4

They Came with Their Songs

And so, they came along with their songs. They sang on the sugarcane fields what they remembered from the *deswa*. They pieced together morceaux as co-workers of the *petite bande* in which they were engaged on a verbal contract. In those days of the still forested Mauritius, with habitations far from each other, they sang as they traversed roads or footpaths and forests or through tall sugarcane fields. They would sing on their poor estate camps in their small thatched huts, to lull a baby to sleep, to make an *arak* (अर्क) to the *sooraj devta*, or a *gorlage* to the *mahabir sami* Veer Hanuman, who would protect them from monstrous difficulties or the village *Kalimayi (Maha Kalimayi)* which was often a piece of stone streaked with *sindur* or the *'sato debis'*, seven protective sisters, who would give them the strength to face the untold and unseen and unknown fortitudes. Songs would express their feelings of desolation, would be their solace and constant companions.

Geet Gawai Group Formation

As new immigrants, the enlarged part of the family migration, poured into Mauritius always on demand from the ravenous planters, more stabilising rites and rituals and village folk songs would be in a process of engaging the socio-cultural fabric of the society.

Occasions of marriage on a sugar estate camp or newly created Indian villages by the free immigrants, known as Old Immigrants after termination of their contracts in the outskirts of the sugar estates, would call for women who knew or remembered from memory the ceremonial songs or *sanskar geet*. Thus, little groups would be formed to give impetus and encouragement, for oral traditions are the most preserved legacies of humankind. The songs come out when occasion demands. Thus, one would nudge the other *'Gaw ge', 'gawa sa gé'* (Sing. Do sing you all!) and the bold one with good remembrance capacity would lead the others.

Those Brave Women

Women immigrants were a stabilising force for the labour community. There arose among them entrepreneurs and *sirdarines*. They bound the family together and upheld the time-honoured values and civilisational ethos of the great Bharat Mata they had left behind. They mastered their destinies. They had strength and endurance and the capacity to bear untold hardships, humiliations and oppressions.

Enterprising Women

Female immigration was in fact *"a means of the quality of recruits in the sense that family men were considered more likely to make good and steady labourers, whilst their wives would assure their domestic well-being and produce a future generation of workers."**

□

* Select Documents, Volume 2, Mahatma Gandhi Institute, 1994.

5

Development of Geet Gawai in Mauritius

"The way the indentured recruitment system worked, especially in India, it not only transported workers, but also carried with them the Indian values and culture."

"The notion of Jahaji remained at the heart of their Indian identity."

"In spite of several generations of indentured these workers have maintained their cultural ethos and values, including languages, literature and festivals."

"In many ways, they have presented some of the old cultural practices which are no more prevalent even in India."

...Some of the best examples of this extraordinary preservation are seen in UNESCO's recognition of Aapravasi Ghat, Port Louis as heritage of mankind and Indentured Labour Route Project and preservation of *Geet Gawai* style of Bhojpuri folk in Mauritius as intangible (cultural) heritage."*

As the *Girmitiyas* bought new lands, after the termination of their five-year contract with their respective sugar estates, they constructed their village space based on the model of what they left back home. They thus recreated their customs and traditions, rites and rituals, songs and games.

The Kathaka Samhita, a component of the *Rig Veda* (xii–I) says that eight women whose husbands are alive should feed the priests and sing appropriate songs to the tune of a drum and the

---

* Concept Paper of International Conference on Centenary Commemoration of Abolition of Indentureship, 20–22 April, 2017; At Indira Gandhi National Centre for the Art (IGNCA)—(organised by ARSP, IGNCA and ICCR)

Veena (lute) and four women may also dance.

The modern *Geetharines* use a copper pitcher—the *lotas* which they hit rhythmically with two spoons one in each hand, on the rim of the *lota* and accompanied by a *dholak* and on which they dance the *jhumar*.

Geet Gawai

"Traditional folk music has been defined in several ways: as music transmitted orally, music with unknown composers, or music performed by custom over a long period of time." The term is also derived from the German *volk* that is "people as a whole". Sometimes it is also referred to as *"old songs with no known composers."* Yet another definition says that "of music that has been submitted to an evolutionary process of oral transmission... the fashioning and re-fashioning of the music by the community that give it its folk character."

Folk songs reveal one side of a 'cultural dichotomy' with the other side found in the lower layer of society—culturally and socially stratified societies also known as 'popular cultures'. In short *'folk music is what the people sing'* (Charles Seeger).

The voyage of the *Geet Gawai* across time and space is part and parcel of an extraordinary saga of human tribulation. It symbolises the genius of mankind in the transmission of its thoughts, ideas and emotions as expressions of humanity, not necessarily written, in difficult and challenging situations, such as the immigration and its dynamics. The *Girmitiya* movement or indentured labour movement that originated on 2 November, 1834 in the wake of the abolition of slavery in the nineteenth century expanded right to the beginning of 20th century. It witnessed the setting up of a new cultural fabric based on the original matrix, way back in India, in the case of *Geet Gawai,* in the Bhojpuri belt of the then Presidency of Oudh, Bengal, Bihar and Orissa during the British Raj in India.

Thus the Aapravasi Ghat as the first stepping stone to Mauritius for the incoming *Girmitiyas* is indeed a "unique place in space and time." It is a living shrine of homage "that tells a moving saga of perseverance and courage." "Each of the sixteen steps of this site is witness to the legacy of the heroic architects of modern

Mauritius." "Literature depends mainly on words but makes use of sound, rhythm, form and such like methods."*

"When an individual migrates, there is never a beginning from scratch. The past travels with him in the form of memories, myths, histories and connections...there is a living relationship with it," continues Jasbir Jain. "As indentured or contractual labour, they were to convert the Mauritian forests into gardens with their hands." John de Lingen qualified them as *'cyclops'* for the efforts they made in the attempt."**

The *Geet Gawai* has been successfully preserved in Mauritius over the last 188 years and reflects a remarkable resilience of Bhojpuri as a *Girmitiya* language of culture, communication and as a vehicle of national and international intangible cultural heritage. Like water, soft and vital, it has made its way percolating from the eastern part of India through the port of Calcutta to Mauritius and from Mauritius it has made its way to the intangible cultural heritage of the whole of humanity—astounding journey.

The Mauritius Bhojpuri folk songs—*Geet Gawai* was inscribed on 1 December, 2016 on the UNESCO Representative List of the Intangible Cultural Heritage of Humanity at the 11th session of the UNESCO Intergovernmental Committee for the Safeguarding of the Intangible Cultural Heritage in Addis Ababa, Ethiopia.

Originally a community singing activity, with the inscription at UNESCO, *Geet Gawai* gains in esteem not only as a Mauritian patrimony, but is part of the international cultural heritage of humanity.

With the inscription, the Government of Mauritius has the obligation by law to safeguard the practices and other elements, such as representations, expressions, knowledge and skills associated with the Bhojpuri folk songs—*Geet Gawai*. It is called upon to give a periodical report to the Intergovernmental Committee of UNESCO for the safeguarding of the intangible cultural heritage, *Geet Gawai*.

---

* Introduction to Jasbir Jain in Films, Literature and Culture, Rawat Publications, Institute for Research in Inter-disciplinary Studies, Jaipur, 2017.

** And Came the Indians by Nivriti Seetohul, 1 Nov., 2017, Mauritius Times.

The Indian Indentured Labour System

It is incredible how people from diverse regions, spanning and sprawling over the vast geographical States of Uttar Pradesh, Bihar, Chattisgarh, Jharkhand and parts of Bengal and Orissa brought from 26 districts during a period of 90 years (2 November, 1834–31 May, 1924) could have recreated and preserved over distance and time and kept intact hundreds of songs in oral form of several genres and varieties with centuries of historical background in an alien environment!

The *traversée* from Calcutta port was traumatising. Right from the Bhowanipore Depot, the first depot of Indian indentured labour particularly set up to house the Mauritius-bound immigrating labourers under contract in the 'Great Experiment' in the Calcutta Maidan, they walked across the *maidan* and along the Adi Ganga river or Tolly Nullah to the waiting coolie ships in the middle of the Hoogly river, tributary of the Ganges. It was tough and rough. Yet in this grim voyage into the chasm of the unknown, men and women in particular were able to retain in their collective memories, hundreds of songs that are traceable to vast regions of the eastern Gangetic Plains. A voyage that stripped them of their dignity. But the songs reflect the ability, stamina, force and determination of the *Girmitiyas* to survive and perpetuate what constitute the vitals of their very existence. It is interesting to note how migrants coming in successive waves from thousands of diverse villages over thousands of miles and distributed in over three hundred sugar estate camps over an area of 720 square miles, one as remote from the other, could have got together to form groups and evolve a common singing pattern.

The singing groups could have been family members and neighbours, friends and acquaintances. This evolution is indeed remarkable. What is significant is that the migrants came in different batches and their distribution at the Aapravasi Ghat, then known commonly as the Coolie Ghat and originally known as La Place Immigration or Immigration Square in Port Louis harbour, took them to the remotest estate camps, separated by mountain ranges, rivers and valleys and forest lands.

In my studies of the *Geet Gawai* group of Petit Raffray

Geet Gawai School—women folk singers come from as diverse villages—as from Mahebourg, south of Mauritius, Bambous, west of the island, Medine, Camp de Masque, Camp Ithier in the east and several villages of the north...

During the immigration period, the women came single or married, accompanying their husbands. They lived in barracks, back to back on estate camps *(Hugh Tinker)*. Their origin from 26 districts of varying geographical zones reflect distinctive linguistic traits.* Over the generations, the collective singing at weddings was passed on from generation to generation. But a distinct pattern evolved all over Mauritius to give the *Geet Gawai* a uniqueness unmatched anywhere in the Indian diaspora. Not even to be found in the places of origin, from Bihar and eastern Uttar Pradesh. I cannot say that the songs are only Bhojpuri in origin and style, content and rhythm, for I have heard similar songs in Maithili, Magahi, Awadhi and other sister dialects such as Bajrika and Angika. These merge one with the other and coalesce, though the dialects change. Is it not said in the Gangetic Plains that:

"Kos kos par pani badle la
Char kos par bani!"

How women singers coming from varied districts with distinct villages in the Gangetic Plains, with different linguistic dialects such as Maithli, Awadhi, Magahi, Bhojpuri and others, could have evolved a single pattern of singing that has become so unique to Mauritius, is indeed baffling.

The *Geet Gawai* gradually took shape in Mauritius over the long decades of immigration and post immigration. Women groups got structured into small groups in almost all the villages and urban areas of Mauritius. As the social mobility slowly took place and economic growth became noticeable, people shifted from sugar estates to villages which they recreated, based on the pattern back home and also moved to urban areas. But they took the *Geet Gawai* wherever they went. It became a familiar feature of the cultural space of the whole of Mauritius. The *Geetharines*, the tradition bearers of *Geet Gawai* developed on Mauritian soil the

* The Bhojpuri Traditions of Mauritius and Speak Bhojpuri by Sarita Boodhoo.

melody of life and its ever vibrant and intensive rhythms, which they had known back in their distant villages, left behind. They found a new *mati* to which they would get so attached and which would nurture not only the tradition of verbal form brought from India, but new variants based on the old original ones.

The *Petit Morcellement* of 1860 followed by the *Grand Morcellement* of the 1880's, parcelling of poor arable lands by plantocrats further accelerated this process of social mobility. Though originally the plantocrats parcelled out their waste, unproductive, remote lands, the immigrants and their descendants ever thirsty for land, '*mati*', saved their meagre earnings to buy land. In a few decades, 40 per cent of land owners were of Indian indentured origin. Thus their economy too improved.

Though there has been a culture shock with the shattering break in the life of the *Girmitiyas* uprooted drastically from their soil, *mati* and from centuries of old beliefs, practices and life, they managed nonetheless to implant the same in their new land and created for themselves a new cultural landscape. They retained their way of living and implanted their songs on new land, nourished by the Mauritian environment, sun, climate, air and soil.

The Origin

The *Geet Gawai* originally developed as a pre-wedding tradition of singing *sanskar geets*. But different *sanskar geets* are also sung at different rites and the ceremony of marriage.*

Though *Geet Gawai* retains the originality of the Bhojpuri songs with the Indian root, yet it developed a new Mauritian flavour. Lyrics retain originality but also have been recreated with reference to local scenes, politics and political figures as well as using a mixed Mauritian Bhojpuri and a few Creole words. However, it is remarkable that the beginning songs of the pre-marriage ceremony are all in pure *desi* Bhojpuri. They have been so well preserved in their originality, that many of them are sung till date on both sides of the Indian Ocean. And they retain the original languorous tunes.

---

* Mrs. Chandramani Singh's 'Marriage Songs from Bhojpuri Region', Kitab Mahal, Jaipur, First Edition, 1979.

Immigration

"For the individual migrants, also the journey overseas entailed a momentous time, of change, an embarkation to a new life and one from which the majority would not return".

"Between 1844 and 1857 in the early period of *Girmitiya,* most young people of the age group of 21-25 were recruited."*

But after that date, migrants were encouraged to come with their families both nuclear and extended. In quite a few cases, many a *Girmitiya,* once accustomed to the long travails of sea voyage and becoming familiar with the new way of life in Mauritius, would return to his native village to bring his family or even recruit new labour.**

In this process, a home away from home was recreated and a pattern of the cultural village life with all its values, traditions and customs, village worship and songs, games, food, art forms...were transplanted to Mauritius.***

As new bondings developed, the leisure of these migrants and their descendants entailed the recitation of *Ramayana* verses, staging of *Indrasabhas* (street plays) and *Ram Leelas* and recollecting from memoirs, oral traditions and different types of folk songs especially.

From among the vast amount of folk songs and folk tales from such a huge geographical space as the Bengal, Oudh, Bihar, Orissa Presidency, a new oral form developed in Mauritius which obtains different genres. Over the years some were lost, such as the *Alha Uddal*. The *birha* songs need to be revived. However, a good number were retained among which are: festive songs such as *holi, godna* song (tattooing), *jantsar* songs (crushing of grains on hand-driven *djanta,* the mill-stone), *janeo (thread-giving ceremony or upanayana),* birth-songs (*lalnas, sohar*), *harparawri* (or rain-songs).

It is from this whole gamut of collective memories that the *Geet Gawai* emerged as the principal heritage oral tradition in Mauritius. This must have been due to the entrenched attachment

---

* P11, MGI Archives.

** Marina Carter, 2000.

*** Sarita Boodhoo, 1999.

to and practice of singing songs at marriage times.[*] As the new immigrants married their children, they called upon elderly family members and neighbours to sing. Younger women or children picked up the tradition as they accompanied the elders to the *Geet Gawai.*

And thus developed one of the most visible and audible forms of oral Bhojpuri singing accompanying the different marriage rites, rituals and customs in Mauritius. They became also the most forceful and visible form of feminine representation and expression. Despite themselves. The *Geet Gawai* session was in fact exclusively feminine. No man dared to cross the boundary. Without knowing, the *dadis* and *nanis* of yore created a strong circuit of camaraderie and knitted bondings where the elders' rule prevailed and guided the younger ones. They practised within the four walls of the village thatched huts with cowdung *lipai* floors and walls. From these small beginnings developed the groups of women who perpetuated and kept alive the numerous genres of Bhojpuri oral songs. But principally marriage songs became more embedded in Mauritius.

Till the 1970s, wedding songs were sung prior to the actual wedding ceremony for several days continuously over a week. They were known as *aath mangras (*eight days auspiciousness*), sat (*seven*) mangras* or *teen (3) mangras. Mangra is* from *mangalachar,* initial benedictory recitations or songs marking the commencement of a ceremony.[**] Eventually, with modernity and new economic demands, lifestyles changed. Time factor claiming leisures—the custom dwindled to only one day of singing pre-wedding songs, which is performed normally on Friday nights as the Saturday is reserved for *tilak* and *haldi* ceremonies and the main nuptial rites are generally perfomed on Sundays. This has been as practical as the weekend is convenient for preparation and the *pandits* do match their horoscopes too to suit. Actually the practice of holding marriages at night changed with the *World Wars* when night curfews were imposed and compelled the Indians to celebrate the marriages during daytime. As weekends

* Chandramani Singh: Marriage Songs from Bhojpuri Region, Kitab Mahal, Jaipur, First Edition, 1979.

** Allied Chambers, India, S.S. Parikh, Ed., 1993.

were normally holidays, it best suited one and all.

Camaraderie among the women singing the marriage songs developed. In these gatherings, they cracked jokes, discussed the village happenings and other family gossips in a hushed low voice in between the songs when they decided to take a pause. Amazing is the energy that emerged and the vibrations created. Old ladies used to show their '*kala*' in *jhumar* dancing, while singing. Men were not allowed in these sessions but sometimes young boys deemed innocent and harmless in a purely feminine world, would sit on the '*machan*' and watch and absorb the scenes. These young boys, grown up, developed a strong affinity with *Geet Gawai* and sing at the weddings too. But the male voices do not carry the same ethos, melody and sentiments as female voices do. The songs and dances would last till the early hours of the morning. Incredible, the spirit they had! Although they worked for long hours in the sugarcane fields and also tended their cows, goats and family which was numerous, went to fetch water from the river over long distances or firewood from the jungle for cooking, still they had the energy to sing and dance vigorously the whole night, playing the *dholak* whose beats excited the women to swing and swirl their hips – '*kamardolawa*' with great force and energy wearing their many layered *Lahenga* studded with folds and folds of laces that would put to shame even the modern *'misses'* and fashion designers!–to the general mirth and hilarity which would work up to a crescendo.

The *Geetharines* are definitely a non-elite group. But they have now found a place of honour and made a niche for themselves even in the elite society.

The Songs Speak

In the early days, the singing was carried out on estate camps. But later with the creation of villages by the Old Immigrants, the singing groups moved from one village to another. This was all on foot. There were few houses and they had to venture in the dark. They kept singing all the way and implored the village deity, the *kalimayis* to protect them.

In today's Mauritius transportation is provided by hosting families.

Early *Girmitiyas*

The conditions in which the early *girmitiyas* were living were harsh and repressive. On top of that in the early phase of indentureship, few women were recruited. Women recruits were less than 5 per cent before 1843. Because the planters wanted above all 'able-bodied men to till the soil'* But there were complaints from single male *girmitiyas* who found life unbearable without a family life. Others were compelled to marry non-Indians. Some even committed suicide due to the hard conditions of life, loneliness and lack of a suitable stable domestic family life. In 1855, Lord John Russell who served as Prime Minister of UK as from 1846 but also served as Secretary of State for Colonies in 1855, even addressed a warning through a despatch to the authorities in Mauritius and the Caribbean Countries that the British government would stop Indian emigration unless provisions were made to recruit a good number of women (Carter : 88). The result was that by 1850s women recruits exceeded 40 per cent - 50 per cent of the male recruits at times. Bonuses were given to encourage family migration. Thus a congenial family life started to be built which facilitated and encouraged all social norms, customs and traditions to be practised. The authorities in Mauritius realised the advantages of a stable family immigration early. They proposed that "*natives of India should have...the grant of a Bonus when they arrive with their own families and others from the same village (ensuring) in this manner regular settlers and a great saving to the Community.*"** Over the years extended members of families which included grand-parents, aunts, uncles and in-laws could be noted on the register at Immigration Office. This ensured a balanced life of the Indian population in Mauritius.

The repressive conditions of work on the sugar estates, the prying eyes of *sirdars* and the planters were another menace to the safety and protection of women of the labourer's family. Many a story is told about the new bride being taken away to the Estate Mansion on demand by the *'saheb'*. It has led to many tragedies

---

* Across the Kala Pani– The Bihari Presence in Mauritius– Marina Carter 2000: 88.

** Across the Kala Pani– The Bihari Presence in Mauritius– Marina Carter 2000: 88.

and woes. Yet the reconstruction of a stable family and socio-cultural life prevailed as time went on.

Even when a married couple came to Mauritius from the Calcutta port having contracted a union validated by Hindu rites, rituals and customs they were subjected to a lot of insecurities on the estate camps. "*Sirdars*, planters and overseers posed a formidable threat to a man's control over his wife."* Men were punished and removed to prison as a mere pretext to separate them from their wives. The lone women were left vulnerable and exposed to the menacing advances and exploitation of the malignant *sirdars*, overseers and planters. Sexual harassment has been a bane of mankind. Not that it has diminished. But on the dense sugarcane fields and isolated estate camps, these were more menacing.

There was outside pressure on the sugar estates and pressure at home too. The work was demanding and backbreaking. Therefore the society of 1800 and 1900 in which these tradition bearers and *girmitiya* women lived were not an enviable environment. Besides the dominance, oppression, suppression prevailing outside at work, the women had little personal freedom within the four walls of their own home. Here they were subjected to the family hierarchy often they were hushed into silence and had no say in decisions. The concept of female suppression has been a subject of studies all over the world. In the context of sugar plantations in the diaspora and with particular reference to Mauritius, it meant the "interlocking complex of lower status" in society in general and in the home sphere.**

The control and dominance at home was and still exists to a lesser degree today despite democratisation and the International Women's movement set up by UNESCO in 1975 and other feminist groups. This was another hurdle faced by the *girmitiya* women and *Geetharines.* And in those dark days of despair, life must have meant little or no freedom at all for the toiling women. Education

---

* Across the Kala Pani– The Bihari Presence in Mauritius– Marina Carter 2000: 92 and Colonial Despatches.

** The Nature and Causes of Female Suppression by Abigail Stewart and David G. Winter University of Chicago Press Journals Signs Vol 2 No. 3 (spring 1977) pp. 531-553

came much later. Still much later came Adult Suffrage in 1948.

Despite all these forms of suppression the *Geet Gawai* prevailed.

The senior ladies being the dominant voices in the group, ruled the roost. The younger ones followed and were apprentices. In the old days they used to wear large lahanga pator and odnis and *'peignoires' (pahanwar)* a loose type of blouse with long sleeves and exposed their jewellery – the *sikris jhumjhumias,* the *chan,* the *guirneas* (guinea coins tied in a black thread around the neck, the *mope* and other *karnphuls* and *jhumkas.* And *peijans* around their feet. The jewellery gave them a sense of pride and fulfillment and of being loved by their *marad.*

The *Geetharines* Brought the Songs in Their DNA

The songs speak. The *Geetharines* brought these songs in their DNA. The songs reveal messages, coded messages to the new bride and bridegroom, how to integrate the family and society. For marriage is a social responsibility. It is the pillar of the society. The *Geet Gawai* serves to bring a bridge between the bride's and bridegroom's bachelorhood and a new rite of passage. These messages are a means to make the passage from one phase of life to another as smooth as possible. And in which not only the family members are involved but the whole extended family and the village community. Such messages are given through these melodious songs. So many of these messages are implied. The songs narrate to beautiful tunes and catching melodies the love and romance of Shiv and Parvati, and how to adjust in difficult situations such as in the *'Purain Pata Par Suteli Gaura Dei'* a famous Mahadeo song shared till this date by both sides of the Indian Ocean. In this song Shiva is found by Gaura Dei to have married another woman who is no other but Gaura's own sister!

It only is a reflection of situations that may crop up later on in the marriage and the song shows a way of coping with it.

The bride is entering a new rite of passage. New situational developments are bound to take place in the new couple's life. Nothing is static. People change. How are they going to cope with these growing changes in their own personalities? How are they to integrate a joint family system? So the message is passed on through jokes, anecdotes in a soft tenderly manner through songs sung collectively. In the songs, question is asked where the bride is going to. What type of adjustments she has to make? Therefore the songs reveal a whole new world, a pedagogy which cannot be obtained through books or from lectures and workshops. So the songs speak strongly. The messages are clear and strong which may not be obtained elsewhere.

The amorous and catching tunes, the group dynamism, the teasing and togetherness stitch together an unseen thread of life in the bride's and bridegroom's consciousness, and stand as a soft power warning of unforeseen situations that may crop up later in their life.

□

6

Setting up of the Mauritius Bhojpuri Institute

At one time it was being felt that the Bhojpuri folk songs brought by our forefathers and foremothers were dying. That one by one as the elderly custodians of this rich heritage died, it signified the end of a tradition. While this is not totally true yet concern needs to be addressed as many rare genres have disappeared over the years with the dying tradition bearers. That the Government set up the Bhojpuri Speaking Union in 2012 and subsequently the *Geet Gawai* gained recognition by UNESCO in 2016 has given a new ray of hope to the Bhojpuri rich heritage and Bhojpuri language as its vehicle. Still an adequate unit has to be financed to repertories these old songs. And provide a valuable safe repository for these rare Bhojpuri songs as well as conduct an inventory of the existing tradition bearers. My cry has remained unheard in the desert for decades so far.

The Bhojpuri culture itself had been left to languish in the backwaters of Mauritian cultural life for over a century and a half. When in 1982, I set up the Mauritius Bhojpuri Institute to give it a boost, the institutionalisation of Bhojpuri at grass roots level gave it wide scale esteem and recognition. Bhojpuri is now gaining significant attention after a long period of *'laisser pour compte'* in the sub-soil of Mauritian consciousness. It is now slowly coming to its own. With the opening of the Mauritius Bhojpuri Institute, Bhojpuri language and its folk songs gained official recognition and valuation. We conducted hundreds of *Bhojpuri weeks* all over the island to give impetus to Bhojpuri language and its cultural heritage.

This rich colourful and romantic language, the *lingua franca* of a sizeable proportion of the Mauritian nation and the base and feeder of several words and terms utilised in creole, has a rich potential, nurtured by the tears, sweat and blood of the toiling masses amidst tales of woe, untold suffering, oppression and suppression.

Bhojpuri is the voice of the soul of the toiling masses. It has been stifled for over 150 years. It expresses the agonies and pangs of the woe-begone times of *'Corvée'* and back breaking work from sunrise to sunset of the *girmitiyas.* This voice is encapsulated in the rhythmical, soul-stirring, hauntingly compelling Bhojpuri folksongs preserved and sung by our *Geetharines,* the tradition bearers.

We have in Mauritius a rich tradition of not only Bhojpuri folk songs and dance but fables – *kissa kahani*, anecdotes, proverbs and sayings that still need to be given official acknowledgement. There are also other genres of folk singing such as the *Gammat*, in which singers mostly male challenge each other with their musicians in a live interlocking singing duel. The modern *gammat* singers have drawn their compositions largely from the popular *Geet Gawai* songs which they have adapted to musical instruments! It is interesting to note that through a proposal by the Minister of Arts and Cultural Heritage. Honourable Avinash Teeluck, the Cabinet approved on Friday 11 February, 2022, the commemoration of Gammat Event by the Ministry annually to pay homage to a great iconic singer Sona Noyan known as the Gammat King of Mauritius on his death anniversary every 9 February.

Genres such as *birhas, godna,* and *alha uddal* are almost lost. It is to the credit of the *Geetharines*, the venerable tradition bearers who despite great social and economic difficulties and poor living conditions, have without schooling or little schooling and formal education, kept a good number of these genres alive.

The richest collection of songs preserved in the throats of our *Geetharines* from generation to generation are the Bhojpuri marriage songs. These are associated with the pre-wedding wedding and post-wedding rituals and traditions.

At the Mauritius Bhojpuri Institute, we gave encouragement

to a new wave of Bhojpuri singers, such as Kishore Taucoory, Deven Jodhun, Ravin Jairam, Deven Makhan and others. Late Meera Mohun was already established as a fine versatile Hindi and Bhojpuri singer, even before she came to the Mauritius Bhojpuri Institute. It is after the audio cassette of 25 bhojpuri songs produced at a memorable historical ballet of two and a half hours on 19 September, 1982 by the Mauritius Bhojpuri Institute, that Bhojpuri language and its Intangible Cultural Heritage gained significant recognition and appreciation at national level. A remarkable catharsis occurred which led to the setting up of new Bhojpuri groups such as the *Bhojpuri Boys* and *Baja Baje* Groups which again used a number of *Geet Gawai* songs in their new artistic renderings. Thereafter, a new impetus developed.

At the Mahatma Gandhi Institite, Dr. Suchita Ramdin, then Head of Department of Bhojpuri Folklore and Oral Traditions had created history by launching a Long Playing Record the "*Swarna Chakra*" in early 1982 through some dozen of Bhojpuri songs incorporating marriage songs on modern instrumental music. Thereafter these songs were played at every Hindu marriage. The *Geetharines* however were yet to be given due recognition.

□

7

Creation of *Geet Gawai* Schools

The first Bhojpuri Speaking Union *Geet Gawai* School was set up in October 2013 at Petit Raffray. Since there are 52 *Geet Gawai* Schools all over Mauritius

On 27 October, 2013, I undertook to give a boost up to this extraordinary heritage music of Mauritius by opening a *Geet Gawai* School at Petit Raffray. 80 women mostly housewives enrolled with great enthusiasm and interest to learn the traditional Bhojpuri folk singing. The opening of a non-formal school gave the tradition bearers a new status in society and in their own eyes. To date 52 *Geet Gawai* Schools are in operation all over the island under the *Bhojpuri Speaking Union.* The teachers are traditional singers who have learnt the songs by heart from their *dadis, nanis, phouphous (buas)* and others at a young age. They accompanied elders to *Geet Gawai* sessions. They are the *guruwaines* or teachers *par excellence*. The younger women students at the *Geet Gawai Schools,* learn by taking notes. Voluntary classes in value education, Indian Indenture immigration history, Bhojpuri language, music and women empowerment are also given at these *Geet Gawai Schools.* In this, assistance is obtained from the Indian High Commission in Mauritius in providing workshops by vising artists from India. The Social Welfare Centres set up by the Government of Mauritius in all villages are obtained free of charge as venues for the classes.

The *Petit Raffray Geet Gawai* School reflects an incredible community dynamism and networking, ever since its inception on 27 October, 2013. Originally, a meeting of some 13 members at a gathering at Mrs. Heywantee Lochan's (veteran *Geet Gawai* tradition bearer) residence in Goodlands, it crystalized in a non – formal school at the Social Welfare Centre of Petit Raffray village in the north of Mauritius in the district of Rivière du Rempart. I appointed Mrs. Dhundevi (Rita Poonith) Poonuth as Head. of the School approved by the Board of the BSU. She gathered tradition bearers of several villages to register themselves. From 80, the *Geet Gawai* groups have multiplied to thousands of members in the 52 Bhojpuri Speaking Union *Geet Gawai* Schools that have been launched in various places of Mauritius.

There are seven *guruwaines* who teach the songs from memory. The students take down notes and memorize the songs and practise them until they are able to sing without copy and in groups at public performances. The *Geet Gawai* is a group performance. They learn the associated rituals and customs such as practised with *sandhya, mandar puja* and *dharti bandhal* for example. They are also taught the significance behind each ritual and custom and also the meaning of each song and its importance in society. Besides the Director and Chairperson of the Bhojpuri Speaking Union organizes regular skilling, leadership courses to empower the singers and which include themes such as research and history of Indentured Immigration, the origin of Bhojpuri language, literature and culture.

The setting up of the *Geet Gawai Schools* by the Bhojpuri Speaking Union has given a larger non Bhojpuri audience the possibility to enjoy and appreciate *Geet Gawai* taking it outside the sphere of its traditional audience, the family and its members.

"There is a definite commitment in choreographing the Bhojpuri linguistic and cultural heritage as a national patrimony."

The *Geet Gawai* School of Petit Raffray in the North of Mauritius had performed at the 50th National Independence Day Celebrations on 12 March, 2018 to a national audience. It is also regularly called upon to perform at the *Girmitiya Diwas,* Indian Arrival Day on 2 November at Aapravasi Ghat. It is also incorporated in stage theatrical performances. The Bhojpuri Speaking Union organized the first ever stage performance of the *Geet Gawai* on a large scale in collaboration with the Indian High Commission and the Indira Gandhi Centre for Indian Culture on

9th October 2016 in Phoenix at the IGCIC Auditorium even before it was inscribed at UNESCO on 1 December of that same year. The BSU has been conducting annual *Geet Gawai* events regularly to mark the inscription. The *Geetharines* of *Geet Gawai Schools* also gave a performance at the International Women's Day on 8 March, 2020 for the Ministry of Gender Equality and Family Welfare.

The Mauritius Broadcasting Corporation has given much visibility and audibility to the *Geet Gawai* through its dedicated 24 hour Bhojpuri Television Channel which was opened in 2013. Recently a private Radio Station *Radio Plus* has given the *Geet Gawai* a new avenue of audibility and encouraged new groups to perform and participate in its competitions which are broadcast live on the private Radio to a large cosmopolitan listeners. The Bhojpuri Speaking Union Website, YouTube on Internet have also facilitated and popularized the *Geet Gawai* among an internet prone younger generation. Thereby ensuring its revitalization and practice among the youth. However, as said earlier distortion of the original tradition of *Geet Gawai* singing is an ever present menace.

The *Bhojpuri Speaking Union* under the aegis of the Ministry of Arts and Cultural Heritage has moreover envisaged the teachings and performances of *Geet Gawai* in pre-primary, primary, secondary and tertiary levels to ensure transmission to younger generations at both formal and non-formal levels.

Tradition bearers seem to have moved very much away from the marginalized strands of society of yore– Today they very much have a space of their own.

In preserving the *Geet Gawai*, the practitioners have not only perpetuated an intangible cultural heritage of humanity but also contributed to the sustainable development of the country. They have contributed towards the laying of the fabrics of the cultural life of Mauritius, by creating an environment of peace, harmony and solidarity through their heritage music.

□

8

Empowerment: Uniting Hub of Community

Empowerment

It is against such a historical colonial background of total repression and suppression vertically and horizontally, that the emergence of the Bhojpuri *women group singing* should be placed. That the women tradition bearers were called upon to sing at marriages was considered as part of a social custom and tradition. Therefore it had the stamp and approval of society and members of the family. It had been practised for centuries in the native place back home and was being reconstituted in a new space, with difficult societal dislocation.

But it also gave the singing women a space all their own. It was an opportunity to write their own script and narrative silently in their performance, unperceived, and unnoticed by the larger society. It was a *'force de frappe'* that could not be imagined by any, not even the severe male dominance that prevailed.

Here was one moment of respite for these women. Empowerment came to them without their knowing it like the still waters of the floods that overcome the sleeping villages in silence. The word *empowerment* is a term that has come into existence in the last two decades – *'Mahila Sashaktikaran'*, a strong symbolical term came into being since 2014 when Shri Narendra Modiji, Prime Minister of India chose to give women their own rights. But the *Geetharines* were doing it, slowly empowering themselves over almost a century and a half despite being unaware of its power. The group singing was a cementing and binding force which acted as a catharsis for their momentary liberation through *'leisure'* activity – a *semi – religious – social – cultural expression.** Leisure as such hardly existed for them. Throughout those early periods of eight days or five days of continuous evening and late night gatherings and singing among women, they were assimilating a new force, where they forged an indescribable union, a strong bonding and sang and joked and enjoyed among women until the marriage ceremony was over. This tradition was passed on from generation to generation. They took the liberty to do so in their own circle. Here they could tease the male members of the family too. It was approved by society. After their hard days' work in the sugarcane fields, they could relax and express their suppressed feelings, thoughts and emotions, through singing soulfully. In doing so, they were passing on knowledge and skill and the tradition and heritage unknowingly. They selected their songs. The songs were *debi debta geet.* They knew these songs by heart and in what order to sing and why to sing it. The singing itself liberated them. Most of the present day women singers have been either sugarcane field workers or machinists and supervisors in textile and other factories that came up in the rural areas in the 1970s since industrialisation.

The *Geetharines* have gained in respect not only in their own eyes, but in the eyes of their family members, in the local community, society in general and at national and international level. They have forged an identity for themselves since the setting up of the *Geet Gawai Schools* and the recognition gained by UNESCO as an Intangible Cultural Heritage of Humanity.

Self-Supporting Socio-Economic Group

The *Geet Gawai* women, the *Geetharines* have constituted themselves as a self-supporting socio-economic group. The *Geet Gawai* ladies are being empowered to stand on their own feet socially and economically too to contribute better to sustainable development as well as transmitting of knowledge and skill and heritage to younger generation. They are encouraged to be skilled in public speaking and express their views and opinions. They have classes in poetry and writing short stories, slam, street plays,

* 'Leisure' article, Sarita Boodhoo: 1995.

folk performing arts, choreography, dance, as well as are inducted in human value education and coping with modern day problems of society such as drugs, domestic violence and indiscipline among youngsters, thus engaging the youth in commitment towards society. Encouraging respect for elders and preparedness for harmonious living at home and in society also form part of the curriculum. Focus is also laid on integrating and creating awareness about protection of the environment, coping with climate change, promoting cultural tourism, engaging in small and medium industries, such as pottery, flower arrangements, making of '*Chattai*' from '*Vacoas*' plants, reintroduction of kitchen gardens and other knowledge inculcating activities.

They are much sought after to perform at individual family, official and social functions. They also have developed a non-professional catering service, cooking for large gatherings at religious, wedding functions in families. They have developed a veritable non-formal domestic activity, a non-formal Small and Medium Enterprise. This has given them a new identity and self-esteem as well as an added revenue. Formerly as per tradition, when women sang at family ceremonies they were given a token. It was known as *'neg'* and formed part of the tradition. Nowadays they are paid an allowance when called upon to perform as they have to cater for transport as well. They may still get a *neg*, over and above a handsome allowance. *Neg* is given out of a certain affection and joy to the *Geetharines* by the head of the family.

In this space of the *Geetharines*, there was no place for the dominant male member of the family. But jokes were targeted at them too. Nonetheless, jokes and *'pleasanteries'* with sexual overtones were shared in the intimacy of the women circle, the singers, the neighbours and family members. The *'domkach'* custom that takes place when the *baraat* has left home for the bride's place expresses that release of energy through games and teasings and songs, around the bridegroom's mother. The women of the *'Geet Gawai toli'* would have their belly full of laughter and openness which they could not enjoy elsewhere. Women had to cover their head, and not seen to be showing their teeth in public or infront of senior members of the family.

Ka Khi Khi Khi Khi karat Hawa sa? (Women were not to be seen laughing aloud in public. But among themselves, they unleashed their pent up, suppressed feelings. So once all male members had left for the *'barat'* with the *Dulha*, the bridegroom's house environment is usually quiet. To fill the emptiness and waiting for the marriage party to come back with the bride, the women group assembles round the bridegroom's mother and enjoys teasing songs and games.

The *Geet Gawai* As a Uniting Hub of the Community

As the tradition bearers continue to assemble together and the demand keeps growing, more groups are being formed around the cultural manifestations of singing the marriage songs. As a component of the marriage ceremony, *Geet Gawai singing* is deeply rooted and embedded. Marriage itself is a socially binding sacrament and a parental obligation. It is undoubtedly certain therefore that now that *Geet Gawai* is an inscribed intangible cultural heritage of humanity with UNESCO its future existence and practice has a certainty of permanency. As a social platform for family gatherings including extended families, friends, young and old alike, and community at large, *Geet Gawai* continues to exert its impact as a cohesive sound and unifying force through its music and dance and accessories of rituals and customs. It acts as a mobile community hub constantly providing a social platform for family and community interaction. As such it manifests a remarkably forceful living dynamism and acts as a matrix for societal and human psychological connectivity and bonding. It is moreover through this dynamic force constantly being re-energized drawing communities together into a hub, that a cultural bridge is being created locally and abroad especially in the diaspora and mother country i.e. India. However, UNESCO warns of the danger of too much exposure to tourism, modernity and commercialization which tend to distort it.

The Singing Style

The *Geet Gawai* carries a grace and vibrancy that is unique in itself. The graceful manner of singing of the women in chorus is soul-stirring. It creates a *halo* of the music of the sphere. It articulates thoughts, feelings and expressions that exude a remarkable spontaneity. It keeps permanently transmitting the universal values of love, joy, happiness and goodness and sharing tenderness and togetherness. Thereby ensuring viability of family and community ties and helping sustainable and healthy societal development.

On the other hand, the inscription of *Geet Gawai* at UNESCO demands periodical reporting by the State Party, in this case Mauritius, which has a definite obligation towards its maintenance, continuity and safeguarding its intrinsic values, above all ensuring its correct and appropriate transmission to younger generations in formal and non–formal ways. With the evolution of the cultural and social and economic scenes in Mauritius, new groups have emerged, with a new background but who manifest the same definite love for heritage culture. *However the danger of distortion and misrepresentation is an ever potential threat.*

As a regulatory body the National Heritage Fund guided by UNESCO provides certain measures and guidelines towards its continuity and safeguard.

As a central element in the Hindu marriage, *Geet Gawai* ensures viability and visibility. Growing public demand for performances in public on public platforms, have seen to the *Geet Gawai* getting out of the cloistered four wall atmosphere of yore especially after independence and principally with the setting up of the *NGO Mauritius Bhojpuri Institute* in 1982 and creation of a *Department of Bhojpuri Language and Folk Lore and Oral Traditions at the Mahatma Gandhi Institute* in 1982 of which I have written elsewhere.

Singing as a Therapy and Group Dynamism

The *student practitioners* come from several villages. The Petit Raffray *Geet Gawai* School may encompass 20–23 different villages.

At the beginning, women desiring to learn the *Geet Gawai* came as far as a distance of 71 kms from Mahebourg on the South Coast of Mauritius, changing three or four buses at times, to come to the school situated in the north at Petit Raffray, leaving home at 6 a.m. to reach the school by 9.30 a.m. Seeing this earnest desire and enthusiasm, the Bhojpuri Speaking Union took the decision to open more schools to tap upon local *guruwaine* teachers in the vicinity and enroll new students.

Women who were depressed having family problems or having undergone death of a husband or other close relatives and other such tragedies have after coming to the *Geet Gawai* School recovered their joy of living and happiness. It has been like a therapy. The singing itself and ability to focus the mind on the different types of songs, memorizing them and practising them acted as a catharsis and cure.

Being at the *Geet Gawai* School has given the formerly home confined women a social outlet, approved by their family members and respected by society. Performances on the national television and at public national and international events has earned them respectability and recognition. Thus they have gained a new status in public, at home and in society which they did not enjoy before. As part of the *Geet Gawai* School, they have developed a group bonding, a sense of belonging, an earthy connectedness and learnt the value of sharing and camaraderie beyond the confines of family.

Leisure

During the immigration period, there was hardly any leisure in the life of the *girmitias.* They reinvigorated themselves or broke the routine of their "*back – breaking*" work through the singing sessions together with their mothers, mothers–in–law on celebrations such as marriage or birth of a child and other such joyful rites of passage. This gave them an opportunity to socialize, to relax and sing, tease each other, gossip among women. Their singing would end up late in the night with the climax heightened with the hip swinging songs and dance of *jhumar* (circle dance) accompanied rhythmically by the beating of the *dholak* (drum).

As they sing together in an ensemble, the women singers gather a lot of energy from each other. Their stamina, enthusiasm, patience, zeal and ability of memorizing is indeed incredible and unbelievable. They can sing for hours at length and never show a sign of fatigue. They start from around seven in the evening and the session of singing and dancing lasts till two and at times three in the morning. And the next day they are out at work in the fields or in the factories. A surge of captivating and infectious energy wells up in them and seems to pass on to all the others in the group like an electric current. Some of the singing ladies, the *Geetharines*, are above 70 years of age and even above 80 and still have an extraordinary reserve of energy and stamina.

□

9

Women Tradition Bearers Profiles of *Geetharines*

Profiles of some of the *Geetharines*/ *Guruwaines* (Teachers)

The *Geetharines* at the *Geet Gawai School of Petit Raffray* in North Mauritius range from 23 to 84 in age!

We give below the profiles of some of these *guruwaines* or traditional teachers. They are all rural brought up simple ladies with modest background.

- **Mrs. Leela Devi Sookun** (aged 64) of Terre Rouge a village in the North of the country. She was working in a textile factory and was inspired from her women coworkers and colleagues to sing. She deepened her knowledge in *Geet Gawai*, by learning from the elders.
- **Late Mrs. Sacoontalah Foolchand** (aged 70) of Terre Rouge village too learnt the art of *Geet Gawai* since the age of nine from her *Dadi* whom she used to accompany to sing during marriage ceremonies. At the age of 37, feeling quite confident with her repertoire and able to lead a group of her own, she started with her own team of women singing having thoroughly mastered the oral art form.
- **Mrs. Seeta Devi Dany** aged 65, is from Petit Raffray village in the north of Mauritius. She is a national singer and participates in regional and national functions and *Geet Gawai* singing competitions. She is creative and versatile and is adept at *dholak* playing, singing and dancing. Her children are married, some of whom are settled in U.K. and doing well.

- **Mrs. Heymawtee Lochun** is aged 75 to date. She resides in Goodlands. She was initiated in *Geet Gawai* since her tender age following her elders to wedding singing sessions. At the age of 20 she put up a full – fledged *"toli"*, group of women folk singers. Her style of dancing the *jhumar* is graceful. She is simply superb as a tradition bearer.
- **Mrs. Kamlowtee Manik** aged 70, comes from the village of L'Esperance, Piton. She learnt the *Geet Gawai* from the *Geetharines* of her village.
- **Mrs. Biprowsee Champa Lagooni** aged 75, lives on the outskirt of Port Louis, Capital of Mauritius, in the village of Crêve Coeur at the foot of the *Pieter Both* or *Mooria Pahar* mountain. She has a huge repertoire of songs in her memory. She learnt *Geet Gawai* from her grandmother since the age of nine and was always singing these songs while playing with her friends. She knows songs associated with the thread giving ceremony of *Yagyopavitra* known also as *Janeo, Harparawri* (Rain songs to invoke Lord Indra during drought), *Gopal gari* (sweet teasing songs). *Jhumar*, forms part of the genres in her long list.
- **Mrs. Teewantee Bundhoo** aged 60, comes also from the village of Terre Rouge off Port Louis city. She worked as a labourer on sugarcane plantations and learnt *Geet Gawai* from her colleagues at work on the sugarcane fields. She is also adept in cooking large scale food at weddings and other festivals. She later worked in textile factories.

All these *Guruwaines* come every week to the *Geet Gawai* School at Petit Raffray to initiate newcomers.

A tribute is paid to the inestimable contribution of these tradition bearers.

The richest collection of oral songs are preserved in the throats of our tradition bearers from generation to generation.

- **The Head of the *Geet Gawai School* Mrs. Dhundevi Poonuth (Mrs. Rita Poonith)** aged 62 comes from a background where for generations women have been singing in her family. Hailing from the village of Piton in the north, she was married at age of fifteen in the village of Petit Raffray also in the North. She got married while still doing her schooling. She has a family of her own. Her husband late Mr. Suresh Poonuth held a good senior administrative post as a Nursing Cadre in the Sir Seewoosagur Ramgoolam Northern Hospital. This did not prevent Rita from continuing to pursue her singing activities. She also was a voluntary school teacher of Hindi at local Hindi *Baithka – Pathshala.* Her *nani* Mrs. Jasodya Kalidin was known in her native village as *Geetharine* Kalidin. She in turn learnt the *Geet Gawai* songs from her *dadi* who was a *girmitiya* (indentured immigrant). Her *dadi* was always singing while performing her work in the sugarcane fields, or carrying fodder or firewood on her head or fetching water from the ponds *(pokhra)* or the *innar,* village wells. As they had to walk long distances to do these hard chores, she sang on the way and taught these songs to fellow women labourer – workers, to ease the burden. Mrs. Rita Poonith's own mother, Mrs. Sonia Conhye from L'Amaury (North of Mauritius) also learnt these traditional songs from her mother Mrs. Jasodya Kalidin – *Geetharine.* Mrs. Sonia Conhye started work on the sugarcane fields since the tender age of six as a child labour on the '*tabissement*' – establishment or sugar estate together with her mother Mrs. Jasodya Kalidin, until her retirement as a labourer at age of 66. She died in 2009 at the age of 86. She was a respected lady in the village who had imbibed a lot of '*Sanskar*' from her mother, Jasodya Kalidin, who had a huge memory of traditional Bhojpuri songs. Mrs. Rita Poonith is the fifth generation in this lineage. Women from all over the North of the island used to go to her mother's place to learn marriage songs at her feet. Mrs. Rita Poonith accumulated this family heritage which was latent in her. As she grew up among a family of four brothers and sisters, the house was full of mirth and they were always singing with *dholak* and *lota* playing at festive family occasions. One day in 2004 she came across the Hindi weekly Newspaper '*Jan Vani*' which carried a Bhojpuri song:

"Hom bhaile jaap bhaile
Dhumwa akash gaile"

This aroused in her the dormant inheritance of her mother and her *nani.* It created a *déclic* and she started visiting elderly ladies in search of rare Bhojpuri songs. She toured some 35 villages meeting various singing groups of *Geet Gawai.* She came across hundreds of potent *Geet Gawai* performers.

The rare stamina, enthusiasm, patience, zeal and ability of memorizing of these *Geetharines* is indeed amazing.

- **Another testimony of a Geetharine: Mrs. Lilo Mathur from Bambous**

This *Geetharine* comes from Bambous village in the Black River district of western Mauritius. She was born on 24 March 1953. She spent most of her childhood close to her maternal and paternal grandmothers *(dadi and nani)*. They were *Geet Gawai* singers and she used to accompany them wherever they went to perform on wedding occasions. As Mrs. Lilo Mathur was quite well versed in Hindi, she wrote down these songs and learnt them. She was also a Hindi teacher at the local *Hindi Pathshala.* In 1979, she created a group called *Pushpanjali Sanskritik Sangh*. She gradually learnt the *Geet Gawai songs – lalna, sohar, parchawan, haldi songs, sabadh and harparawri.* Her *phouphous* (father's sisters) too helped her. One day the team who was to sing at a pre-wedding ceremony at the village of Vallée des Prêtes did not turn up. She was called upon to replace. Since then she put up her own group of *Geet Gawai* singers. She has brought out several CDs and performed at various national and regional programmes.

In China, *Zhu Zheqin* Cantonese born singer, after her world acclaimed Tibetan inspired albums *Sister Drum* and *Voices from the Sky,* made it her mission to help preserve China's traditional ethnic music. In 2009, she became UNDP ambassador and she travelled through some of China's remotest regions. She took along with her a film crew, a photographer and a writer. In this way, she recorded more than a thousand folk songs. Zhu said: "China today is basically all western things...(Newsweek 29 November, 2010). *"Zhu's lesson that China should draw on its diverse roots "to make sure our cultural transmission does not stop"* should be a bell that rings a warning for Mauritius too".*

Indeed some years back, Prof Helen Myers a renowned American musicologist having worked for 20 years on the Bhojpuri folk songs of the village Felicity in Trinidad and Tobago came to Mauritius to make a comparative note. She interviewed several

---

* *Mauritius Times– 14 October, 2011– Sarita Boodhoo.*

tradition bearers among whom Manty Ramodhin who is from the village Morcellement St André in the North and a *'guruwaine' Geetharine* of the *Geet Gawai School of Petit Raffray.* She brought along with her sophisticated digital recording apparatus and an assistant Shri Umesh Sharma from the Gangetic plains to help her with the wordings and interpretations!

Some *Geetharines* like Tiwantee Bohorun of Cap Malheureux (Northern Coastal region, aged 74, testified to me, that when she would go for *Geet Gawai* sessions, her husband used to shut the door in her face, to prevent her from going. Somehow, she would manage to dodge him and go!

Jamoontee Ganawree of L'Esperance, Piton aged 82, mother of Leela Devi Sookun, *Geetharine* with *Bhojpuri Speaking Union Geet Gawai School* also faced great hurdles when she would go to sing! The house door would be shut and she would have to face the reprimand of the husband. But on the day of the session, she would hide behind the house and when the friends would come, she would join the group in the dark night and surrounded by the sugarcane fields, they would go to sing. They would carry a *hanswa* (sickle) on the shoulder as a precautionary self-defence weapon and carry a *'chirag'* petrol lamp in the hand!

□

10

The Types of Bhojpuri Folk Songs Preserved in Mauritius

Classification

Bhojpuri folk songs can be classified as per **(a) sacraments, (b) seasons, (c) festivals and fasts, (d) work and labour and (e) various unclassified types (*Upadhyaya* 1988: 20)**

In Mauritius one can distinguish songs such as those that

- *Retain the original characteristics of the songs brought by the earlier waves of girmitiyas.*
- *Those songs that have retained the same tune and substance but have taken on local colours having been exposed to other cultures. Mauritius being a multi ethnic and multi-cultural nation. As new waves of immigrants assimilated with the descendants of the old immigrants who had already lost touch with the original customs and traditions, a new Bhojpuri singing pattern developed on the Mauritian soil.*
- *Then a third category of Bhojpuri songs can be discerned: those that have retained the essence but with new lyrics with Mauritian Bhojpuri and blended Bhojpuri tune with creole music or sega.*
- *The fourth category noticeable is that created by new generations of Mauritian tradition bearers who compose their songs in Mauritian Bhojpuri. Nonetheless they do retain the traditional essence.*

In an essay on the music of the folk songs, Bruno Nettl (Coffin 1968:41) says, *"Some singers are creative, they like to improve and elaborate a tune. More frequently, singers are forgetful and delete material from a song."*

Singers may further combine materials from two different songs. A singer may change an existing song and adapt it to other style or other music she has learnt and with which she feels familiar or she would like to experiment and create a new text. This often happens with the *Geet Gawai* ladies in their rendering of traditional Bhojpuri songs.

Now when a tune is passed on from one shore to another over a sea voyage of 30-35 days, over a distance of 5808 Kms (3912 nautical miles) and also with migrants coming in different waves from a wide geographical area encompassing several sister dialects and thousands of villages, backgrounds and having been implanted in a new soil, change is bound to happen.

We must also take into consideration that since the first wave of *girmitiya* immigration, officially recorded as from 2 November, 1834, 188 years in time have elapsed, creating more changes and distortions.

"Thus the folk singers have improvised upon the traditional heritage and created their own repertoire with a Mauritian colouring and flavour, often with some creole words ingrained in it". (*The Bhojpuri Marriage Songs of Mauritius and Their Message*). The Bhojpuri folk songs of Mauritius are a treasure house of life experience and contain symbolic messages. They are an expression of the aesthetics of life. They also relate to societal moods and patterns, beliefs and practices that have been inherited. This is the basis of the very great bonding that prevails in Bhojpuri society. As these songs are sung at specific rites of passage, namely, *vivah sanskar,* birth rites, *namkaran sanskar,* or other public festive occasions and religious celebrations, such as *Divali, Ganga Asnan, Maha Shivaratri,* they give a supportive dimension to the occasions, creating a sense of auspiciousness, cementing further the family ties and highlighting interactions between members of the community. In these cases, they are projected on stage and to a wider audience other than the inner circle of the family. They are further broadcast on the National Television, radio and also available in You Tube. The tradition bearers are seen as carriers and promoters of heritage. They have an important role in taking the ancestral legacy forward and assuring its continuity.

The songs vary in texture and rhythm. The repertoires of the *Geetharines* reflect the innate capacity to innovate while keeping the original essence.

As Mauritius moved from agricultural essentially monocrop sugar based economy to industrial life as from the 1970s and from there into a rapidly evolving modern society with financial services, tourism and digitalised society into an upper middle-income economy and now, in the 21st century, into a higher Income Economy with a globalised outlook, there was a period of transition when it looked as if these songs were being given less importance. The singers too dwindled in esteem being considered *ganwar* – rustic.

However with the efforts of the Mauritius Bhojpuri Institute, and the setting up of the Bhojpuri Speaking Union the *Geet Gawai* gathered a new momentum. With a new life line. With its inscription at UNESCO as an intangible cultural heritage of humanity, it gained further in esteem, visibility and acceptability.

The Types of Songs

The *Geet Gawai* is an intrinsic part of the lives of the practitioners. They breathe and live it. It is rooted in their lives. There is usually a group of ten or twelve women led by a main or lead singer who sets the tone of the whole singing ensemble. She is succeeded by others, who take turn to sing or lead. When they start their singing session, they first make an offering to the *Dharti mata/Mother Earth. "Pehle main sumiron dharti mata ke..."* They touch the floor and ask for the *ashirwaad* (blessings) of *Dharti mata.* They also take the *ashirwaad* of all the elders by touching their feet and then start performing.

The *Geet Gawai* depicts the different stages of life cycle and the rites of passage such as those involving arrival of the baby in the family. The birth, name giving, *mundan sanskar* (tonsure), first food eating of baby, *sohar* songs, *jantsar* and all the songs involved with pre – wedding, wedding and post – wedding rites and rituals and customs at both the bride and bridegroom's place, depict thus a harmonious blend creating an auspiciousness. The women gather in a chamber provided by the lady of the house. Women of the family and neighborhood well dressed in traditional attire, come to join the group or listen. They group themselves in a semicircular style and a space is made in the middle for the *'jhumar'* dance.

The sequence of *Geet Gawai* singing at a wedding entails the *'Lagan Kholna'* or simply *'Lagan Ke Geet'* – The turmeric is brought from the bridegroom's place to the bride's place at the time of the *Tilak* Ceremony in a *bandhawa*. This is a white square cotton material with red floral motifs used in Hindu marriages in Mauritius for generations now since the Immigration period. The raw turmeric from both bride's and bridegroom's are then mixed in a sort of game by minimum of 5 married women. With their end of sari *anchara* or *pallu* (end of sari) they cover their head, they sit on their feet squatting in a semi-circle. They wear vermilion in their mid-hair parting. As they sort out the turmeric pieces and unhusked rice, and *dub* (*durva*) grass women sing songs of *lagan* that is to announce the auspicious coming together of man and woman in a new life. The women apply *sindur* to each other's hair parting and oil as a *'sumangal'* sign of being happily married. It may be a group of five or seven married women who do the *Lagan Kholai.* There is much mirth and rejoicing in the atmosphere. Usually the family sets the tone of the coming wedding ceremony by offering *neota* (invitation to the gods and goddesses, to the Ganges- any river or sea). *Neota geet* is thus sung during the *Geet Gawai* session.

The *lagan kholna* song and its accompanying ritual is followed by:

(1) ***Neota Geet***

(2) ***Sumiran Geet***

(3) ***The Sandhya Songs***

(4) ***The Debi Debta Geet***

(5) ***The Suhag Geet***

(6) ***Mahadeo Songs***

(7) ***The Sukar Geet***

These are the invocation songs preserved from the original songs brought from India and are sung in chorus without the accompaniment of musical instruments.

They are then followed by a whole series of lilting *Jhumar* songs after the *Dholak/Mandar Puja* and *Dharti-Bandhal Geet* accompanied by musical instruments.

(8) ***Dholak Puja or Mandar (Madar) Puja***

(9) ***Jhumar Geet***

The Musical Instruments

In so far as types of musical instruments used are concerned we have to guard it against modernity, over commercialization and overexposure.

Musical Instruments Used

- ***Dholak* – Wood**
- **Copper *Lota* and two spoons**
- ***Chimta* – Brass**
- **Capsule Tops in a wire string**
- ***Lakritaal* – Wood**

The ***genres*** include a large variety of Bhojpuri folk songs which reflect the moods, memories, stories and myths from hoary past such as from the Shiv Purana, the Ramayana and Krishna Leela, the Bhagwatam, and other Puranas as well as songs related to environment and nature, family bonding and jewellery. The instruments that accompany the songs are simple and rudimentary. The *dholak* from India has been retained. It is an Indian drum used for centuries indeed millennia to accompany women in their singing. Household items such as *lota* (copper or brass) container or pitcher, hit with two spoons on the rim to produce rhythmical sound and two pieces of wood known as *lakritaal* fabricated by the women themselves which they hit one against the other to produce a musical sound and rhythmic beats have been adopted. The *Geetharines* also use clapping of hands during the *Jhumar* dances. According to Smt. Padmashri Malini Awasthi, renowned Indian folk artist, on her visit to Mauritius in the India Week in 2015 organised by the Indian High Commission, in the Gangetic plains too, the village folks used to play the *lota* as a musical instrument. On that occasion, she also conducted workshops for the *Geetharines*. In fact in the old days the kitchen utensil *thali* was beaten with the hand to announce the birth of a son!

Mauritian women have been innovative. Since they could not avail of *chimta* or *jhals* they pierced dozens of steel or tin bottle tops which they even paint in different colours and string them together in a circular thin wire and jingle it to produce musical sound. This they shake and thereby produce an extraordinary rhythmic sound. These instruments have been recognized by UNESCO as basic musical instruments to accompany a *Geet Gawai* session. The *Geet Gawai* extends to the early morning sometimes when the cocks crow to announce that dawn is approaching!

Rasas in *Geet Gawai*

The Bhojpuri folk songs of *Geet Gawai* carry a flavour of all the nine ancient Indian *Rasas* originating in the Sanskrit *Natya Shastra*, attributed to Bharat Muni who composed it around 200 BC. But it was the Kashmiri saivite philosopher Abhinavgupta around 950 AD-1020 AD who developed it in drama, songs and other performing arts. The primary goal of the *rasas* is 'to transport' the audience into a parallel reality. That is why the Bhojpuri *Geet Gawai* have a sort of a captivating lingering effect on the listeners as well, like a spell transporting them to another level of reality.

These *rasas* are aesthetic in nature and evoke an emotion or feeling in the *listener 'but which cannot be described.'* These *rasas* are created by *bhav* that is conveyed by the singer/singers. They thus echo a resonance in the heart of the listeners who can then connect instantly to the song with emotion. Each *rasa* is said to have a presiding deity.

The *rasas* convey a sort of an unknown '*taste*', an essence, and '*a different consciousness*'. The *rasas* are enumerated as:

(1) Sringar- Romance; (2) Hasya- Laughter, Mirth; (3) Raudra- Fury (4) Karuna- Compassion, Mercy; (5) Bibhatsana-Disgust, aversion; (6) Bhay- Fear; (7) Veer- Heroism; (8) Adbhut-Wonder, amazement.

The ninth one is *Shant*- Peace or tranquillity, said to have been added by later authors. The Bhojpuri folk songs – *Geet Gawai* are more than a set of songs to amuse or entertain. They can be said to be an invocation to the gods and goddesses, with the appropriate musical sounds to convey these divine resonances and correct emotional accompaniment. That is why the *Geetharines* always insist that *'bhav se chahein la gawe ke'*: one must sing with *bhav*, the right emotional accompaniment.

When the *Geetharines* sing, they sing in chorus, repeating in a drawling style after a lead singer. Their singing is marked by conspicuously full and rich sounds or tones. This style of singing intensifies the *bhav* and the *rasas* add to make the resulting collective singing achieve that *'different consciousness'* which pervades the atmosphere as mentioned in the Natya Shastra or by Abhinavagupta and also in the *Rig Veda* and the *Atharva Veda*. The reinforcement or prolongation of the sounds of the *Geet Gawai* songs create a synchronous vibration in the milieu. This enhanced vibration produced serves to lift the singers and listeners to a '*new reality*', a '*parallel reality*'.

□

11

The Different Genres of Sanskar Geet Associated with Marriage

Sanskar Geet: Origin

It is remarkable to go deep into the hoary past to discover the origin of *sanskar geets* or *Geet Gawai.* They have their origin in the *gathas* of yore sung by *sutas* or folk singers as early as the Rig Vedic period. It is mentioned in the Rig Veda that *gathas* are ritual songs. They serve not only to bring an atmosphere of auspiciousness but also to provide or "conjure" a certain charm, spell at the time of the wedding ceremony to protect the bride and bridegroom.*

It is mentioned in the *Kathaka Samhita* a component of the Rig Veda (xii-1) that eight women whose husbands are alive should feed the priests and sing appropriate songs to the tune of a drum and the *Veena* known as *Vana* in the early Vedic period.** *Manava Grihya Sutra*, an ancient domestic manual says that four women whose husbands are alive should play on the *nadi* (drum).

During the ritual *Indrani Karma,* the rite dedicated to the Goddess Earth, women tradition bearers were enjoined to sing and dance so that the Goddess of Earth who is also the Goddess of fertility would descend and give her blessings to the bride.

"The village people continuously received a smattering of higher knowledge through Puranic tales, songs and dances. The very same cultural ideas provided inspiration to the city gentry... The flow of culture was not from cities to villages, but rather the

---

* Kanya Dan...Sarita Boodhoo 1993.

** Kanya Dan...Sarita Boodhoo 1993.

other way round." Says Acharya Dr. Hazari Prasad Dwivedi in a foreword to Chandramani Singh's book *'Marriage songs from Bhojpuri Region'* He adds: "The extollers of India's culture did not start from the cities to reach its villages, but from villages to the cities. The Indian culture was conserved by unlettered rural saints".

The danger of globalization and modernization towards obliterating "touching expressions of folk life...and preservation of "these precious songs" was felt by Acharya Dr. Hazari Prasad Dwivedi in those early days. He felt they "should be compiled and preserved". This is why UNESCO brought up the 2003 Convention to protect the intangible cultural heritage of humanity. He added "some of our old traditional songs are in danger of being lost in oblivion".*

Bhojpuri Marriage Songs Associated with Different Rites and Rituals

As a compendium of human experience, the *Bhojpuri folk songs* of Mauritius carry a number of highly symbolic messages. They are amorphous in nature, being expressive of a mood, and depict the aesthetics of life. They also seem to reflect the social mores and patterns, the religious beliefs and the ramification of family ties in *Bhojpuri society*. They support the various rituals and customs associated with rites of passage, and highlight the interactions between members of the community. They give credence and support to the folk as tradition - bearers and transmitters of culture.

Among the sixteen sacraments that regulate the life of a Hindu, marriage is one of the most important. These life cycle ceremonies, such as at the birth of a child, the tonsure, the sacred thread ceremony, marriage and death, are accompanied by a number of *Bhojpuri folk songs*. A traditional Hindu marriage is a very elaborate affair, consisting of a vast gamut of ceremonies. In my book *Kanya Dan, The Whys of Hindu Marriage Rituals (1993)*, details of these ceremonies are elaborated upon.

In many ceremonies, especially the preliminaries, large groups of women sing together to the rhythm of *dholak* (two-faced

* Chandramani Singh: Marriage Songs from Bhojpuri Region p. 6, 1979.

drum) and cymbals. In Mauritius, the women use copper pitcher which they hit rhythmically with two spoons. These *Bhojpuri* songs create an auspicious atmosphere around the marriage set-up and the homes of brides and bridegrooms. As the wedding day approaches, the tone heightens and joy lurks in the heart of one and all.

The *Bhojpuri* marriage songs can be classified as those accompanying the pre-wedding, the wedding and the post-wedding rites.

These marriage songs having their origin in the *gathas*, that is, ritual songs that have been propagated by folk singers since the early Vedic period (they are mentioned regularly in the Rig Veda written some 5000 years ago [Upadhyaya, 1975:11]), create an atmosphere of gaiety.

Songs of marriage settlement are known as *barachia* songs (Boodhoo, 1993:135). In Indian societies, marriages are generally settled by parents. The foremost of the procedures of *Bhojpuri* marriage is the selection of a suitable bridegroom by the father of a girl (Padaruth, 1985:34). After he has made the selection, the *barachia* ceremony is held. *Barachia* literally means 'protection of the bridegroom', or, more crudely speaking, the reservation the *'Roka'* of the bridegroom. This initial step reflects the solemn determination of both parties on the consummation of the marriage.

Songs associated with the *tilak* ceremony relate to the betrothal. The formal acceptance of the bridegroom is marked by a ceremony in which the bride's father or brother applies a *tilak*, or red mark, to the forehead of the groom as a mark of acceptance. Women sing joyous songs to mark this event. They describe the ceremony in detail, and mention the various gifts that are brought for the bridegroom by the bride's party. This marks the formal integration of both families.

Dowry Songs

The custom of dowry is no longer practised in Mauritius, though a symbolical token is offered at the *tilak vidhi*.

The following Bhojpuri song implies that *dahej* is expected.

It is a dialogue between the *dadi,* paternal grandmother who teasingly asks the grandson

"Hansi hansi pucchela
Dulha ke dadi
Se nati ka tohra milal dahej"

"Laughingly the dadi asks her grandson what had he received as dahej. To which he replies:

"Marowa mein milal dadi
Kanya kumari
Kohbar mein milal dahej"

"That in the maroh (wedding pavilion) in front of the panch public audience I received the bride and in the privacy of the inner chamber *kohbar I got the dahej (in the intimacy of the family)."*

Once the marriage has been practically settled, both sides start to make hectic preparations which involve many rites and rituals. These are all accompanied by folk songs, always sung by groups of women, usually and the songs are all sung in chorus. These preparations involve the digging of earth to make the Vedi (the sacred ritual space for the wedding ceremony), the preparation of the marriage canopy, and the setting up of the marriage pole where the marriage takes place.

The digging of the earth song is striking:

Outhou outhou matiya ho
Iyari se piyari ho
Tohar bina kaissan biyah
Ehi je matiya ke
Vediya bana weh la
Tohar bina kaisaan biyah

O Earth, arise. Take the yellow colour [when the turmeric paste is applied] as an auspicious sign. How can the marriage take place without your presence? After all, it is with this earth only that the wedding Vedi [the sacred ritual nuptial place] will be made for the nuptial fire. How is the wedding possible without you?

This song shows the importance of getting pure earth for the nuptial ceremonial site. Every offering needs to be of the purest, from the fresh dawn flower, to the virgin bride, the new set of clothes, etc. In the *padhatis,* a commentary of ancient Hindu scriptures, it is mentioned:

"On the ninth, seventh, fifth or third day before marriage in an auspicious moment, with music and dancing, earth should be fetched from a place to the north or east of the house, for growing sprouts, in a pot of clay or a basket of bamboo."

(Pandey, 1987:209)

Sprouts signify fertility, a new life. In Mauritius to this day, a bit of clay is dug out after due rituals have been performed to the accompaniment of music and singing, and is placed in a bamboo basket carried by the bride or bridegroom's sister or paternal aunt. This ceremony is known as the "*matikor* and is accompanied by women singing.

The next ceremony, which involves a good number of women singing, is the *hardi*, or applying-of-turmeric-paste ceremony. Both the bride and bridegroom undergo this ceremony before the marriage bath. Smearing of the bride and bridegroom at their respective homes with an ointment of mustard oil and turmeric root paste is an old Indian tradition that prepares them for the crisis in the life of an individual. And the individual has to be duly prepared to enter this new situation, in this case, the householder's life. Turmeric is health-giving and hygienic, purificatory and beautifying (Pandey, 1987:210). The application of turmeric paste to the limbs and face of the bride and bridegroom at their respective homes, first by the priest, then by the male members of the family, and finally by the female members beginning with the mother, is always accompanied by women singing in chorus to heighten the auspiciousness of the occasion. The utmost care is taken to protect the bride and bridegroom from any impending danger or negative feelings. Only married men and women are allowed to apply the turmeric paste.

Pehli hardi more bipra
Chadhawe la bipra chadhawe lan
Pache sajjan sab log
Awaroo sajjan sab log
Pahle hardi more baba
Chadhawe lan
Pache sajjan sab log
Awaroo sajjan sab log

First of all may the priest apply the turmeric paste, then follow all others. First of all may my father apply the turmeric paste, then follow the others.

The agnates apply the paste first, followed by all the other relatives and friends. The song is repeated according to the relation of the person (to the bride or bridegroom) applying the paste.

Songs are also sung by women singers at the time of the welcoming of the bridegroom and his party by the bride's people or the bride herself. These are known as *Parchawan Geet.*

Prem se aarti outarji bar byahan aye

I discovered two *aartis – parchawan* in Smt. Bhagyawati Devi Makhansingh Gayasingh's book *'Vivah Mangal'* published on 15 September, 1936 by Pandit Gayasingh Khelawonsingh. But she started writing it in 1910 and went on campaigning for the uplift of women till her demise in 1918, almost for 8 years as she has mentioned herself in the Introduction to the book.

Some verses have been forwarded. The song has endured 112 years and is still very popular. I published the current version in *Kanya Dan the Whys of Hindu Marriage Rituals* in 1993.

Parchawan Geet

Mangal Gaan

Gawahou mangal charji
Bar bhyahan aaye
Dalo gale jai malaji
Var bhyahan aaye
Mangal murti, soondar surti
Karjor Namaste souna wahou
Var bhyahan aaye
Soondar thar kapur ki bati
Prem se aarti outarahou
Var bhyahan aaye
Shoubh din shoubh ghadi
Aaj tou lana
Karhou soumangal charji
Var bhyahan aaye
Dekhat Chandra chakor

Sukhi bhaye
Teissé he dulhan aaj ji
Surya samouha kumud
Sakuchani
Dekhat Chandra vikasji
Bar bhyahan aaye
Var dulhan donon howein chiranjiv
Sukh pawahou jag mahiji
Bar bhyahan aaye
Prem se aarti outaro ji
Bar bhyahan aayé

At the giving away of the daughter ceremony known as *Kanya Dan*, women also sing to accompany the solemn ritual. This is known as the Kanya Dan Geet.

Kanya Dan Geet

The *Kanya Dan* ceremony is the most touching and auspicious moment in a Hindu nuptial. The 'gift of the daughter' is no ordinary gift. In the rite of the passage of marriage, the bride is befittingly being handed over by her father to the bridegroom as his '*ardhangini*'. It is a transfer of power. The term '*dan*' should not be taken in the *mundane* meaning of a simple gift. (Kanya Dan, 1993)

"While giving away his daughter, the bride's father mentions certain conditions:

"Dharma charthe cha kame cha
Nati charitvya twa yeyam"
"My daughter, Sir is not to be
By-passed in the attainment of
Health, desire and piety"

(Kanya Dan, 1993)

The following Bhojpuri folk song that women sing accompanying this solemn ceremony is revealing of the state of mind and feeling of the father at the time of Kanya Dan. The father is full of emotions. The song also reveals the fact that at the time child marriage was being practised. The child bride sits on her father's lap (in the song). This song was given to me by Mrs. Manty Ramodhin *geetharine* aged 78 on Thursday 10 March 2022 who sang it over the phone for me.

कन्या दान गीत	**Kanya Dan Geet**	**(Gift of the Daughter Rite of Passage)**
झिरी झिरी नदिया	Jhiri Jhiri Nadiya	The slender stream is Flowing
हो बाबा के बहे	Ho baba ke bahe	O, father's river is
ल सेंवार	La seinwar	Carrying the seinwar (a river grass)
ताही नदिया	Tahi nadiya	In that river
आवा हो	Awa ho	The daughter is
बेटी	Beti	Having her (bridal)
करे ला असनान	Kare la asanan	Bath
असनान करी	Asanan kari	Having taken her
हो बेटी	Ho beti	Bath the daughter
बैठे ला	Baithe la	(bride) sits on
बाबा हो जांग (2)	Baba ho jaang (2)	Father's thigh
जंगिया के बइसल	Jangiya ke baissal	Sitting on father's
हो बेटी	Ho beti	Thigh O daughter
पवित्रा होई गइल	Pavitra hoyi gail	You have blessed me
हांठ ले सिंदूर वा	Hanth le sindurwa	Take the sindur box
हो बेटी	Ho beti	O daughter and
खोईंचा वा पकल	Khoincha wa pakal	place it in the
हो पान	Ho pan	"khoincha" with Blossomed betel Leaves.
सिगुरल सिगुरल	Sigural sigural	The daughter
जंगिया के	Jangiya ke	Clings to her
बइसल हो बेटी	Baissal ho beti	Father, sitting
पवित्रा हो जाई	Pavitra ho jaayi	on his thigh Making him Blessed.

दुनों नइना बहे ला	Dunon naina bahe la	Both my eyes
बेटी नयनवा	Beti nayanwa	are filled
धरे हो लोर	Dhare ho lor	O Daughter with
बाबा देवे ला	Baba dewe la	Tears for I am
कन्या दान	Kanya dan	Performing your Kanya Dan.
अम्मा केंवरिया	Amma keinwariya	Mother is standing
धरले हो थार	Dharle ho thaar	Holding the Door
दूनों नैनन धरे	Dunon nainan dhare	Her two eyes
दूनों लोर	Dunon lor	Brimming with tears
आगे कत हू न देखू	Aage kat hun na dekhu	I will not now see
नेपुर झनझन कार	Nepur (nupur) jhanjhankar	You, nor hear the melodious Sound of your anklets
कत हू न देखी बेटी	Kat hun na dekhi ho beti	Nor will I see
सुरतिया हो तोहर	Suratiya ho tohar	O daughter your face
चुप ही कू चुप अम्मा	Chuphi ku chup Ammna	O Mother do not cry
हो हमार	Ho hamar	Do not cause further delay O mother of mine
पांचल के दियाहल	Panchal ke diyahal	You have given me to
तेहू लेले जाई	Tehu lele jayi	My husband in front of The *panch (*public witness), he is taking Me with him
चुप ही कू चुप अम्मा हो	Chup hi ku chup amma ho	O mother of mine
हमार	Hamar	Be calm and undisturbed
पाँच के दियाहल	Panch ke diyahal	The one who has married
सेहू लेले जाई	sehu lele jayi	me infront of the *panch*
आगे जवन वा	Aage jawanwa	(witness Public) he is taking

रहिया घूमें हो	Rahiya ghumein ho	me with him
अम्मा साथे चलऽ	Amma sathe chala	The mother accompanied
हो जाई	Ho jayi	the *doli* till the road
एक बन गइले	Ek ban gaile	Having crossed one forest
दुही बन हो जाई	Doliya dui ban ho jayi	Having crossed the second
डोलिया उघारी हो	Doliya ughari ho	Forest the bride lifts the veil
देखे भैया चलल	Dekhe bhaiya chalal	of the *doli* (sedan) she sees her
हो आई	Ho jayi	Brother coming along.
भेंट ही गइलन	Bheint hi gailan	The Brother asked the wayfarers
राह के चलल	Raha ke chalal	about the whereabout of
हो जाई	Ho jayi	his sister's *doli.* The wayfarers
एही राहे देख ला	Ehi rahe dekhla	indicated to him- This is the
हो भैया डोली	Ho bhaiya doli	way the *doli* went *O brother.*
चलल हो जाई	Chalal ho jayi	Yes, O brother, we
देख ला लोग	Dekhla log	saw the *doli* going this way
में देखली हो	Mein dekhli ho	
भैया डोली	Bhaiya doli	
चलल हो जाई	Chalal ho jayi	
ओही डोलिया में	Ohi doliya mein	In that *doli*, O brother
हो भैया,	Ho bhaiya	Sits your sister crying,
बहिन तोहे	Bahin tohe	
रोवे तोहर	Rowe tohar	
फेरी जाऊ	Pheri jawou	The sister tells her brother
फेरी जाऊ	Pheri jawou	Go back my brother
भैया हो हमार	Bhaiya ho hamar(2)	Go back O brother of mine(2)

जाई समूझैयऽ	Jayi samujhaiya	Go back home and persuade
अम्मा हो हमार	Amma ho hamar	My mother convince my *dadi*
दादी हो हमार	Dadi ho hamar	(paternal grand-mother)
चाची हो हमार	Chachi ho hamar	Talk to my *chachi* (paternal
अहो जाई	Aho jayi	uncle's wife) O brother go and persuade my
समूझैय	Samoujhaiye	
फुफू हो हमार	Phuphu ho hamar	*Phouphou* (paternal aunt)
अहो जाई	Aho jayi	O please brother go back and explain
समुझैया भौजी	Samujhaiya bhowji	to my *bhowji* (sister-in-law)
हो हमार	Ho hamar	
बहिन हो हमार	Bahin ho hamar	Explain to my *bahine* (sister)
जिन कर पाँच के	Jin kar panch ke	That the one who has married
बियाहल हो जाई	Biyahal ho jayi	me infront of the *panch* (the people)
भैया सेहू लेले जाई	Bhaiya sehu lele jayi	O brother he is now taking me with him
जिन कर दोर बंधल	Jin kar dor bandhal	To whom I tied the knots who put
हो सेंदुर भैया	Ho seindur bhaiya	The *sindur* (vermilion) In my mid hair parting
सेहू लेले हो जाई	Sehu lele ho jayi	He is the one who is taking me

The Lighting of the Sacred Fire: Homa Bhaile

The lighting of the sacred fire around which the bride and groom move four times to make the marriage vow is another important rite also accompanied by women singing. This is followed by the application of the vermilion powder on the bride's mid-hair parting by the bridegroom.

It should be underlined that Hindu ceremony cannot be performed without lighting the fire. The fire is considered as the central witness, and symbolizes the fire of life from the conception of the child to its end, when the body is consumed by fire. As the sacrificial fire is lighted, women sing in chorus:

Homa bhaile jap bhaile
Dhumwa akash gaile
Baba ke dev sab anand bhaile
Aju ghar wa jag bhaile
Sorahi gay ke ghiv howein
Am ke lakariya howein
Amwa ke palawa bipre homa kaile
Aju gharwa jag bhaile

With lighting of the sacrificial fire and the chanting of the sacred mantras [verses], the family gods are pleased as the smoke rises heavenwards. Father's gods and deities are all blissful and pleased, that they have been thus honoured. And they bless the house. The environment is purified and exudes fragrance. The sacrificial fire is lit with purest of clarified butter from the best of cows and the choicest of wood [that is, mango twigs, one of the nine sacred woods]. And the priest uses the mango leaf to offer the oblations. The house is blessed.

Fire also burns the impurities of the ego in man. In the sacrificial fire, the bride and the bridegroom burn all their impurities, and make themselves fit for the responsibilities of a new life.

Another ceremony where women sing songs is the *chumawan* or touching with rice ceremony (Boodhoo, 1993:91). This is performed with the rice held in the performer's hands, with which she touches the bride's or bridegroom's hand, knees and shoulders; the rice is then thrown behind their back. It is done three, five or seven times. Five married women whose husbands are alive perform this ceremony. They are close relatives of the bride or bridegroom. Rice is a sign of fertility. It is auspicious as it is an essential food grain and one of the essential elements in the sixteen modes of offering to the Gods.

Man bhara chumiya amma
Dil bhara chumiya ho
Hriday se diha na ashishji
Man bhara chumiya chachi
Dil bhara chumiya ho
Hriday se diha na ashisji

Do the chumawan [touching with rice], O mother of the bride/bridegroom, with all your heart, and shower your blessings wholeheartedly. Likewise, do the touching with rice ceremony, O aunt [paternal uncle's wife] of bride/bridegroom, and give your wholehearted blessings...

Blessings are showered to ensure that all goes well in the new life of the couple. At every step negative forces are warded off. The ceremony is symbolic of the fact that the bride and bridegroom will never be in need of food, and will always be prosperous. "May all the limbs be healthy and protected and function properly." It is also a sign of affection, as well as suggestive of blessings for fertility.

The post-wedding songs herald the bride's departure for her future home. They are very emotional pathetic refrains that symbolize the separation of the bride from her family and her integration into a new family, where she will raise children of her own. She is enjoined to respect her father-in-law and mother-in-law, and to bear her tribulations with patience and stoically.

After the marriage, the bride's parents give a reception to the bridegroom's party. A sumptuous feast is offered. The food is served on fresh banana leaves. On this occasion, women of the bride's family sing pungent songs known as *garis*

Marriage being an important family and social event, invitations must be handled with great care. They are a very important aspect of marriage preparation, and it is highly essential to invite, among others, (1) the gods and goddesses of the family, (2) the other deities of the shrine, (3) the river Ganges (or any local substitute, sea or lake), (4) the village mother-deity known as *kalimai*, (5) the ancestors, (6) the relatives and friends.

Furthermore, it is equally essential to have both divine and folk witnesses to the marriage ceremonies. The invitation known as *neota* is first given to the family gods and goddesses and the other deities. Marriage is a lifelong engagement, a social responsibility. The integration of the new couple in society needs to be handled properly. Every precaution must be taken to ward off obstacles so that all goes well in the couple's new life.

The invitation song says:

Dharti bhi newanti la
Brahma bhi newanti la
Newti lewe dharti seshanagji

I invite the Mother Earth, I invite the God Brahma [one of the trilogy of the Hindu pantheon], I invite the mother Earth and the serpent God.

A few days before the wedding, a great festive mood pervades the whole household, as mentioned earlier. A joyous atmosphere, nostalgic in essence, hovers over the house of the bride and bridegroom, indescribable in nature. This atmosphere is heightened by women singing. It is a must for the woman of the house to invite personally the womenfolk of the village or locality to the singing session one or two days before the wedding.

If the women from the neighbourhood are not properly invited, they may not attend the singing session. It may be tantamount to slighting. The singing session is known as *Sandhya*, that is, it is derived from the songs sung in the morning or evening. The songs are dedicated to the gods and goddesses who are invoked to attend the nuptials to give their blessings (Singh, 1979:23). After the dinner, the woman of the house and the neighbourhood gather in a room amidst much excitement. They sing several sets of pre-marriage songs.

These simple womenfolk, who do not normally take an active part in politics, and who may be unlettered by western standards, are highly conscious of political developments. Their collective wisdom is an inheritance of a rich cultural history. Ingenious and creative, they create songs that reflect the current moods. Singers even take the names of the politicians of the day.

Jugnauth je bole Vacoas hamar ba
Ham boli la Mahabharat hamar ba
Boodhoo je bole Belle Terre hamar ba
Ham boli la Mahabharat hamar ba

Jugnauth [Sir Aneerood Jugnauth, Prime Minister of Mauritius] says that Vacoas is his [he lives at Vacoas], but we say that Mahabharat [epic ancient scripture] is ours. Boodhoo [former Deputy Prime Minister] says that Belle Terre [his native village] is his, but we say that Mahabharat is ours.

(Boodhoo, 1993:157)

These folk traditions have been handed down from generation to generation intact, or recreated in different variants and tunes, or readapted to Mauritian situations. However, modernity is a threat to the preservation and promotion of these valuable treasures of mankind's cultural heritage, as folk culture takes a back seat in the face of the electronic culture of the mass media.

They symbolize the aesthetic feelings and moods of the folk, their social, political and cultural interactions. They reveal the folk's cultural dimensions and traditional values. They also reflect the various stages of the rites of passage, in this case marriage, and mirror the realities of life.

These marriage folk songs, like other Bhojpuri folk songs, have a lofty literary significance and may be described as hidden culture. They have been inspired from ancient Hindu Scriptures such as the Puranas and Vedas.

These songs are known to be socially carrying a message reflecting the socio political environment of the time. The singers were mostly sugarcane workers. Their lives were woven around the sugar factory, the harsh treatment meted out to them and the suppression that prevailed.

□

12

Explanation of the Tilak Song

This is a rare *tilak* song, given to me by Mrs. Manty Ramodhin of village Morcellement St Andre in the North of the Island.

The *tilak* ceremony marks the officialisation of the betrothal. *Tilak* itself is an ornamental or religious mark that signifies the acceptance of the boy as the bridegroom by the girl's party. It is denoted by a vermilion or sandal mark over the forehead. The *tilak* ceremony symbolises an official given word of honour that the marriage is concretised. *Tilak* symbolises that the boy is ready for marriage.

The *tilak* is applied to the bridegroom's forehead by the girl's brother at a formal ceremony held at the bridegroom's place. It marks the beginning of the wedding ceremony. The bride's party composed mainly of the bride's father, bride's brother, the barber, the Brahman (Priest) and other close relatives and family friends who go to the bridegroom's house to apply the *tilak* on his forehead. *"It is a high form of respect and marks the official acceptance of the bridegroom by the bride's family"*[*]

"In Mauritius the tilak ceremony used to be held one month before the marriage ceremony took place." "At that time only the Brahman and barber (nao) accompanied the main male members of the bride's family."[*] Nowadays it is held closer to the wedding day, most often on the eve.

Many songs are found in Mauritius associated with the *tilak*. The bride's brother honours the bridegroom with the gifts he has brought also known as '*tilak*'. Which signifies the acceptance. These gifts include clothings, fruits, sweets, *thali,*

** Kanya Dan, Sarita Boodhoo, p. 185.

lota, katora set, a garland, flowers and above all *token money*. *Tilak* money used to be negotiated earlier in India and Mauritius. If the bridegroom's party were not satisfied with the '*tilak*' an unending negotiation would be held between the two parties before coming to a final agreement to the satisfaction of both parties. In some cases, the agreement having failed, the bride's party returned and the marriage would be called off. Therefore the *tilak* marks indeed a very determining and crucial step in the concretisation of the marriage. In Mauritius the *tilak* is only a symbolical token sum of coins nowadays. Formerly gold and silver coins were used.

Once accepted, the items mentioned above are first offered to the presiding deities at the *Vedi* or marriage altar before being offered to the *dulha*, while the Brahmans chant *Vedic* mantras and *Geetharines* sing the *tilak* songs. These are known as '*Chadhawas*' offerings. Thus the *tilak* ceremony is known as '*Tilak Chadhawe*'.

In this very rare song of *tilak*, the bride's father assumes the role of Raja Janak and takes the *tilak* accompanied by his priest and his people and musicians to go to the bridegroom's father's place here denoted as Raja Dasruth.

Arriving at the bridegroom's father's place, the bride's father is told by the bridegroom's father that he will not accept the *tilak* as his son here symbolised as Lord Ram (Raja Ramchander) is still not of marriageable age.

But the bridegroom in the song overhears the conversation and tells his father that he is ready to accept the '*tilak*' and the '*luchmee*'– the token money should not be returned. Thereupon the bridegroom's father makes immediate arrangement for the *tilak* ceremony and asks the priest, Brahman and *nao* barber to bring the best of the marriage ceremonial items from Ayodhya such as the *haris*, the pitcher *kalash*, the *pidha*, the lamp all in gold. But the bridegroom tells his father that they are but ordinary mortals and as such a small mango branch would symbolise the *haris*, a copper *kalash* would do, the *pidha* low stool can be made of sandal wood, and an ordinary earthen lamp with four faces would do for the ceremony.

Tilak Songs

Each *tilak* ceremony and offering of clothes, fruits, flowers, garlands and other gifts are accompanied by throaty *tilak* songs which are sung by old ladies of the family and other women of the neighbourhood. They describe all the rituals and different aspects of the ceremonial.

तिलक गीत – Tilak Song

(Song given by Mrs. Manty Ramodhin)

भोजपुरी	Roman Translation	English Translation
कहांवा से आवे ला आजन बाजन अवरू सज्जन सब लोग अवरू जनक राजा ? आपण सज्जन लेले ? हाँथे तिलक लेले आवे ला ?	Kahawa se Awe la aajan Bajan Awarou sajjan sab log Awarou Janak Raja? Apan sajjan lele? Hanth tilak lele Awe la?	Where is the Sound of music coming from? And where are these people coming from? And is coming also Raja Janak Accompanied by his people With "*tilak*" in his hand?
**अटइनी* से पूछे ला *बटोही* (बटइनी) से पूछे अवरू कुइया पनिहारीनू (2) कहाँ बसे दसरथ दुवरिया तिलक लेले जाईब	Attaini se puche la Batohi (battaini) se puche Awarou kuunya Paniharinou (2) Kahan basse Dasruth duwariya Tilak lele Jayib	He is asking this one He is asking the wayfarers He is asking the women pulling Water from the well Where is the dwelling of King Dasruth? I am coming with Tilak (For Raja Ramchandra)
हमरो बतवाऽ ए..... कहाँ बसत दसरथ दुवरिया तिलक लेले जाई हो	Hamro batawah Eh... Kahan basat Dasruth Duwariya Tilak lele jai ho	Show me the way O you travellers Where is Raja Dasruth's dwelling I am coming with Tilak
एक बन जाइये जनईला दुही बने जइये अवरू तीसर बन द्वार में होमा का झंडा हो	Ek ban jaiye janaila Duhi bane jaiye Awarou tissar ban Dwar mein homa ka Jhanda ho	Once You cross one forest, Then you cross a second forest And the third forest Infront of his Dwelling You will find a *homa* flag fluttering

अमवा जे होवे धावत फल इमली झतपति फूलS ताही तरे खरा भैलS जनक राजा हाँथे तिलक अपने सज्जन लेले	Amwa je howe Dhawat phal Imli jhatpati phul Tahi tare Khara bhail Janak Raja Hathe tilak Lele Apne sajjan Lele	Under the fully ladden mango trees And also Tamarind In bloom The Raja Janak Stood thereby With Tilak in his Hand
दसरथ दसरथ पुकारी दसरथ नाहीं बोले ला झार झरोका पर चढ़े बोले राजा दसरथ मोहे बेटा लइका गढ़ेरवा तिलक नाहीं लेवी	Dasruth Dasruth pukari Dasruth nahin bole la Jhar Jharoka par Chadhe bole Raja Dasruth Mohe beta laika Gadherwa Tilak nahin lewi	He calls for Dasruth Dasruth does not reply Dasruth peeps from the Window and says: my son is Yet a child He will not accept the Tilak
चौका चढ़ी बेटा रामचंद्र पिताजी से अरज करे दुवारे लछमिया जानी तू घुमइया हमरो मन वा तिलक तिलक हम लेई	Chowka chadhi Beta Ramchandra Pitaji se Araj kare Duware luchmiya Jani tu ghumaiya Hamro man wa Tilak Tilak ham lei	Raja Ramchandra stands on the platform and pleads With his Father Luchmi has come Don't send her away I am eager to Have the Tilak I will accept the Tilak
बांस वा कटाई दसरथ खंबा वा गढ़इलक बीचे बीचे बेदिया बंधाई रवर ही कटायी के माँडोवा छवाइई बीचे बीचे बेदिया बंधाई हो	Bans wa katayi Dasruth Khanbawa Gadhailak Biche biche Bediya Bandhayi Khar hi Katayi Ke madhowa chawaiyi Biche biche bediya Bandhayi ho	Dasruth had bamboo poles cut To make a *marhoh* In the middle He had a *Vedi* (marriage altar made) He got the *kush* grass for a seat He got the marriage altar-the *Vedi* made

औरु राजा दसरथ ताही चढ़े बइसे राजा रामचंद्र	Auroo Raja Dasruth Tahi chadhe Baisse Raja Ramchander	And Raja Dasruth Climbed the Vedi There is sitting Raja Ramchander
धाव हो नववा धाव हो बीप्र अयोध्या चली जाय एही अयोध्या में सोने के हरीस धाई हरीस लेले आवा हो	Dhawa ho nawwa Dhawa ho Bipra Ayodhya chali jai Ehi Ayodhya mein Sone ke haris Dhayi haris lele Awa	Run O Nao Run O Priest Go to Ayodhya In that same Ayodhya There is a golden "*haris*" Bring that "*haris*"
चौका चढ़ी बैसे राजा रामचंद्र पिता से अरज करे सोने के हरीस वा मानूस वा कहाँ पायी आम के हरीस वा गढ़ाई	Chowka chadhi Baisse Raja Ramchander Pita se araj kare Sone ke haris wa Manus wa Kahan payi Aam ke Haris wa Gadhayi	On the platform Sits Raja Ramchander He begs his father Where will man Get a golden "*haris*"? Let us have A common mango *haris* For the ceremony
धाव हो बीप्र धाव हो दीहली धाई अयोध्या में जायी कलश लेले अवऽ	Dhawa ho Bipra Dhawa ho Dihali Dhayi Ayodhya Mein jayi Kalash lele aawa	O run O Priest Run O Priest Go to Ayodhya And bring a *kalash (ceremonial pitcher)* From there
धाव हो बीप्र धाव हो नववा एही अयोध्या में सोने के दीपक लेले आवा	Dhaw ho Bipra Dhawa ho Nawa Ehi Ayodhya mein Sone ke Deepak Lele awa	Go Priest Go O Barber To Ayodhya Bring the Golden Lamp From there

सोने के दीपक मानूस कहाँ पहिये	Sone ke Deepak Manus kahan Pahiye	Where will man Get a golden lamp?
माटी के दियरा बराओ सोने के दीपक मानूस कहाँ पइहें	Mati ke diyara Barawa Sone ke Deepak Manus kahan Paihein	Let us do with An earthen lamp Where will man Find a Golden Lamp?
कंचन सूता के बाती बनाई सरसो के तेल झलकायी चौमुख दियारा बराई	Kanchan suta Ke bati banayi Sarso ke tel Jhalkayi Chowmukh diyara Barayi	Take the golden cotton wick And the mustard oil And light the Four faced Lamp

Note: Please refer to:

"Puchele attaini battaini Kunya pani bharani ho"

*"पूछेले अटइनी बटइनी कुइयाँ पनिभरनी हो"**

This seems to be a common verse in many songs of the Bhojpuri belt. He asks the dwellers on the outskirts of the village, as well as wayfarers, and the village women filling water from the village well.

There is a great resemblance between these verses from the *tilak* song of Mauritius and the verse given above from the *Sohar* Geet. Here also we see an example of an *onomatopoeia.* The word *Atala* is also a Sanskrit word that means a settlement of butchers.** It may be also that *Attaini/Attaili* is devrived from *Atala*.

□

* From Bhojpuri Sanskar Geet no 51 of Sohar, p. 60: 1977.

** Allied Chambers: Allied Pvt. Ltd. New Delhi.

13

The Bollywood Impact on Bhojpuri Folk Songs and Vice-Versa

Bollywood Impact

The Bollywood too has had its impact on the Bhojpuri songs sung at *Geet Gawai* – In the 1940s and 1950s, *Nadiya ke paar* (1948) was a great Hindi movie starring Dilip Kumar and Kamini Kaushal. All the eight songs of the film became very popular and they were written by Moti 'BA' a great Bhojpuri Scholar from Deoria in Uttar Pradesh. His full name was Motilal Upadhyay. The music composer was Ramchandra Narhar Chitalkar. The songs had the vibrancy of the Bhojpuri language and the film became an instant hit. Since then, every Bollywood film carries at least one Bhojpuri tune based song. The song – *'Dil leke bhaga, daga dege bhaga, kaisse bedardi se, Dil more laga'* was an instant hit and was immediately adopted by the *Geet Gawai* women singing groups of Mauritius. This song still forms part of their repertoire and sung to this day at pre-wedding ceremonies. So powerful has been its hold on the village folk consciousness, it reflects the dynamics of folk songs and in this case the hold of Bhojpuri folk songs on Indian Cinema.

Hindustani Semi Classical Music

Hindustani Semi Classical Music is one of the many forms of art music that have their roots in particular regional cultures. The roots of the classical music of India are found in the Vedic literature of Hinduism and the ancient *Natyashastra*, the classical Sanskrit text on performance arts by Bharat Muni. *Sangita* became a distant genre of art in a form equivalent to contemporary music. The ***Samveda*** composed thousands of years ago are entirely structured to melodic themes. Sections of the ***Rig Veda*** are set to music.

Link with Bhojpuri Folk Music

The Hindustani Semi Classical Music has a great link to the Bhojpuri traditional folk music brought by our forefathers the *Girmitiya* Indentured labourers. The Classical Hindustani Music has several Gharanas. Dr. Nishi Gupta, a PhD in Classical Hindustani Music from Benares Hindu University, conducted workshops in June 2017 for the *Geetharines* on behalf of the Bhojpuri Speaking Union. She showed the deep link between the Hindustani Classical Music to the Bhojpuri traditional folk music. The illustrations she gave were derived from the Benares *Gharanas* and other Bihari *Gharanas*. The Bhojpuri Folk and Semi-Classical Music includes among others:

"Dadra, Chaiti, Kajri, Thumri, Dhamaal, Hori,
Chowtaal, Jhumar, Sohar, Phagwa, Birha, Pachra,
Jatsar, Harparawri, Nirgun, Alha Uddal."

Impact of Bhojpuri Folk Music on Bollywood/Hindi Cinema Music

The Bhojpuri Folk Music has a great impact on Bollywood/ Hindi Film Music. Some Hindi Film Songs influenced by Bhojpuri Folk Music are provided here for the benefit of readers.

1. Baiju Bawra –
   - (a) Dur koi gaye
   - (b) Mohe bhool gaye sawariya
   - (c) Jhoole mein pawan ke
   - (d) Tu ganga ki mauj mein
2. Dabangg – Munni badnaam
3. Bunty aur Bubli – Kajra re
4. Pakeezah – Hamari na maanon sipahiya se pucho ; Inhi logon ne ; Nazariya ki mari ; Thare rahiyo, etc.
5. CID – Boojh mera kya naam re Nadi kinare gaon re
6. Babul – Jaddu bhare nainon mein
7. Nagin – Jadugar Saiyan Chodo Mori Baiya; Mann dole mera tan dole

8. Barsaat – Hawa mein udhta jaaye more lal dupatta
9. Bahar – Saiyyan dil mein aana re
10. Ganga Jamuna – Do hanson ka joda; Nain lad jaihe to manwa kasak hoi be kari; Dhoondo dhoondo re sajna
11. Ganga Maiya Tohe Piyari Charaibo – All songs which are in Bhojpuri language
12. Mere Mehboob – Jaaneman ek nazar dekhle
13. Ratan – Ankhiyaan milake Jiya bharmaa ke
14. Nadiya Ke Paar of Dilip Kumar 1948 – All songs including More Raja ho, Ho gori ho chori kahan chali ho, etc
15. Albela – Shyam dhale khidki tale
16. Madhumati – Zulmi sang aankh ladi; Daya re daya chaidh gaye re paapi bichuaa
17. Kala Pani – Nazar lagi raja tore bangle par
18. Bol Bacchan – Chalao na nainon se ban re
19. Shabnam featuring Dilip Kumar 1949 – Most songs
20. Baghbaan – Holi khele raghuveera
21. Silsila – Rang Barse
22. Milan – Saawan ke mahina, paawan kare shor
23. Guide – Piya to se naina laagi re
24. Bandhan – Bina badra ke bijuria kaise chamke
25. Hum Aapke Hai Kaun – Didi tera dewar deewana

Many Music Directors of the Hindi Cinema have used Bhojpuri folk tunes and impovised upon them.

The Zarina Factor and *Geet Gawai*

In the 1930s and 1940s the phenomena of Hindi cinema had reached the Mauritian shores too. Photos of popular dancers and heroines were sold in the Central Market in Port Louis and they were plastered on the walls of the poor people's huts.

Zarina was one such dancer. Even the historian journalist Pandit Atmaram Vishwanath who was called by Manilal Doctor to be editor of his newspaper '*The Hindustani*' wrote in his book '*Hindu Mauritius*' in 1936 (re edited by Pahlad Ramsurrun in English 2012) that '*somewhere the photos of Zarina are hanging and somewhere that of Sulochana*'.

Not only that, I am told that many local *Geetharines* rose to copy the Hindi cinema dancer Zarina and perform at pre wedding sessions of rich and wealthy Indians such as at the residence of the great Dookhee Ganga Families in Gros Billot, New Grove Mauritius. These local *Geetharines* were themselves known as '*Zarinas*'. "There were several *Zarinas*", Mrs. Narvada Damyantee Jodhun (85 years old) of Petite Riviere told me. During her childhood, she had seen the *Geet Gawai* dancing of one such *Zarina* at the fabulous marriages held in the Ganga family at Gros Billot.

Mrs. Narvada Jodhun hails from the Dookhee Ganga family of New Grove Mr. Hurryduth Krishnanand Sreekeesoon, Mrs. Narvada Jodhun's eldest brother, a former school teacher born in 1936, living at Gros Billot, Rose Belle told me about one *Zarina* who was living in the village and who came to dance in family weddings of the Great Dookhee Ganga.

"Ego nachaniya rahal".
(There was a dancer)
She was beautiful and
A wonderful *Jhumar* dancer.
"Ou ego *Zarina* rahal"

Mrs. Narvada Jodhun and Mr. Hurryduth Sreekeesoon are great grandchildren of the wealthy philanthropic Dookhee Ganga who rose from a poor Immigrant's son to be one of the greatest and most impressive Indian small planters of Mauritius.

□

14

Bhojpuri Folk Songs and Caste References

Another interesting development worth noting is that the *Geet Gawai* singers could be hailing from different caste groups. This has helped to eliminate caste and class barriers, though each one in the group knows to which caste group each one belongs too. And everybody else too is aware in the village of which caste the other belongs. But there is no issue so far as socialising is concerned, singing together, eating together and sharing each other's food too as Chandramani Singh states in her Foreword in her book *'Marriage Songs from Bhojpuri Region'.*

As their voices blended together in one feminine ensemble, caste 'appurtenance' retreated in the background momentarily. As all the singers sat huddled together on gunny bags in the earlier stages and later on mats or *chattai,* nowadays on carpets, rugs and chairs., there was no difference of caste felt. Those unable to sit on the floor would bring along their small wooden *pirhas* and nowadays raffia plastic chairs.

Caste References in the Songs

Some of the Bhojpuri songs contain caste references but nothing pejoratively. It only indicates the particular trade or work being performed as in the following song, sung on the occasion of applying of *haldi paste* (turmeric) on the bride or bridegroom prior to the actual marriage ceremony.

"Koirine koirine tu hu mori rani ho
Kahanwa ke hardi
Uparjan aju ho

Hamro ho Mahadeo/ beti (or beta)
ho atti sukumar/sukumari ho
Sahalo na jala
Hardiya ke jhaak..."

"It is asked in the song: O Cultivator, Koirine, implying the cultivating caste you too are dear to me (my rani) from where have you acquired the hardi because my son (Mahadeo)/ daughter is very tender and soft. He/she may not be able to bear the pungent smell of the hardi mixed with tel (sarso – mustard)."

The *haldi ceremony* entails the availability of turmeric cultivated by the *koirine,* the cultivator. To the turmeric is added oil to make of it a good paste to apply on the body parts of the bride or bridegroom as a purification and embellishment custom.

So the next verse of the *haldi* song makes an appeal to the *telline* (the oil presser)

"Telline, telline, tuhu mori rani ho
Kahanwa ke telwa
Uparjan ho
Humro Mahadeo/beti/beta (according to the situation)
atti sukumar/sukumari
Sahalo na jala
Telwa ke jhak (pungent smell) ..."

"Oh oil presser, you are a darling (my rani) from where have you acquired the oil (pressed from which seed – in this case it used to be mustard (karwa tel). My son Mahadeo /or/ daughter is very soft and tender. He/she may not be able to tolerate the pungent smell of the oil."

In preparation for the Bhojpuri ballet *Parbatia* in 1982, I went to Richelieu a small village in Petite Rivière on the western outskirt of Port Louis. It was on 20 August, 1982 in the evening where a *Geet Gawai* session was being held. I was astounded by the richness and the originality of their songs. The *Petite Rivière* group was unique, in fact each singing group has its own particularity. I got several rare songs from them. One was *Tahi tare Morwa ho Nahai.* Surprisingly this song speaks of a Brahmin boy who obviously has fallen in love with a non Brahmin girl and the song is a complete story of a reply and answer between the boy and the girl which leads to a happy conclusion.

Brahman Chokarwa

ब्राह्मण छोकरवा	Brahman chokarwa	The Brahman Boy
ताही तरे	Tahi(tahi) tare	The peacock sitting
मोर वा हो नहाई (2)	(Chahi tare) Morwa ho nahayi	Under the shade(of a tree) Is having a bath
जेहू तोहर मोरवा	Jehu tohar Morwa	If your peacock can
कैलऽ असनन वा	Kaila asananwa	have a bath under
बूँद वा हो एक	Boondwa ho ek	the shade of a tree You may kindly Give me a drop of water
पनिया पियाय (2)	Paniya piyaye	
ताही तरे मोर वा हो नहाय।	Tahi tare morwa Ho nahayi	The peacock is having a bath under the shade of a tree
कैसे पियय बो में	Kaissey piyaye bo mein	How can I make
पनिया	Paniya	you drink (this) water?
ना जानू जतिया हो तोहर (2)	Na janou jatiya	when I do not know
	Ho tohar	your caste?
हम हू तो होइहे हो	Hum hu to hoyi hein ho	I am a Brahmin boy
ब्राह्मण छोकरवा (2)	Brahman chokarwa (2)	please give me (a handful of water)
बूँद वाहो एक पनिया पियाय।	Boondwa ho ek paniya piyaye	
जब तू हव्वे हो	Jab tuhu howe ho	How do I know you are
ब्राह्मण छोकरवा (2)	Brahman chokarwa	a Brahmin boy?
ना देखू गलवे में जनेव	Na dekhu galawey Mein Janeo	when I do not see the Sacred thread (*janeo*) Around your neck?

नन्ही उमरिया में	Nanhi umariya mein	I lost my parents
माइ बाप हो मर गइल (2)	Mai baap ho margail	at a very young age
केही दाले गलवे	Kehi dale galwey	Who would do
में जनेव (2)	mein janeo	My thread giving ceremony?
जेहू तोहर माईबाप के	Jehu tohar mai baap ke	If I were to rear
गैया चरइबबों (2)	Gaiya chadhai bon	your parents' cows
हसियान हो नइहर वा	Hansihan ho naihar wa	The people of my village
के लोग (2)	ke log	will ridicule (laugh at me) Mock at me
जब तोहर हांसिये	Jab tohar hansiyeh	If the people of your
नइहर वा के लोग वा	Naihar wa ke logwa	Village will ridicule (Make fun of you)
तोहर लेके उर बो में आकास	Tohar leke ourbo mein Aakash	I will take you with me
तोहरो लेके खील बो पताल	Toharo leke khil bo pataal	And fly to heaven
हमर अइबो हो पताल	Hamar aibo ho pataal	And take you even To the nether world

Lagan Geet

लगन गीत

आव–आव सगुनि (2)
आव–आव सगुनि सगुनवा लेले हो आव।
तोहरो जे हो सगुनियाँ सगुनयां होखेला हो बियाह
आव आव हो नववा (2)
आव आव हो नववा महावर लेले हो आव,
आव आव हो नववा (2)
आव आव हो नववा दुबिया लेले आव।
तोहरो जे हो महावर, होखे ला हो बियाह।
तोहरो जे हो दुबिया होखे ला हो बियाह।

आव आव हो कोइरीन धनवाँ लेले आव।
आव आव हो कोइरीन हरदिया लेले आव।
तोहरो जे हो धनवाँ होखे ला हो बियाह।
तोहरो जे हो हरदिया होखे ला हो बियाह।
आव आव हो तमोलिन, आव आव हो तमोलिन
आव आव हो तमोलिन पनवाँ लेले हो आव।
तोहरो जे हो पनवाँ होखे लाहो बियाह।
आव आव हो मालिन फूलवा लेले आव।
तोहरो जे हो फूलवा देखे ला हो बियाह।
तोहरो जे हो हरवा देखे ला हो बियाह।
आव आव हो दुल्हा सेंदूरवा लेले हो आव।
तोहरो जे हो सेंदूरवा होखे ला हो बियाह।
आव आव हो तेलिन तेलवा लेले आव।
आव आव हो तेलिन (2)
तोहरो जे हो तेलवा होखे ला हो बियाह।
आव आव हो लच्छमी (2)
आव आव हो लच्छमी मोहर लेले आव।
तोहरो जे हो मोहरवा होके ला हो बियाह।
आव –आव सातो सोहागिन (2)
आव –आव सातो सोहागिन बैसऽ अंगन मोरिया। खोल हो लगनियाँ।
तोहरो जे हो खोलल लगनिया होखे ला हो बियाह।
आव आव हो बिप्र वेदवा (2)
आव आव हो बिप्र वेदवा लेले आव।
तोहरो जे हो वेदवा के मंत्र होखे ला हो बियाह।*

Roman Transliteration of Lagan Geet by Sarita Boodhoo

Awa- awa *sagooni sagoona*wa lele ho awa.
Tohro je ho *sagoonyan sagoonawan* hokhle la ho biyaah.

---

* पुरखों की जीती जागती परंपरा
(भोजपुरी गीत गवाय)
Purkhon Ki Jiti Jagti Parampara
(Bhojpuri *Geet Gawai*)

–Mrs. Beegaylutchmee Ramloll Luchmun

Awa ho *nowwa (2)*
Awa ho *nowwa mahavar* lele awa,
Awa ho *nowwa (2)*
Awa ho *nowwa doobiya* lele ho awa.
Ho *nowwa doobiya* lele ho awa
Tohro je ho *mahawar*, hokhe la ho biyah.
Tohro je ho *doobiya* hokhe la ho biyah.
Awa awa ho *koirine* dhanawan lele awa.
Awa awa ho *koirine (2)*
Ho *koirine* dhanawan lele awa.
Awa awa ho *Koirine haradiya* lele awa.
Ho *Koirine haradiya* lele awa.
Tohro je ho *dhanawan* hokhe la ho biyah.
Awa awa ho *Koirine (2)*
Tohro je ho *haradiya* hokhe la ho biyah.
Awa awa ho *tamoline (2)*
Ho *tamoline panawan* lele ho awa.
Tohro je ho panawan
Hokhe la ho biyah.
Awa awa ho *Maline* (2)
Awa awa ho *Maline phoolawa* lele ho awa.
Tohro je ho *phoolawa* hokhe la ho biyah.
Tohro je ho *harawa* hokhe la ho biyah.
Awa awa ho *dulha* (2)
Awa awa ho *dulha sindoora* lele ho awa.
Awa awa ho *teline* (2)
Tohro je ho *sindorawa* hokhe la ho biyah.
Awa awa ho *teline telawa* lele awa.
Tohro je ho *telawa* hokhe la ho biyah.
Awa awa ho *luchmee* (2)
Awa awa ho *luchmee mohara* lele ho awa.
Tohro je ho *moharawa* hokhe la ho biyah.
Awa-awa saato *sohagine* (2)
Awa-awa saato *sohagine* baiysa angan moriya khola ho laganiyan.
Tohro je ho kholal *laganiyan* hokhe la ho biyah.
Awa ho *bipra* (2)

Awa ho *bipra vedawa* lele awa.
Tohro je ho *vedawa* ke *mantra* hokhe la ho biyah.

The Lagan Geet

Translation in English & Explanation
(By Dr. Sarita Boodhoo)

This song that accompanies the ceremony known as *Sagun* or *Lagan* marks the auspicious beginning of the marriage ceremony. The *Lagan Kholai* is held at the bride's place. The *Lagan* has been sent by the bridegroom's party. *Saguna* is a Sanskrit word that means "with attributes" or with "qualities". It is a good omen. What augurs well- the auspiciousness!

Come O, *Saguna*,
Bring the good omen.
O thanks to you, O *sagun*
The wedding is being held.
Come O, *nao* (barber)
Bring the *mahavar* (red colour)
Come O, *nao* (barber)
Bring the *doobiya…dub* (*durva* sacred/grass)
O Mahavar (red colour of auspiciousness)
With your colour paste
(the limbs of the bride/bridegroom) hands and feet will be
Embellished/Decorated for the wedding.
Come O *Koirine(cultivator)*
Bring the *dhan* (unhusked rice/paddy)
O *Koirine* bring the *turmeric* and
With your *paddy*, the wedding
Will be celebrated
With your *turmeric* (applied on
Bride's/bridegroom's body).
Come O *tamoline*
(the one who grows betel plants or is a seller of betel)
Bring the betel leaf (*Paan* preparation)
With the *paan*, the ingredient will be
Complete for the wedding.
Come O *gardener*

Bring the flowers
With your flowers, the
Wedding ceremony will be complete
With your flowers (the bride's/bridegroom's
Garland will be made.
Come O *dulha* (bridegroom)
Bring the *Sindorra* (vermilion box)
With your *Sindur* (red powder)
The wedding will be complete.
Come O Oil Presser bring the oil
With your oil (coconut, mustard)
The turmeric paste will be prepared
For the wedding ceremony.
Come O Goddess of Light/ Wealth
Pouring the *mohar*, the golden coins
With your golden coins (for offering)
Will the wedding ceremony be completed
Come O seven married women (*Suhagin*)
Come and sit around and open the
Lagan (sent by the groom)
When you perform the *Lagan Kholai*
(Opening of Lagan),
The wedding will be completed
Come O *Priest*, do bring the *Vedas*
With your *Veda mantras*,
The wedding ceremony will be sanctified.
The *Lagan Kholai* is held at the bride's place.

In this *Lagan* geet references are made to several specific caste groups who are involved in different activities such as the barber, who is to bring the red colour *mahavar* which he will apply on the bridegroom's hands and feet. The barber will also bring the sacred *dub* or *durva* grass with which turmeric paste will be applied. The agriculturalist who grows the rice will bring the unhusked rice for offering and also the turmeric for making the turmeric *(haldi)* paste. The cultivator of betel plants or seller of betel is asked to bring the betel leaves for without betel leaves the *Paan* cannot be made. The gardener is enjoined to bring the flowers with which the bridal *Jaimalas* (garlands) will be made. The Oil Presser is asked to bring the oil to mix with the turmeric paste for application on the bride's and bridegroom's limbs.

But besides these specific caste groups, without whom the wedding ceremony cannot be completed, reference in the song is also made to the *Dulha* himself, the bridegroom, the principle actor–who will bring the *Sindur* (vermilion) in a *sindora* (vermilion box) and from which he will apply the vermilion in the mid hair parting of the bride. The Goddess of Wealth Luxmi too is invited to bring the *Mohar* (gold coins) for offering to the Gods.

And finally the seven married ladies are invited to come and sit on the floor in a circular form with the *lagan* placed in the middle and are requested to open the '*Lagan*' the auspicious rice, turmeric, *dub* and coin 'package' in a '*rumal*' sent by the bridegroom's side. These will be assorted and used in the '*haldi*' ceremony of the bride. The *Lagan* geet is sung while they perform this auspicious custom. Thus several castes are involved and contribute to the success of the marriage ceremony.*

Castes Recorded on the Register of Immigrants

Castes recorded on the Register of Immigrants alighting from the *Nimrod* at the Immigration Depot, Port Louis on 21 January, 1873: As an illustration of castes brought to Mauritius, I am giving for the benefit of readers a study, I made of the passengers travelling by the sailing ship *'Nimrod'* without any hierarchical order. Many of these castes have disappeared or merged in other dominant *'Varnas'* or changed their appelations. as per this table–

---

* पुरखों की जीती जागती परंपरा
(भोजपुरी गीत गवाय)
Purkhon Ki Jiti Jagti Parampara
(Bhojpuri *Geet Gawai*)

–Mrs. Beegaylutchmee Ramloll Luchmun

1. Sonar	26. Kumhar
2. Rajhbur	27. Lohar
3. Brahmin	28. Shur
4. Bhooeea	29. Gosain
5. Brahmi	30 Tailee
6. Ahir	31. Ajoree
7. Jantee	32. Ghuttoa
8. Koyree	33. Jhatwar
9. Malla (Malhah)	34. Kutowar
10. Hajjam	35. Bania
11. Chamar	36. Bhoochar
12. Dosaud	37. Bohelia
13. Pasee	38. Mochee
14. Kahar	39. Mooshar
15. Kanoo	40. Ateet
16. Jally	41. Darjee
17. Koormee	42. Bajdee
18. Gowalla	43. Chuttree
19. Kyrtt/Kaytt	44. Mallee
20. Kaudoo	45. Mateer (Muslim)
21. Rajput	46. Pathan (Muslim)
22. Patona	47. Patua
23. Napith	48. Kundan
24. Fautee	49. Sudgope
25. Brou	50. Kaibutta

For obvious reasons, I have omitted mentioning the names of the indentured immigrants who arrived on board the ***Nimrod***.

□

15

The Haldi Ceremony

The ***haldi*** (***hardi*** in Mauritian Bhojpuri) is the ceremony of applying of turmeric paste on the limbs of the bride and bridegroom at their respective homes prior to the marriage bath. Smearing of the *dulha* and *dulhan* at their respective homes with an ointment of mustard oil and turmeric root paste is an ancient Indian tradition. Marriage is a rite of passage that unfolds a new phase of life for man and woman. "Every rite of passage opens up a crisis in the life of an individual"*

The individual entering a marriage, enters a sort of a social contact. She/He has to be prepared thoroughly to enter this new situation of life, i.e. the householder's life. Turmeric is health – giving and hygienic, purificatory and beautifying.**

The Hardi Songs

Haldi is often pronounced as *hardi* and means turmeric. It takes its name from the colour emitted by the root of the turmeric plant. It is derived from Sanskrit *halad*. The custom of applying a *hardi* paste on different limbs of the body of the bride and bridegroom at their respective places by the married family members and relatives and friends is mentioned in ancient marriage manuals and is known as *haridra lepana.**** It is also mentioned in *Folk Culture and Oral Tradition* by *S.L. Srivastava, p. 98.* As well as by L.P. Vidyarthi and Ganesh Chaubey in *Bihar in Folk Study* p. 228.

---

* Dr. (Mrs.) Sarita Boodhoo, Kanya Dan, the Whys' of Hindu Marriage Rituals, 1993.

** Pandey Rajbali, 1987:210

*** Dr. Rajbali Pandey in Hindu Samskaras, p. 210.

Smearing of the bride and the bridegroom with an ointment from turmeric root paste mixed with mustard oil also known as *ubtan* is an old Indian tradition popular in all Indian states. By virtue of its yellow colour, turmeric stands as a spiritual plant giving a divine glow. Yellow is an auspicious colour.

Hardi is also applied at the time of the *Janeo* or *Upanayana Sanskar* and *moondan* (tonsure) *sanskar* and other *sanskars* as well. The elder ladies of the family and *Geetharines* bring out their *Hardi* songs from their repertoire to accompany the *Hardi* ceremony.

"Pehele haradiya more bipre
Chadhawe lan
Pacche sajan sab log"
"First of all the priest
Applies the hardi,
Followed thereafter
By all others"

"It is the officiating priest who has the honour of applying the *hardi* first of all and the others follow suit, led by the brides'/ bridegroom's father on behalf of the men folk and the bride's/ bridegroom's mother on behalf of the women folk".*

The application of the turmeric paste first by the father and male members of the family and then by the mother followed by the female members of the family is always accompanied by women singing in chorus to lighten the entry into this new phase of life. It also heightens the auspiciousness of the occasion. Even the grower of the turmeric (*Koirine*) plant and the maker of the oil (*telline*) to be applied are enjoined to be careful because the bride or bridegroom are very young, soft and tender (*Sukumar, Sukumari*)

"Koirine koirine tu hu mori rani ho
Kahanwa ke hardi
Uparjan aju ho
Hamro ho Mahadeo/ beti (or beta)
ho atti sukumar/sukumari ho
Sahalo na jala
Hardiya ke jhaak..."

---

* Kanya Dan, Sarita Boodhoo, 1993.

"It is asked in the song: O Cultivator, Koirine, implying the cultivating caste you too are dear to me (my rani) from where have you acquired the hardi because my son (Mahadeo)/ daughter is very tender and soft. He/she may not be able to bear the pungent smell of the hardi mixed with tel (sarso- mustard)."

The *haldi ceremony* entails the availability of turmeric cultivated by the *koirine,* the cultivator. To the turmeric is added oil to make of it a good paste to apply on the body parts of the bride or bridegroom as a purification and embellishment custom.

So the next verse of the *haldi* song makes an appeal to the *telline* (the oil presser)

"Telline, telline, tuhu mori rani ho
Kahanwa ke telwa
Uparjan ho
Humro Mahadeo/beti/beta (according to the situation)
atti sukumar/sukumari
Sahalo na jala"

These 2 *haldi* songs are from *Bhojpuri Sanskar Geet. Edited by Shri Hans Kumar Tiwari and Shri Radha Vallabh Sharma. Published by Bihar Rashtrabhasha Parishad Patna- 1977. (p 202- Songs no 43&44 Hardi Chadhayi)* They reveal a stunning similarity to the *Haldi* songs sung in Mauritius as written above.

भोजपुरी	Roman Script
केई जे हरदी उपराजेला केई बेसाहेला ए ए कवन दुल्हा के सिरवा चढ़ावेला हरदी सोहावन ए	Keyi je hardi uparajela Keyi besahela eh Eh kawan dulha ke sirwa Charhawela Hardi sohawon eh
कोइरीनि हरदी उपराजेले कवन देव बेसाहेले ए ए कवन दुल्हा के सिरवा चढ़ावेले हरदी सोहावन ए	Koirini hardi ouparajele Kawan deo besahe le eh Eh kawan dulha ke Sirwa chadhawele Hardi sohawon eh

भोजपुरी	Roman Translation
1. कोइरिन कोइरिन तुहू मोरे रानी कहंवा के हरदी सुबासओ ना जानी	Koirine koirine tuhu more Rani Kahanwa ke hardi subaswo Na jani
2. तेलिन तेलिन तुहू मोरे रानी कहंवा के तेलवा सुबासओ ना जानी	Teline teline tuhu more Rani Kahanwa ke telwa subaswo Na jani
3. हमरा कवन बाबू बढ़ सुकुवाँर सहलो ना जाला हरदिया के झाँक	Hamara kawan babu badh sukuwanr Sahalo na jala haradiya Ke jhank
4. हमरा कवन बाबू बढ़ सुकुवाँर सहलो ना जाला तेलवा के झाँक।।	Hamara kawan babu badh sukuwanr Sahalo na jala telwa Ke jhank

□

16

Jewellery in Bhojpuri Folk Songs

Jewellery

Jewellery features abundantly in many of the Bhojpuri folk songs in the *geetharine's repertoires.*

"nanad more sone
Ke chidhainya
Accha aacha gahana
Banade bhaiya
Sonara
Pehne la bhowji
Nirekhe la bhaiya"

The song goes on to enumerate the different types of jewellery such as *chan* (worn on the wrists), *phuli* (nose ring), *aierine* (earrings), *har* (necklace), *peijan* (payal).

Throughout the *girmitiya* diaspora it has been noted that the men folk saved their meagre income to buy jewellery for their wives. This provoked envy and also was frowned upon by others outside the community. It was held that the revenue of the country was being wasted.

The love for jewellery by the Indian Indentured women/ wives is known throughout the diaspora. It was looked down upon with envy in the West Indies because of the fabulous sum of money spent on these jewelleries. In Mauritius too, this aspect of the Indian life is mentioned in Governor's Ordinances and Despatches and notaries' deeds also make mention of jewellery left behind as legacy or bequeathed to a bride during marriages during the immigration period.

In 1855, the Indian population had reached 121,000. Indian

women on the estate camps were bestowed with *"more valuable jewels and other ornaments which are with those abandoned creatures, the ruling passion..."* Extract from a letter, written on 5th October, 1855 by the Governor James Macaulay Higginson to the Secretary of State for Colonies, Sir William Molesworth.

Jewellers' Shops

When Nicholas Pike the American Ambassador visited Mauritius in 1868, he made many observations:

"Jewellers' shops abound, from the grand establishment in the *chaussée* (Author's note- today's Chauss*é*e Street in Port- Louis), where you may gratify your taste in French gold and jewels, and lighten your pocket of fabulous sums, to the little rooms, a few feet square, where an Indian works all day mending trinkets for his country women, or boring heels in gold and silver coins, for necklaces for these *same jewel-loving dames.*" (Reference to the most prized *guirneas.*)

"When marriages took place between the children of the new elite of the indentured community – the *sirdars* and small tradesmen – the sums and gifts involved were so costly as to necessitate the drawing up of a legal contract."*

Thus in 1874, a marriage contract was drawn up between Ramessur and Soodale at the notary Maingard's office. The *dulha* was the son of Ramchurn, *Sirdar* from Pamplemousses in North of Mauritius. As for the *dulhin*, Soodale, she was the daughter of Beeroo, the immigrant. She was a child bride. Both of them had been born in India and had come very early, maybe in the 1860s with their migrating parents as part of the scheme of migrating families encouraged by the Mauritian government.

As per the notary contract, Soodale received 45 rings or necklaces of silver and gold worth 100 *piastres.* Besides jewellery, she also received clothes and other goods: 1 cow and 4 goats and a cash sum of 150 *piastres.*

The Sanderson Report of 1910, gives an extract of a Report of Mr. Muir Mackenzie.**

---

* Across the Kalapani– P. 105. 1999.

** Select Documents an Indian Immigration– Mauritius 1834–1926 Volume 3. Mahatma Gandhi Institute 1999.

"On the roads, especially on Sundays and holidays, Indians are to be seen in large numbers... the women well supplied with ornaments."

Love for Jewellery Across the Girmitiya Diaspora

Basdeo Mangru's book *'The Elusive El Dorado – Essays on the Indian Experience in Guyana'* published by the University Press of America Inc, Lanham, Maryland, 2005 clearly indicates how attached to jewellery were the Indian migrants. No wonder then that they feature so often in the Bhojpuri songs of the *Geet Gawai* repertoire. Writes Basdeo Mangru (page 74)." *"The anti – immigrationists also strongly objected to the Indian disposition to melt down silver coins to make jewelry with which they bedecked their wives and children and to their repatriation with small fortunes. The astounding array of jewelry worn generally by Indian women appeared conspicuous indeed. Referring to the gaudy silver jewelry worn by a "beautifully – modeled" Indian woman, a contemporary estimated that "three or four pounds in the weight of sterling silver had been permanently withdrawn from circulation to be beaten and molded for her ornamentation and adornment". Such conspicuous display of apparent wealth and prosperity seemed to infuriate anti-immigrationists who charged that immigration benefited only Indian workers and sugar planters, and that both the introduction and repatriation of Indians impoverished the colony".* If this was true for Guyana, it was true for Mauritius too and for Fiji, Suriname, Trinidad and South Africa.

Guirnea

In Mauritius the *guirnea (guinea)* phenomenon is well documented at the Indian Immigration Museum of the Mahatma Gandhi Institute, so deeply entrenched it is in Mauritian Indian Society.

"The guinea was a former British gold coin which was first minted in 1663 from gold imported from West Africa. It was replaced by the sovereign in 1817. The term guinea persisted though and the old Indian immigrants as well as the new ones saw in it a mark of status. Their wives wearing a whole range of guinea coins around the neck symbolized the possession of wealth

of the husband which gained him a pride of place in the community. The Bhojpurias rushed to the sonar jeweler in Port Louis with their savings to turn them into gold guirnis. The term guirni is a transformation of guinea which the girmitiyas could not pronounce. The term sovereign pronounced souverain in creole came to denote the same." *

Many *jhumar* songs composed in Mauritius talk of the pride of the immigrant's woman possessing a string of *guinea* around her neck out of which she proudly distributes to her grand-children.

"Galé ke guirnea
Gira ta ta giré de
Patli kamariya dola ta
Ta dole de"
The 'guirnea' (guinea) gold coin necklace may fall, let it fall...
Because my slender hip is swinging (with the beat of the drum)
Let it swing...
"Mata Saraswati ke
Pan phul chadhaibo (2)
Aho Saraswati Bhavani
Bich mein pheilawe
Mohar mala
Aho Saraswati Bhavani"

"I offer betel leaves and flowers
To Mother Saraswati
O, Saraswati Bhavani
I also spread infront of you
A garland of gold coins
O Saraswati Bhavani."

□

* The Guirni Necklace: A Tangible Cultural Heritage Dr. Sarita Boodhoo– article in Mauritius Times of 26 May, 2017

17

Family Bonding Relationships in Bhojpuri Songs

In many of the *Bhojpuri* songs references are made to the close bonding and togetherness that prevail in a Hindu Bhojpuri family. These relationships are highlighted in the songs.

Each particular member of the family from the patriarch, the *dada* to the youngest members has a role to play in the wedding. It reflects the happy close knit family ties that prevail in the Bhojpuri family life which the *girmitiyas* brought and maintained in Mauritius despite the oceans crossed and several centuries since they left their ancestral land.

They have maintained these close bondings till date which are reflected in the songs. Not only close family kinships but every member of the village community also is involved in one way or the other. For the village members are like members of an extended family.

The *Suhag* Song reflects all these different family relationships. Likewise other songs like the *Haris geet* and *Lagan* reflects the roles to be played by each member of the community in the wedding.

Nanad more sone ke chidiya
Acha acha gahana banade bhaiya sonara
Pehne la bhowji nirekhe la bhaiya
Acha acha churiya banade bhaiya sonara
Pehne la bhowji nireke la bhaiya

My husband's sister says: "my sister-in-law is a golden bird. O brother jeweller, please make beautiful ornaments for her, wearing which my brother's wife will bewitch him. O brother jeweller, make beautiful bracelets, earrings, necklace and so on, which my brother's wife will wear to bewitch him."

The song reflects the relationships between the husband's sister and his wife. The joint-family system at times led to a great deal of tension and conflict among family members. These songs tend to alleviate such feelings and throw a teasing light on these frictions in relationships.

Imli Ghontai Song
Song provided by Mrs. Manty Ramodhin

The *Imli Ghontai* song illustrates very poignantly the family bonding especially the strong ties between brothers and sisters. After marriage the sister leaves the parental abode for another dwelling. In the old days, daughters were married young while still in their childhood. The brother was a strong link. At the time of the marriage, he or all other brothers would give the '*lawa*' (puffed rice) to the sister which she and bridegroom would together pour into the consummating sacred fire-Agni- the principal witness to the wedding rites and rituals.

The brother/brothers assure the sister that he/they will always support her though she is going away and will assure that she will never be in lack of any food grains in her new abode. When the sister now has a family of her own, she is set to marry her own children, the brother and his wife again have an important role to play. The sister sometimes forgets to send an invitation to her brother to come and attend her child's marriage.

Sometimes sisters and brothers are crossed with each other. In many families the sister-in-law *bhowji* or brothers's wife is a cause for the rift between brother and sister and sometimes the sister (*nanad*) herself is jealous of the brother's love and care for his wife. But at the time of marriage they forget these family frictions. She begs of him to come and let bygones be bygones.

The *imli* or *amli ghontai* is one such custom in a Bhojpuri marriage ceremony, which takes place at the bride's and bridegroom's place prior to the proper wedding ceremony. *Imli* means tamarind. And *ghontai* means to swallow. It is known as

Imli Ghontai (tamarind) or *Amli Ghontai. Amli* are small tender mango leave studs. The mango is a sacred plant and its leaves, fruits and bark are auspicious. At the time of the *Imli* or *Amli Ghontai* ceremony, the bride or bridegroom's mother sits behind her or him on a low bench and holds her hands or his hands from behind. She gives her/him blessings.

At this time the *Mamou/Mama* or Mother's brother again stands here with gifts of clothes and money to assure the sister that he will support her as he did at the time of her own marriage. He pours drops of water in the palm of her right hand which she drinks and he says '*jourail bahine*'? Are you content my sister? And she answers '*Han, jurail*!' 'Yes I am content'. Many beautiful Bhojpuri songs were sung by women at the time of *Imli (Amli) Ghontai* ceremony. We give for your benefit such an *Imli (Amli) Ghontai* song sung by women while the ceremony is being held.

The bride at her residence and the bridegroom at his place sit in front of their respective mother in the *maroh*, marriage pavilion. The mother wears the beautifully decorated *pat mawri*, crown, on her head that the son will soon wear to proceed for his wedding. In the meantime the *nao* (barber) paints the feet, toes, fingertips and nails of both the mother and her child with red coloured liquid known as *mahavar* or *alta*. The *nahachu nonkh tungana* ceremony is held at this juncture (ceremonial cutting of nail).

What takes place in the *Imli Ghontai* ceremony? The mother sitting on a *pidha*, a low stool, behind her son/daughter covers his/her eyes with her hands. This is symbolical of the mother seating her son/daughter in her lap actually. She covers his head/her head with her *anchal*. The boy/girl too sits on a *pidha* or low stool between his/her mother's legs. The groom's/bride's maternal uncle, *mama* – *mamou* in Mauritius-offers a mango leaf to his nephew/niece. The bridegroom/bride bites a little piece of the stem of the mango leaf which he/she then spits in his/her mother's cupped right hand stretched in front of him/her. The uncle pours a little water on this, in her cupped outstretched right hand. The mother makes a symbolical gesture of sipping this water. This water poured in the mother's right hand is symbolical and pregnant with meaning. It is to remind her that it was this water that he had given her at the time of her own wedding, many years ago. Water is symbolical of life.

This water giving ceremony started in the *laja homa* ceremony when she was getting married. And he had made a protection vow with the sacred water at the time to protect her. Now that her own child is getting married, he reminds her of his promise made on her wedding day of supporting her all along in life. And now that her child has reached marriageable age and is entering a new rite of passage, he is there by her side to look after his nephew/ or niece – the result of the water he had offered her – that is her progeny. She has done well, he seems to say, and has produced children of her own. She had had a prosperous life for which he had blessed her on her wedding day. Now that she is marrying her own child, he is there by her child this time. This ceremony signifies the interest that the agnatic lineage of a woman takes in her even after her marriage and consequently her absorption into another family, and years later when her own child has grown up and has reached marriageable age.

The maternal uncle gives a sari to his sister on this occasion to congratulate her. The bridegroom's/bride's mother is shown a lot of affection. Not one, but all her brothers bring saris for her and if the brothers are no more or absent, their wives replace them. Sisters are also known to be doing the *imli ghontai* ceremony. Late Pandit Jugdish Sharma of d'Epinay gave one explanation for the term *imli*. According to him, *imli* may be corrupt form of *amli*, derived from *aam* (Sanskrit-Aamr), that is, mango since the tender twigs of the mango leaves are utilised in the ceremony. *Amli* may be the leaf of mango that she offers her son/daughter as a sign of affection which he/she returns in turn. *Amli* is also significant of what is close to the heart, that is the heart's desire of a mother is being fulfilled when her child has reached marriageable age and is about to enter a new life of his/her own.

After the *imli ghontai* ceremony, the *pat mawri* is removed from the mother's forehead and tied to the bridegroom's. He is now ready for proceeding to the bride's residence. The elderly ladies of the family and neighbourhood sing songs on the occasion.

Special references are made to the bond that exists between the mother and her brother.

(*Courtesy Kanya Dan, the Whys of Hindu Marriage Rituals: Sarita Boodhoo, 1993*)

इमली घोटाई गीत (आमली घोंटाई)
Song obtained from Mrs. Manty Ramodhin

भोजपुरी	Roman Script	English Translation
भैया जे होवे बजनिया बाजन बजावऽ हो सुनिये नैहर वा के लोग इमली (आमली) घोंटाई अइहें	Bhaiya je howe Bajaniya Bajan bajawa ho Suniye naihar wa Ke log Imli ghontai aihe	If only my brother were here O musicians Do play the music Listen O you My *naihar* folks Of my ancestral Village
अगन/अगहन नेवती ला** ***पगहन नेवती ला ***अवरू बीरन भैया***	Agan/Agahan neoti la Pagahan neoti la Awaroo biran bhaiya	I have invited others I have invited countless other guests But I have not invited my own brother?
हमरो पाहुचत चंदा देर होइए तोहर पाहुचत सुबह घड़ी	Hamaro pahuchat Chanda der hoiye Tohar pahuchat Subah ghadi	It will take me time To reach there! O Moon You will reach very fast
लेवु लू चंदा हाँथे नेवता भैया के नेवता देले आवा	Lewou lou Chanda Hanthe neota Bhaiya ke neot Dele awa	Take O Moon The "*neota*" invitation In your own hands And extend invitation to My brother (on my behalf)
अगन नेवती पगहन नेवती ***अवरू बीरन भैया** (2) अगन लोग चल आईल बीरहन लोग चल आईल	Agan newati Pagahan newati Awarou biran bhaiya (2) Agan log chal aiyila Birhan log chal aiyila	I have invited others I have invited countless others But not my own brother! All the others have come

तभो नाहीं सुहागन मोरे मढ़वा एक हो न अपना बीना	Tabho nahin suhagan More madhwa (marwa) Ek ho na apana bina	Still the "*maroh*" (marriage pavilion) looks empty Without the presence of my own brother
हमरो पहुचत सुबह साम हो जायी तोहरों पहुचत चंदा घड़ी घंटा लग जायी	Hamaro pahuchat Subah sam ho jayi Toharo pahuchat Chanda Ghadi ghanta lag jayi	It will take me time You O Moon will reach In less than No time
हाँथ वा में लेबो चंदा नेवता भैया/भौजी के हाँथ दीहिया	Hanth wa mein lebon Chanda neota Bhaiya/bhowji ke hanth Dihiya	Go O Moon Take the invitation and Extend to my brother/ sister-in-law
उजर घोड़ा चित का बर द्वारे में थार भईले	Oujar ghora Chit ka bar Dwarey mein Thar bhaile	O the beautiful red spotted white horse is standing In front of the gate
भैया जे आवेला घोड़ा चढ़ी भौजी आवे ला डोली में	Bhaiya je awela Ghora chadi Bhowji awe la Doli mein	O my brother has come On horse back My sister-in-law Is also here in Her palanquin
रच एक बहिनी चौका बिरमावऽ भैया/भौजी आहि गैले अब माँड़वा सोहावन बा	Rach ek bahini Chowka birmawa Bhaiya bhowji Aahi gaile Ab, (marohawa) Sohawan ba	O Sister (says the brother) Remain seated in the Chowka and wait Your brother and sister- in-law Have arrived
आही गैलन भैया/भौजी अब मरोहवा सोहावन बा	Aahi gailan Bhaiya bhowji Ab marohwa Sohawan ba	My brother has come My sister-in-law has come Now the pavilion Is blessed
लेवी आवा चेरिया हो	Lewi awa Cheriya ho	O maid servant Go and bring

सोने के परात भैया के ही पाँव वा पखारब हो	Sone ke parat Bhaiya ke hi Paawa pakharab ho	The golden platter so that I can wash my brother's feet (And honour him)
आही गैलन भैया भौजी अब माँड़वा व सोहावन बा	Aahi gailan Bhaiya bhowji Ab madhowa Sohagan ba	Now my brother/sister-in-law have come Now the (maroh) marriage pavilion is blessed

Note: **Agan-pronounced as Agahan in the song. Likewise we have agahan pagahan. Agan is a Sanskrit word. Also aganiya, which means innumerable, countless. Pagahan is a word used to match agan. It is an onomatopoeia. That is the formation of a word from a sound associated with what is named and the use of such a word next to it or before it. These words have rhetorical effect (Oxford Dictionary).*

Agahan pagahan: In the above song the sister says I have invited countless other guests but not my own brother.

*** Biran Bhaiya: "biran is term used by a sister for her brother" Allied Chambers Hindi English Dictionary. Allied Publishers Pvt Ltd 2008 New Delhi.*

इमली घोंटाई (आमली)
Second Song on Imli Ghontai

भोजपुरी	Roman Script	English Translation
चौका चढ़ी बैसेलन 'कौशल्या' बहिन भैया से अरज करे भैया हमरो आमलिया के साद आमली हम चाहिला हो	Chowka chadi baise lan "Kaushaliya" bahin Bhaiya se araj kare Bhaiya hamro Amaliya ke saad Aamli ham Chahila ho	"kaushalya" sister Is seated on the Wedding platform (in the wedding pavilion) She is entreating her brother O brother I want to have The stub of the mango leaf The stub of the mango leaf, I want
***अरबे से आव भैया** ***दरबे से आव हो** लाल पियरी देय के बहिनी के आमली घोंटावे ला हो।	Arbe se aawa bhaiya Darbe se awa ho Lal piyari dei ke Bahini ke aamli Ghontayi la ho	Come O brother Well prepared Come prepared with (money) Bring me the red and yellow Sari And do your Sister's *"Amli" ghontai* ceremony

मोहरो भनजावत बहिनी भैले बड़ी देर हो (2) चुनरी रंगावत बहिनी भैले बड़ी देर हो (2)	Moharo bhanjawat bahini Bhaile badi der ho (2) Chunri rangawat bahini Bhaile badi der ho (2)	Getting the change of Gold coins O sister I got delayed. Getting your *chunri* (sari) Dyed O sister Took time That is why I am late
चारो कोना से आवे चारो हो भैया हो (2) बहिनी के आमली घोंटावे अहो आम के पलौवा से।	Charo kona se awe Charo ho bhaiya ho Bahini ke aamli ghontawe Aho aam ke palawa se	From the four quarters Have come my four brothers To do the "*amli ghontawa*" Ceremony With the tender new mango leaves
बुँदे-बुँदे पनियाँ हो बुँदे-बुँदे जलवा हो अंजूरी में गिरावे भैया बहिनी के हिरदय जुड़ावे ला हो।	Boonde (2) paniya ho Boonde (2) jalwa ho Anjuri mein girawe Bhaiya Bahini ke hirday jurawe la ho	Drop by drop of water Drop by drop of water Brother pours in sister's palm So that her heart is appeased And content

*Note: *For the meaning of 'Arbe se Darbe' in the second song, I consulted four scholars in India for the exact meaning. This is a very old term found in Bhojpuri language of 300- 400 years ago or even much earlier. Finally, I came across a book given to me by the Bhojpuri Academy of Patna during my visit there in 1983. The book is entitled Bhojpuri Sanskar Geet edited by Shri Hans Kumar Tiwari and Shri Radha Vallabh Sharma and published by Bihar Rashtra Bhasha Parishad, Patna in 1977. I came across three Imli Ghontai songs in this book which contain the words 'Arbe se Darbe se' in varied forms such as 'Arpi se aao Darpi se aao' and also 'Arbi se aao and Darbi se aao'. The learned editors of this book have given the meaning of 'Darbe' as meaning 'Pride'. Which means that the brother would come at his sister's place with all the pride, might, power and wealth at his sister's place for the wedding of her child. The word 'Darbe' derives from 'Drava' (dravyam) that is 'wealth'. 'Arbe' is given as a word that is linked to 'Darbe' to give support to the word 'Darbe' as is done in many Bhojpuri, Hindi terms and even in other languages such as English and French.*

□

18

Nature and Environment Gods and Goddesses and Village Spirits The Di Baba

Sayer – from Tribal Influences

The Bhojpuri songs are replete with references to nature and environment, to the gods and goddesses and village spirits such as the Di Baba and Sayer which probably originates from the early wave of tribal migration in the first of the nineteen century.

Di and Sayer

There are many songs where towards the end the *Geetharines* make invocations to *Di* and *Sayer. Di* is a village spirit in many Bhojpuri belt villages. The Di's blessings are taken prior to many ceremonies. I have personally witnessed several years ago in the village of Berkunda in Azamgarh, U.P., at the residence of late Pandit Kuber Misra a scene where a *barati* procession with the *Dulha* go to pay obeisance to the local *Di Baba* before proceeding on to the marriage.

Sayer may be an addition from the many tribes who came to Mauritius in the early phases of immigration such as the Dhangar, the Oraon, the Santhal, and the Ho and so on.

As the women sing they add the names of Brahma, Vishnu, Surya Dev and Di and Sayer, and *Bhulal Chukal* (all those whose names have not been taken). Later on when Ramayana chanting of Tulsidas gained ground, they also added Tulsidas towards the end of any *Geet Gawai* song to give value and status to the song.

"तुलसीदास भलू आसन चरन के हरि चरन चीत लागी"

"Tulsidas bhalu asan charan ke Haricharan chit lagi"

In an article on Tribals in Bihar, Durgadas Mukhopadhyay says in *Indian and Foreign Review:*

"Most villages in Tribal Bihar also have the Sarna or the sacred grove where village's deities are supposed to reside".

"Among the Santal and Hos the sacred grove is known as Jaher. Two of the tallest trees in the grove standing side by side are deemed to be the seat of Marang Buru, the chief spirit of the Santal and his female consort Jaher Burhi or the lady of the grove. During the festivals, Pahan or the village priest offers worship at the sacred grove for the propitiation of the deities".

It may be that over the years, *Jaher* turned to *Sayer* with the twist of the tongue and being handed over by one generation to the next with original tradition bearers forgetting sometime the original line or proper pronunciation of words. In the song *Kanya Dan*, the words *Sigural, Sigural* have been pronounced as *Dugural, Dugural* by some singers which have no meaning and make no sense. But such changes happen in oral songs. I have in my collection the same song by different tradition bearers with different wordings at places.

दी सायेर	Di Sayer	Di Sayer Song
पेहेली में सुमीरों	Pehli mein sumiron	First of all I take the
धरती मैया के	Dharti maiya ke	name of the Mother Earth
बीत्ता भर जगिया	Bitta bhar jagiya	so that she gives me
हमरो के दान दे गे (2)	Hamaro ke daan de ge (2) Bitta bhar jagiya	A hand span of space So I can dance
मैं घुमी फिरी बांधी ला	Main ghumi Phiri bandhila	I go round and round
देव अस्थान के में।	Deva asthan ke main Ghumi Phiri bandhila Deva asthan ke main	And tie the gods and goddesses' at family altar (first in the house) so I get Their protection.
तार बांधे ला मैं	Taar bandhe la main	I tie the stars
धरती ऊपर आस्मान	Dharti uppar asmaan	And the sky above the Earth

मैं घुमी फिरी बांधी ला	Main ghumi Phiri bandhila	I go round and round
देवअस्थान के मैं।	Devasthan ke main	I tie the gods and goddesses' Altar For protection
बहरा में बांधीला	Bahara mein bandhila	I also tie the spirits found
दी सायेर के (2)	Di sayer ke (2)	Outside such as the Di and Sayer
बहरा में बांधीला	Bahara mein bandhila	I also tie the seven (sisters)
सातो देबी के	Sato Debi ke	Goddesses found outside
घरवा में बांधीला	Gharwa mein bandhila	Inside the house I tie the
देवअस्थान गे मैं।(2)	Devasthan ge main(2)	gods and goddesses at the Family altar
मैं बहरा में बांधीला	Main bahara mein bandhila	Outside I tie also the walking
चलते मसान गे मैं।	Chalte masane ge main	Spirits of Dead Bodies
हियाँ वा के धरती	Hiyan wan ke dharti	This land (in this village)
नववा गे मायी (2)	Nawwa ge mayi(2)	Is new to me O Mother (2)
दी सायेर जे	Di Sayer ke	I am not familiar with the
नानू जानी ला हम	Nanun jani la ham	Di and Sayer of this place.
धरती मैया	Dharti maiya	O Mother stay behind me (my Back,) give me your protection
पीठिया पर होइयऽ	Pithiya par hoiyya	O Di and Sayer Spirits
हो सहाय गे मायी	Ho sahaye ge mayi	Stay behind me (my back)
दी सायेर पीठिया पर	Di Sayer pithiya par	Protect me
दीहिया सहाय गे	Dihiya sahaye ge	I turn round and round
मैं घुमी फिरी बांधीला	Main ghumi Phiri bandhila	And tie the
दी सायेर के मैं।	Di Sayer ke main	Di and Sayer (of this new place)

Di, Sayer References in Bhojpuri Songs

This song was given to me on Saturday 19 March, 2022 at 9 a.m. by Mrs. Manty Ramodhin. She told me that when the *Geetharines* go out to sing at a different village other than their own, they feel they are unprotected. Therefore they make a special prayer to propitiate the spirits roaming around in the new village such as the *Di* and *Sayer* to give them their protection and blessings so they can accomplish their singing session without any qualm or fear. Because as they say in their song they are unfamiliar with these spirits and even with the Earth over here (the land). So they ask for their support and protection, to keep them safe from any sort of malefic harm and injury until they complete their *Geet Gawai.* This song has appeared in a different form in the *dharti bandhal geet* also. But here, we are particularly making reference to the frequent occurrence or reference to *Di* and *Sayer* in the Bhojpuri songs found in Mauritius. It could also be a derivation from *Sayed (Baba)* a Muslim saint whose *Darga* is worshipped till date by both Muslims and Hindus.*

□

* Abhishek Kumar: Banaras, District Ghazipur

19

Haris Gadhana

Another song which is sung at the ceremony of the *haris gadhana* is quite significant. It combines the putting together of a small branch of mango plant, a bamboo pole with leaves as a symbol of fertility or some *kush* leaves to place on the *vedi* or wedding altar to represent the *Hari-is* God to give blessings to the bride and bridegroom and to conjure auspiciousness. The *haris* is also the end part of or the beam of a plough.

Geet Gawai women sing at the placement of the *'haris'* at the *vedi.* In this song– Mention is made of *nao,* the barber. It is the barber who used to go and invite the people to the marriage ceremonies and go on several errands for the family in the old days. The barber has traditionally played an important role as a link in the village life, in sharing news and in match making – the *Agwa.* This tradition has perpetuated in Mauritius too. During the immigration period, till recently, the *nao* accompanied the *pandit* to go and extend the marriage invitation.

The word *Agwa* is a strong word in Mauritian *parlance* of the public domain. It has entered the political jargon. When the coalition between two political parties is being contemplated by some go between, he is referred to as an *Agwa*.

In this *Haris* song, it will be observed that each caste is required to play a particular important role, without whom the ceremony would be incomplete.

The *Nai* or *Nao* in Bhojpuri is also referred to as *Napit* since ancient times. It is pronounced as *Nai* in Sanskrit and also spelled as *Nhavi.*

"Because of the ambulatory nature of the profession, which

requires going to patrons' houses, the barber plays an important part in the village life, spreading news and matchmaking."

The *Nai,* known as *Nao* in Mauritius performs certain rituals as the occasion of birth and marriages in Hindu families. This community is also known as *'paramanik'* which is an occupational Hindu caste traditionally engaged in hair cutting. In older times, the *napit* was a social institution. On the occasions of births and marriages of Hindu families, a *napit* used to perform some essential rituals. During the marriage, as well as during the birth ceremonies such as the performance of *mundan sanskar* (removal of baby's original hair/ *tonsure*) the *nao* plays a major role in the domestic rituals.

Modernity

The traditional occupational ritual that a *nao* performs has been passed on from generation to generation. In some families in today's Mauritius, this has been passed down even to daughters, wives or sisters known as *naonine.* Needless to say that the occupation of a *nao* has now been democratised beyond caste appurtenance such as the modern hair dressing saloons which are unisex in service offered. However the presence of a *nao* in ritual ceremonies is a must.

Shri Hemraz Suneram commonly known as Ashok aged 71 told me that he has been practising as a '*nao*' in Hindu rituals since his youth. His father Kanchan Suneram was a barber and also practised as ritual '*nao*' in Hindu ceremonies. This has been a '*khandani*' practice. They lived in a village on the eastern outskirt of Port Louis, Longue Mountain. Ashok moved to Port Louis and has cultivated a wide range of clients who resort to him for various ritual ceremonies. His '*natin*', daughter's daughter, Aswani Inderjeet too has followed in her '*nana's*' footsteps. She accompanied him as a child and learnt to assist him. She has studied till the Higher School Certificate of Cambridge University and works as a clerk in an Insurance company. But she practises as a '*naonine*' on the side.

Haris Geet

This song like thousand others lays stress on Ram and Sita as a couple and reflects the marriage preparations under way at the bridegroom's house.

A dialogue ensues between Lord Ram and his Father, King Dasruth on the ritual materials to be used in the wedding. The *Lokdhara* always refer to the highest personalities. Ayodhya falls within the Awadhi Bhojpuri Maithili belt of India and therefore since thousands of years, it has given rich literary support to the lores, legends and folk literature of the peoples of the surrounding areas. Sita's *maike* or *neihar* or mother's residence Janakpur falls in the present State of Bihar and Ayodhya in Uttar Pradesh.

In the song the *nao*, i.e. the barber, and the *badhai*, i.e. the carpenter, are asked to run to Ayodhya, the Kingdom of Ram, to fetch God's image, all in gold, for the nuptial ceremony and to bless the bride and the bridegroom. The prince Ram tells his Father, Dasruth, 'Listen, Father to these words of mine, it is not in man's destiny or within ordinary mortals reach to have an image of God, all in gold. It is not the luck of common man to have a golden image. Therefore, ordinary man has to make good the void with an image in the form of 'bamboo' that is the *'haris'*.

All the ceremonial items: the *kalash*, the lamp, the seats for the bride or the bridegroom are now placed on the *chowka*. In the same song, reference is made to the above items. The *nao* is asked to bring a golden pot. The prince Ram tells his Father Dasruth in the song that it is not the fate of ordinary man to have a golden ceremonial pot, therefore he asks him to bring an earthen pot instead. And the same reference is made for the lamp. An earthen lamp will do for the common man. Since golden seats are out of question for the nuptials, the *badhai* is asked to make two wooden seats- *pidhas* out of *chandan* or sandal wood. Till today we find that the tradition of making little *pidhas* of sandalwood prevails. If sandalwood is not available then they are made of *kath* wood that is from the jacktree and dipped in turmeric.

Formerly, the *pidha* was made all in one piece. Sandalwood is one of the seven sacred woods used in Hindu rites. Nowadays, more sophisticated handmade *pouffes*, or velvety cushioned seats for the bride and the bridegroom are made. In the Tamil Nadu families, the bride and the bridegroom sit on the floor to this day. Ram here symbolises the *dulha* and Dasruth- the bridegroom's father.

Haris Geet

Dhawa ho nawwa ho
Dhawa ho bariya
Dhayi Ajodhya mein ja
Ohi Ajodhya mein sone ke
Haris wa
Ho sone ke hariswa
Dhayi haris lele awa (2)
Kahe Raja Ramchander
Soonoo Pita Dasruth
Soonoo le ho bachan hamar
Sone ke haris
Manus kahan paihein
Manus kahan paihein
Bans ke haris dharawa
Bans ke haris dharawa
Dhawa ho awa ho
Dhawa ho bariya
Dhayi Ajodhya mein ja
Ohi Ajodhya mein sone ke
Kalas wa
Ho sone ke kalas wa
Ho sone ke kalas wa
Dhayi kalas lele awa
Dhayi kalas lele
Kahe Raja Ramchander
Soonoo Pita Dasruth
Soonoo leho bachan hamar
Sone ke kalas wa
Manus kahan painhein
Manus kahan painhein
Mati ke kalas dharawa
Mati ke kalas dharawa
Dhawa ho nawa ho
Dhawa ho bariya
Dhayi Ajodhya mein ja
Ohi Ajodhya mein

Sone ke deepak wa
Ho sone ke deepak wa
Dhayi deepak lele awa
Dhayi deepak lele awa
Kahe Raja Ramchander
Soonoo Pita Dasruth
Soonoo le ho bachan hamar
Sone deepak ke wa
Manus kahan painhein
Manus kahan painhein
Mati ke diyara barawa
Mati ke diyara barawa
Dhawa ho nawa ho
Dhawa ho bariya
Dhayi Ajodhya mein ja
Ohi Ajodhya mein
Sone ke pidhaya
Sone ke pidhaya
Dhayi pidhaya lele awa
Dhayi pidhaya lele awa
Kahe Raja Ramchander
Soonoo Pita Dasruth
Soonoo le ho bachan hamar
Sone ke pidhariya
Manus kahan painhey
Chandan ke pidhayi dharawa
Chandan ke pidhayi leyawa
Dhawa ho nawa ho
Dhawa ho badhiya
Dhayi Ajodhya mein ja
Ohi Ajodhya mein
Sone ke haris wa
Dhayi haris lele awa
Kahe Raja Ramchander
Soonoo Pita Dasruth
Soonoo le ho bachan hamar
Sone ke haris

Manus kahan painhein
Manus kahan painhein
Bans ke haris dharawa
Bans ke haris dharawa

□

20

Raillery- Gari/Gali Songs

Gali/ Gari Songs

The *Geet Gawai* encompasses many types of songs. Some of them are known as *gali songs,* where teasing of male members of the family takes place during wedding ceremonies specially.

But in the early phase of the setting up of the Arya Samaj movement in Mauritius this was frowned upon. That this type of teasing was acceptable in the society since centuries was not known to urbanized women or leaders from other States of India in those early days of the 20th century. It was not encouraged by the reformist movement. My paternal great aunt, father's '*bua*' Mrs. Bhagwatee Devi Makhansingh Gayasingh in her reformist campaign of uplift of women, undertook to change the songs and composed new songs with didactic import – inserting Swami Dayanand as a towering figure in societal reform. – The song she brought out in a book entitled *'Vivah Mangal'* has endured over a century: *'Prem se aarti outarji bar byahan aye'* composed by her, a welcoming song of the Bridegroom is most touching and full of love and exudes a tremendous fragrance of welcome, loaded with expectations of a new happy married life of togetherness. It is popular to this day in Mauritius. She undertook to polish the songs. Nonetheless, the *gali* songs continued like the *teasing* of the *bhansur* bridegroom's elder brother at the time of offering of gifts to the bride at the *vedi,* the marriage altar. Even Dr. Suchita Ramdin adapted it to music in her '*Swarna Chakra*' album produced by Mahatma Gandhi Institute in the 1980s which became a hit for decades at weddings.

Raillery

Teasing Songs (Good humoured teasing)

After the wedding ceremony, a reception is given to the bridegroom and his party by the girl's parents. A sumptuous feast is held. "On this occasion the women from the bride's family sing pungent songs known as *garis* (literally abuses)".*

Contradictory as this may appear, jokes using words regarded as taboo in polite usage are welcome. They are directed against the bridegroom's kin, calling them by name. These 'victims' enjoy it thoroughly. It is said there is no fun in eating at the bride's residence without being subjected to these abusive and humorous songs (Srivastava, 1974:372). These are teasing and mocking songs meant to taunt the bridegroom's party, and are meant to be taken lightly. These songs are an important medium of socialization and bring a closeness between the bride's and bridegroom's parties. No offence is meant to or taken by the bridegroom's party. At the end of the singing, the bridegroom's father or his elder brother must give a token of money known as '*neg*' to the singing women before they leave, otherwise they may be considered avaricious, and their reputation may suffer.

These jokes with overtones are directed against the bridegroom's kins calling them by names. They too, the targeted persons enjoy the jokes and abuses thoroughly.

The bridegroom's party too enjoys it. At the end of the singing the bride's father or elder brother gives a token of money- ***neg*** – to the *Geetharines* before they leave.

Raillery in Tulsidas's Ram Charit Manas

When one consults the *Ram Charit Manas,* twice Tulsidas makes elaborate mention of this raillery. At the wedding of Ram the hero of the epic Ramayana – to Sita, the *barati* led by Raja Dasruth, Lord Rama's father too had to bear with these *gari* songs, popular custom of raillery. Writes Tulsidas "*the guests started eating and were enraptured to hear songs of raillery.*" This custom was prevalent in the sixteenth century at the time of writing of the Ram Charit Manas and even many centuries before that. Tulsidas adds...

* Sarita Boodhoo, Kanya Dan. The Whys of Hindu Marriage Rituals, Mauritius Bhojpuri Institute, 1993.

"As the dinner was in progress, women rallied in melodious strains at men and women both, mentioning each by name (Jai, 1980:262)

"Panch kawal kari jewan laage
Gari gaan suni ati anurage"

"While eating, hearing the gari/gali song is indeed very pleasing"

Tulsidas adds:

Jewat dehi madhur dhuni gaari
Lei lei nam purush aroo naari"

"As the dinner was in progress, Women railed in melodious strains at men and women both mentioning each by name"

"Samai samai suhawani gaari biraja"

"Even raillery at an opportune time is agreeable and welcome".

And the king Janak too enjoyed it.

"Hansat rao suni sahit samaja."

King Dasruth and his whole party (Barati) felt amused to hear the women's railleries.

" Ehi bidhi sabahi bhojanou kinha,
Aadar sahit aachamanou dinha."

In this way according to tradition They all enjoyed their dinner And did their *achaman* with all due respect"

Baalkanda

Chawpais Between doha 328 -329 from
Tulsidas's 'Ram Charit Manas'

The above reflect how these *Geet Gawai* songs are tradition bound and come from a distant past. So that, even Tulsidas mentions it in detail in the *Balkanda* at the time of Ram's wedding to Sita.

"The names of Ram and Sita come every so often in so many of the *Geet Gawai* songs".*

Shri Narayan Kumar, Director at Antar Rashtriya Sahayog Parishad (ARSP) gave me one beautiful '*gali*' in Maithili, from Mithila belt in North Bihar. This is Sita's birthplace. Women railed:

---

* Kanya Dan: Sarita Boodhoo: 1993.

"राम लखन सन
सुन्दर बर के कोना
क दीय गाढ़ी है
दसरथ गोर
कौशल्या गोरी
राम लखन तक किए
कारी है"

"Women cracked suggestive jokes at Dasruth: That Dasruth and Kaushalya are so fair, but how come then Ram-Lakhan are dark skinned?"

Eh Chiya Bhansur

This is a rare song of *gali* sung at the time the bridegroom's elder brother *bhansur* comes to welcome and honour the bride and brings her clothes, jewellery, flowers, garlands, etc which he first *'chadhawo',* offers to the *vedi* and then gifts to the bride.

At this time women sing to tease him that the different items brought are all borrowed. And make fun and satirize him. No offense is meant. One interesting thing is the different types of jewellery mentioned such as *Karnphul* for ears, *Kangana, batana, jhumka, hansuli, anguthi, bichuwa* (toe rings), *jhabiya, mangtika, bajuban* – All these are different pieces of jewellery of the time. Mention is also made of the *binduri* and *tikuli* and *senura* (the box of *sindur* – vermilion)

Gari Geet

Eh Chiya Bhansur – Oh Shameless Brother-in-law

- ***Eh chiya bhansur toke laaj***
  Nahin lage re
  You shameless brother-in-law (elder brother of bridegroom)
  Aren't you ashamed of yourself?
- ***Mangni ke karnphul***
  Madhowa jhamkawe re
  You bring borrowed earrings and splash/ display them in the marriage pavilion!
- ***Mangni ke kangana ho***
  Mangani ke batana

Mangani ke jhumka
Madhowa jhamkawe ho
Borrowed bracelets
Borrowed bangles
Borrowed (jhumka, earrings)
You display in the
Marriage pavilion?

- ***Mangani ke binduri***
  Mangani ke tikuli
  Madhowa jhamkawe re
  Borrowed Bindi
  Borrowed Tika
  You display in the
  Marriage pavilion
- ***Mangani ke anguthi***
  Mangani ke bichuwa
  Mangani ke jhabiya
  Madhowa jhamkawe re
  Borrowed ring
  Borrowed toe ring
  Borrowed large multi layered laced skirts
  You display in the
  Marriage pavilion!
- ***Mangani ke mangtika***
  Mangani ke senura
  Mangani ke bajuban
  Madhowa jhamkawe re!
  Borrowed head pendant
  Borrowed sindur box
  Borrowed armlet
  You display in the
  Marriage pavilion!
- ***Langadh tang ghisyawat badhe***
  Khapta dant dikhawat badhe
  Kani aankh matkawat badhe
  Phuhar honth bichkawat badhe
  Eh chiya bhansur toke
  Laj nahin lage re!

You are dragging your leg
You are showing your big teeth
You are staring with sightless eyes
You are twisting your ugly lips
You shameless brother-in-law

You have no shame (to display borrowed jewellery, clothes, etc...)

Gali Song from Bihar –*Ramji Se Puche*

भोजपुरी	Roman Script	English Translation
राम जी से पूछे जनकपुर की नारी बता दा *बबुआ लोगवा देत काहे गारी, बता दा बबुआ।।	Ramji se puche Janakpur ki nari Bata da *babua Logwa det kahe gaari Bata da babua	The women of Janakpur Are asking Lord Rama (The bridegroom who has come to Janakpur, Sita's place) O "**babua**" tell us why people (of Janakpur) are giving Gari/ gali (making abusive comments fondly) Tell us O Son-in-law
तोहरा से पुछु मैं ओ धनुषधारी, एक भाई गोर काहे एक काहे कारी बता दा बबुआ लोगवा देत काहे गारी, बता दा बबुआ।।	Tohra se puchu main O dhanusdhari! Ek bhai gor kahe Ek kahe kari Bata da babua Logwa det kahe gari Bata da babua	I am asking you, O Wielder of bow and arch Why is it that one brother is fair skinned And the other one is dark skinned? O Son-in-law The people (of Janakpur) are Questioning/wondering! Tell us O Son-in-law
इ बूढ़ा बाबा के पक्कल पक्कल दाढ़ी, देखन में पातर खाये भर थारी, बता दा बबुआ लोगवा देत काहे गारी, बता दा बबुआ।।	Ee budha baba ke Pakkal pakkal dadhi, Dekhan mein patar Khaye bhar thari, Bata da babua Logwa det kahe gari Bata da babua	One old man with white beard He looks thin, but is devouring the whole plate (leaf) of food! Tell us O Son-in-law Why are the people (of Janakpur) Questioning/wondering? And making abusive comments?

राजा दशरथ जी कइलन होशियारी, एकता मरद पर तीन तीन जो नारी, बता दा बबुआ लोगवा देत काहे गारी, बता दा बबुआ।।	Raja Dasruthji Kaylan hoshiyari, Ekta marad par Teen teen jo nari, Bata da babua Logwa det kahe **gari Bata da babua	The King Dasruth (father of Lord Rama) has been very clever (How has he managed) To have three wives? Tell us O Son-in-law Why the people (of Janakpur) are making abusive comments?
राम जी से पूछे जनकपुर की नारी बता दा बबुआ लोगवा देत काहे गारी, बता दा बबुआ।।	Ramji se puche Janakpur ki nari Bata da babua Logwa det kahe gari, Bata da babua	The women of Janakpur are asking Lord Rama Tell us O Son-in-law Why people are making abusive comments?

This *gali/gari* song is thus very popular in Bihar at the time of the marriage. As mentioned earlier even Tulsidas makes mention of it in the *Ram Charit Manas*. This folk song is in Maithili, sister language of Bhojpuri in North of Bihar around the birth place of Sita, Janakpur. Quite a few *girmitiyas* came to Mauritius from the Maithili speaking region of Bihar during the immigration period. Therefore, there are Maithili origin people in Mauritius.

I obtained this (*gali*) song on Wednesday 11 May, 2022 from Dr. Nitu Kumari Navgeet, Singer of folk songs and Writer (Bihar) by chance. She sang this song as part of her presentation: "*Lok Geeton me Prabhu Shri Ram Aur Mata Sita Ka Jeewan*" at a function held at the World Hindi Secretariat, under the aegis of the Ministry of Education, Tertiary Education, Science and Technology in the context of a one week International seminar in Mauritius by *Sahityik, Sanskritik Shodh Sanstha* of India in collaboration with the High Commission of India.

Note: ****Babua*– A word of endearment for a son, son-in-law/brother-in-law. (Allied Chambers/Ltd. New Delhi, 2008)*

*** **Gali**– Abusive songs sung by women as part of marriage celebrations. (Allied Chambers/Ltd. New Delhi, 2008) in a teasing manner for fun!*

□

21

The Sandhya Songs

The *sandhyas*, evening songs, are invocation songs. *Sandhya* means the time of dawn or dusk, and is derived from the Sanskrit word *sandhi* meaning to *"meet"*- that is, when night meets day and day meets night. At this time in Hindu homes, an invocation (Mookherjee, 1985:70-77) is made to *Sandhya* by lighting an earthen oil-lamp. At *Sandhya,* twilight or dusk, select Vedic hymns have been recited in the morning or evening prayers since the Vedic period. This practice continues till date. No women tradition bearers will start their singing or dancing session unless they have completed the *Sandhya* and other sets of songs dedicated to the gods and goddesses.

In the *Sandhya* songs, the presiding deity of light is ceremoniously invoked with great love and due respect by all members of the singing group. She is requested to leave her daytime residence by the bank of the river to come and take her seat at the family shrine as dusk approaches, so as to bestow auspiciousness upon the family for the happiness of the *'dulha'* (bridegroom) and *'dulhan'* (bride). In all, five *Sandhya* songs are sung:

An example of a Sandhya Geet

"Sanjha bhaile sanjha,
Ghare ghare ghume
Kehi more sanjha manayo ji (2)
Apne mahaliya se nikalelan dada (2)
Ham rowra sanjha manayo ji (2)
Apne mahaliya se nikalelan dadi (2)

Ham rowra sanjha manayo ji (2)
Sanjhé debon sanjhawar,
Parate datwan pani
Baisse ke (debon) sone ke singhasan (2)
Anchara desayi debon,
Phula chitaraya debon
Rase rase beniya dolayo ji (2)
Tohro bhojan sanjha,
Dudh bhat khowa
Gheewa se homiya karayo ji (2)
"Sanjha bhaile sanjha,
Ghare ghare ghume
Kehi more sanjha manayo ji (2)

Lyrics of Sanjha Geet translated by Dr. Sarita Boodhoo

Dusk has arrived
Evening has arrived.
The Goddess of Dusk 'Sanjhaa' is roaming from house to house
Eager to be welcomed, she asks who will welcome me in the house
Lighting of lamp in my honour?
Dada (father's father, grandfather)
comes out of his quarters and says
I will do your (rowra) welcome ceremony, with all the required grace and honour.

In the evening I will make the appropriate offerings
And for your morning requirements (parate) (प्रात:)
(I will offer) Datwan (wooden brush) and water
And I will offer you the golden throne to sit
(Dadi – grandmother comes out of
her quarters and welcomes Sanjha) and says:
I will place my anchara (the end part of my sari)
at your feet and wipe your feet
I will lay flowers at your feet

I will also move the hand fan slowly to make you comfortable

Sanjha, for your meals
I am offering dudh (milk), bhat (cooked rice)
and khowa (milk cake)
And pour ghee (clarified butter) – in sacrificial fire (hom)
(to propitiate you)

Dusk has arrived

The Goddess of Dusk 'Sanjhaa' is roaming from house to house
Eager to be welcomed she asks
who will welcome me in their house,
With lighting of lamp in my honour?"

Amitav Ghosh in his novel *Sea of Poppies,* has quoted a few lines of *'Sanjha'* from the *Bhojpuri Traditions of Mauritius.*

Geet Gawai in Sea of Poppies of Amitav Ghosh

In the *Sea of Poppies:* (John Murray, 2009), Amitav Ghosh internationally well-known Indian English writer, makes his heroine Deeti sing:

"sanjh bhaile
Sanjha ghar ghar ghume
Ke mora sanjh
Manayo ji"

"Twilight whispers
At every door:
Its time
To mark my coming"

The geography of the novel based on Indian Immigration is set partly in Mauritius.

These Bhojpuri lines are taken from Mauritius. In fact they are from Mrs. Sarita Boodhoo's *'Bhojpuri Traditions in Mauritius' 1999*, p. 63, as says the author himself. It reflects the honour and space given to Mauritian *Geet Gawai* Bhojpuri songs on an

International level. By so doing, the famous writer has given cognizance not only to Mauritius as the 'First Post' in the 'great experiment' of *girmitiya* movement but also created awareness worldwide for the rich Bhojpuri literature brought by Indian Indentures.

In Eastern Uttar Pradesh and Bihar, the *sandhya* songs are sung both in the morning and evening. In fact, the morning songs are known as *Parati* from *pratah* meaning morning. (प्रात: Sanskrit)

It will be remembered that in the days when we did not have the luxury of electricity, petrol lamps were lighted and much before that earthen oil lamps were used. The first lamp was always lit in honour of the Goddess of light. The tradition of doing *sandhya,* morning and evening continues in many Hindu families. However, with the rush of modernity, quite a number of Hindu families have dropped this tradition. But in many Hindu homes it is still the practice for one female member of the family to light the lamp at the family shrine. The daughter of the house is guided by elders: '*Jo sanjha baar*' 'Go light the lamp'. The name *sanjha* itself is given to the evening lighting of lamp.

A reference to a *Sanjha* Song from *Bhojpuri Sanskar Geet. Edited by Shri Hanskumar Tiwari and Shri RadhaVallabh Sharma published by Bihar Rashtra Bhasha Parishad Patna, Bihar (1977)* shows a stunning resemblance to the *sanjha* songs preserved in Mauritius.

भोजपुरी	Roman Script	English Translation
सांझा बोलेली माइ हे केकरा घरे आई के मोरा संझा मनाई हे (1)	Sanjha boleli mayi he Kekara ghare aayi Ke mora Sanjha manayi he	Sanjha says O Mother To whose house will I go? Who is that person Who will welcome me (As per the established tradition?)
बोलेली कवन देइ हमरा घरे आई हम रउरा संझा मनाइब हे (2)	Boleli kawan dei Hamra ghare aayi Ham rowra Sanjha Manayib he	Says *so and so* (name of the lady of the house) Devi Come to my House I will welcome you With all the honour due

सांझे देबो सांझबाती पराते देबो बायन इहे मोरा बहुआ के सुलछन हे (3)	Sanjhe debon sanjhbati Parate debon baayan Ihe mora bahuwa ke Sulacchan he	In the evening I will light for you the traditional (earthen) lamp In the morning I will offer you sweetmeats (Prasad) This is the good habit of the daughter-in-law of this house.

□

22

The Mahadeo Songs

Mahadeo Songs

The performers continue with several *Shaadi* songs. They sing five *Mahadeo* Songs – dedicated to Lord Shiva and his romance with his wife Parvati's sister Ganga. With the advent of the Mangal Mahadeo serials on TV channels the *Geetharines* who have preserved these lores and legends of Shiv culled right from the Shiv Purana are noticeably surprised to see their songs being depicted on the small screen, which they have been singing and preserved for centuries from generation to generation.

The *Geetharines* insist that they must sing five *Sandhya Geets,* five *Debi Debta Geets* and five *Mahadeo Geets* at the very beginning of the *Geet Gawai* sessions. They are an invocation. They all sing with one single voice. Singing these songs consecutively at pre wedding occasions create a certain charm and auspiciousness. When properly sung with faith and devotion one feels the divine presence pervading the atmosphere.

Likewise for the song *'Mahadeo: Gai Ke Gobar'*

It is found in exactly the same wordings, style and tune and sung by all *Geet Gawai Geetharines* of Mauritius. I was amazed to hear it being even enacted on stage on several occasions at the annual Antarrashtriya Bhojpuri Mahotsaw put up by Purvanchal Ekta Manch in Baba Deo Nagar, Sector 13, Dwarka, New Delhi by the Batohia group up till 2017.

Further I even heard it sung in the same tune and word for word by Prof. Lal Babu Yadav, a Political Science Professor at University of Jai Prakash Narayan in Chhapra in 2010! and recently on Sunday 18 December, 2022 at Bhikhari Thakur Chowk in Chhapra. Amazing. He had learnt it from his *Dadi*. Moreover, Dr. Sandhya Sinha from Jamshedpur, daughter of famous Bhojpuri *Publisher* and Scholar Writer, Mr. Nagendra Prasad Singh sang *Gai ke Gobar* song which she learnt from her mother Shanti Devi, a school teacher and All India Radio artist from Patna. She published the song in her magazine *Angna* across which I came in 2011 in one of my visits to the Bhojpuri belt of India.

Mahadeo Song: Gai Ke Gobar – The Sacred Cow's Dung

Chandramani Singh says in the Prologue to her Book 'Marriage Songs from the Bhojpuri Region' (1979) (Page 9) – "The women sang five songs in the morning and five in the evening, many composed in praise of natural powers and of ancestors, and then a number dedicated to Lord Shiva and to the Goddess Kali. After this a group of young girls sang marriage songs and in the end there was a 'Jhumar – circle dance'. This is being carried out in Mauritius in exactly the same pattern in the pre – wedding *Geet Gawai* sessions.

Women sing five songs known as *'Parati'* early morning. But in Mauritius, the *Parati* songs have become rare. Only the *Sandhya* songs – ode to the evening goddess is very popular.

As for the Mahadeo song *Gai Ke Gobar* it is well preserved in Mauritius as well as in the Bhojpuri belt of India.

- ***Gai ke gobar***
  Mahadeo
  Angna lipai ke
  Gajmoti ya ho Mahadeo
  Chowka purai
  Suni eh Siva
  Siva ke dohai
  Sunu eh Siva

  The cow dung is used to (It is considered sacred)
  Plaster the yard,
  O Mahadeoo
  We will offer flowers to decorate your seat
  (where the marriage will take place)
  Listen oh Siva
  Give your blessings (entreaty)

- ***Sehi chowka baisse le Mahadeo***
  Gaile alsayi (sleepy) (bored)
  Bahiya laphayi gowra dei
  Dehli jagayi
  Sunu eh siva
  Siva ke dohai (entreaty)
  Sunu eh siva

  It is on this chowka that Mahadeo is sitting.
  And feeling sleepy
  Gauri tries to wake him up
  By extending her arm towards him
  (He gets angry and tries to go away)
  Gauri tells him, Listen O Siva, I entreat you

- ***Tahi chowka baise le Mahadeo***
  Gaile alsai
  Angutha je marile
  Gaura dei, lihal jagayi
  Siva lihali jagayi
  Sunu eh Siva
  Siva ke dohai
  Sunu eh Siva
  Mahadeo was sitting on the chowka square raised platform and feeling sleepy.
  Gaura woke him up with the touch of her finger.
  Siva woke up
  Oh Siva listen

- ***Aan ke maaral he Mahadeo***
  Mane musukai
  Gaura dei ke marle Mahadeo
  Chalale kunhai
  Siva chalale kunhai
  Sunu eh Siva
  Siva ke dohai
  Sunu eh Siva
  When others touch Mahadeo

He just shrugs it off lightly
And smiles to himself
But when Gaura Devi touches him
Mahadeo showed his displeasure and walked away

- ***Bahiya laphayi***
  Gaura dei
  Lihale manayi
  Bahiya laphayi
  Gaura dei
  Lihale manayi
  Siva
  Lihale manayi
  Sunu eh Siva
  Siva ke dohai
  Sunu eh Siva
  Gaura devi stretched her arm towards Siva
  To appease him and get back his love
  Oh Siva
  I entreat you
  Listen oh Siva

- ***Biyahe ke beriya Mahadeo***
  Kuchuwo na payi
  ****Gawano ke beriya Mahadeo***
  Sab kuch payi
  Sunu eh siva
  Siva ke dohai
  Sunu eh Siva
  At the time of the wedding ceremony
  Oh Mahadeo you won't get anything (dowry, gifts)
  It is only at the time of gaona that you will get everything
  Listen oh Siva, I plead with you

- ***Khaye ke thali Mahadeo***
  Anchawe ke lota
  Sute ke palangari Mahadeo
  Odhé ke rajayi

Suni eh Siva
Siva ke dohai
Suni eh Siva

You will be gifted with thalis for food, Mahadeo
And lota for drinking water
And a bed for sleeping, Mahadeo
You will also get a Rajayi (quilt) for cover
Listen oh Siva
I entreat you

- ***Baba dihele hanthi se ghora***
  Bhaiya dhenu gai
  Amma diheli aapan dhiyawa
  Anguri dharai
  Suni eh Siva
  Siva ke dohai
  Suni eh Siva
  My father will give you
  Elephants and horses
  My brother will give you milch cows
  My mother will give you her beloved daughter
  And a ring on your finger
  Oh Siva
  I entreat you
  Do not go away

- ***Kahan tohre baba***
  Gaura dei
  Kahan tohar amma,
  Kahan toharo bhaiya
  Gaura dei?
  Kahan tohro bhowji
  Gaura dei?
  Sunu eh Siva
  Siva ke dohai
  Sunu eh Siva

Where is your Father Gauri?
Where is your Mother?
Where is your Brother Gauri?
Where is your bhowji (Sister-in-law)
Oh Siva
I entreat you

- ***Baba more sabha ho baissela***
Amma more machiya (baissela)
Bhaiya more passa ho khele
Bhowji rasoya ho (2), Mahadeo
Sunu eh Siva
Siva ke dohai
Sunu eh Siva
My Father is there in the Sabha (meeting)
My Mother is sitting on the machiya (raised platform)
My Brother is playing dice
My Sister-in-law (bhowji-bhabhi) is in the kitchen,(cooking)
Oh Siva, I entreat you
Do not go
Listen to me.

Note: *"*Gaona* – In the old days, girls were married very young. They were child brides. After marriage they remained at their parents' house. At the age of puberty, a ceremony was held known as *'gaona'* when she was sent to her in-laws with all the ceremonies and gifts. Her husband came to fetch her.

Purain Pata Par Suteli Gaura Dei

Soomatee Jeebaun was 86 years old when I met her on 5 May, 2014 at her home in Richelieu, Petite Riviere (Black River District). She was born in 1928 and got married in 1943. She was 15 years old when she got married. She is now 95 years old. She sang this song for me on 5 May, 2014.

महादेव गीत

पुरइन पात पर

भोजपुरी	Roman Script	English Translation
1) पुरइन पात पर सुते ली गऊरा देई सपना देखे ला अजगूत	1) Purain paat par Sute li Gaura Dei Sapna dekhe la Ajgut	1) On the Lotus Leaf Sleeps Gauri (Gaura Devi) She sees a strange Dream (unparalled)
2) सांझ बिहान करके गईला महादेव बीति गईले छव ही मास	2) Sanjh bihan karke Gaila Mahadeo Biti gaila chawa Hi maas	2) Mahadeo, You left In the evening saying You will be back tomorrow, But six months have gone by!
3) पुरइन पात पर सुते ली गौरा देई सपना देखे ला अजगूत	3) Purain paat par Sute li Gaura Dei Sapna dekhe la Ajgut	3) On the Lotus Leaf Sleeps Gaura Dei She sees a strange, Unparalleled dream
4) पारा परोसीं तोहर मोरे गोटनी सपना के कर न बिचार	4) Para parosin tohar More gotni Sapna ke kar na bichar	4) She consults The neighbours and her close ones. "Please interpret this strange dream of mine"
5) तू हू हो गौरा देई आनी से ज्ञानी पढ़ल पंडितवा के धिया	5) Tu hu Gaura Dei Aani se Gyani Padhal Panditwa Ke dhiya	5) "You yourself Gaura Dei You are Yourself a learned girl You are yourself Daughter of a Great Pandit!"
6) तू हू गौरा देई आतुर से चतुर अपने से करऽ न विचार।	6) Tu hu Gaura Dei Aatur se chattur Apne se kar na Bichar	6) "You are yourself Gaura Dei A clever girl You try to get the meaning By Yourself!"
7) मोरंग देस बजन एक बाजे सीवजी के होके ला बियाह सीवजी के होके ला बियाह	7) Morang des bajan Ek baje Siwji ke hoke la Biyah Siwji ke hoke la Biyah	7) So she hears the musicians Coming from the *Morang des* (a neighbouring state on the border of Nepal and Purnea District of Bihar) And is coming a barat (With musicians playing beautiful music, it is the marriage party of Sivji)

8) छवा ही मास पर लौटे महादेव दुवारे में डोली लेले थार	8) Chawwa hi Maas par Lowte Mahadeo Duware mein *doli* Lele thaar	8) Mahadeo is back after Six months and brings a *doli* which He gets positioned infront of the house door!
9) सांझ बिहान करके गईले महादेव कहांव गवई ला छवा मास	9) Sanjh bihan karke Gaile Mahadeo Kahanwan gawaila Chawa maas?	9) You left in the evening Saying you would be back the next day! Where were you for Six months Mahadeo?
10) तोहर नैहर गौरा तोहर भइया के बियाह हुवें गवइली छवा मास	10) Tohar naihar Gaura Tohar bhaiya ke biyah Huwein gawaili Chawa maas	10) i went to your *naihar* (parents' house) O Gaura, I went to attend the wedding of your brother. I was there for six months !
11) सीव दुवारे काहे डोली करले थार ?	11) Siwa duware kaahe *Doli* karle thaar	11) But Siva why is there a *doli* (Palanquin) in front of the house?
12)तोहरा से चोरी हम कैली दुसर बियाह	12) Tohra se chori Ham kaili dusar Biyah	12) Hiding from you I had a second marriage!
13) किया हो गौरा देई *चोरनी से चटनी हो(2) किया बानी कोखिया बेहून किया हो महादेव सेवा में चुकली काहे के कैलऽ दुसर बियाह ?	13) Kiya ho Gaura Dei *Chorni se chatni ho (2) Kiya bani kokhiya Behun Kiya ho Mahadeo Sewa mein chukli Kahe kai la Dusar biyah?	13) Gaura asks Mahadeo *Do I hide things from you? Am I a barren woman? O Mahadeo have I failed in my duty towards you? Why did you contract a second Marriage?
14) नाहीं हो गौरा देई *चोरनी से चटनी नाहीं बानी नहीं गौरा देई	14) Nahin ho Gaura Dei *Chorni se chatni Nahin bani Nahin Gaura Dei	14) *No Gaura Dei, you do not hide nor conceal things from me

नाहीं हो कोखिया बेहून नाही सेवा में चुकला भागी कई लन दुसर बियाह	Nahin ho kokhiya Behun Nahin sewa mein chukala Bhagi kai lan Dusar biyah	Nor you are a barren woman Neither have you failed me in your duties as a faithful wife. It is destiny that brought a second wife to me O Gaura Dei
15) पैरु हो गौरा देई इयरी से पियारी सवतिन परिछी भलू लेवो	15) Pairou ho Gaura Dei Iyari se piyari Sawtini parichi Bhalu lewo	15) I am imploring you, Gaura Dei You are a *sohagin* (married woman whose husband is alive) Do welcome your *sawtin* (co wife) with the traditional *arti*
16) डोलिया उठारी जब देखे ला गौरा देई इत बारी बहिनी हमार	16) *Doliya* outhari jab Dekhe la Gaura Dei It bari bahini hamar !	16) When Gauri lifts the curtain from the *Doli* what does she see? She is shocked! "This is but my own sister!"
17) तीन भुवन बहिन बर नाहीं मिलले हो ? **मोरे पीठी दारे लू अंगार !	17) Teen bhuwan bahin Bar nahin milale ho? **More pithi dare loo angar!	17) O sister could you not get a husband in all the three worlds? Why did you have to torture me?
18) एइसन आसीस देबन मोरे बहिनी जूग जूग बढ़े ले एहुवात	18) Eissan aasis deban More bahini Jug jug badhele ehuwaat	18) I will give you such a benediction my sister You will be an *ehuwaat* a married woman always. Live here forever with us (Have the protective presence of your husband)
19) हमरो बालक के खेलइया मोरे बहिनी स्वामी जी के सेज ना जानी जइहा	19) Hamaro balak ke Khelaye more bahini Swamiji ke sej Nahin jani jaiha	19) You will rear/play With my child but you will never approach my husband's bed
20) सार पैसन बहिन गोबर करियऽ दासी तू होइय या हमार	20) Saar paissan bahin Gobar kariya Dasi tu Hoiyya hamaar	20) You will enter the cowshed And bring out the cow dung You will forever be my maid servant
21) मंगिया के जुड़े सूखे रहिया मोर बहिनी कोखिया के रहिया बेहून।	21) Mangiya ke jure sukhe Rahiya more bahini Kokhiya ke rahiya behun!	21) You will beg for your food my sister but you will never have a child of your own!

22) ऐसन असीस तोहरा देबो मोर बहिनी जूग जूग बढे एहवात	22) Eissan asis tohra Debo mor bahini Jug jug badhe *ehuwaat* (2)	22) This is the blessings I give you. My sister You will forever be a married woman (whose husband is alive).

Note: *According to Dr. Chandramani Singh, *(Marriage Songs from Bhojpuri Region: 1979- Kitab Mahal, Jaipur).*

** *मोरे पीठी दारे लू अंगार! / More pithi dare loo angar!* : Literally the meaning is translated as "you have put hot embers on my back" which Dr. Chandramani Singh has interpreted as *"why have you tortured me?"*

This Bhojpuri song is very popular throughout the Bhojpuri belt of India. It has also been sung by Dr. Sandhya Sinha in one of her recent video online programmes (2021). It has been sung by famous Indian Bhojpuri singer Sharda Sinha too.

In this rare song, the story goes that Mahadeo tells his wife *Gaura Dei* that he is going out and will be back the next day. She has a dream. She is sleeping on the leaf of the lotus. In this dream she sees Mahadeo coming back after 6 months with a palanquin and asks her to welcome the new bride who to her utter shock is no other than her own sister Ganga! He makes excuses to her that he had gone to her brother's wedding. She welcomes her co-wife whom she tells that she has but placed a dagger in her back by marrying her (*Gaura's*) own husband. She tells her that you will be always a married woman so long as her husband is alive. But she will never share his bed and will instead live in the cowshed and will be looking after her own (Gaura's) Child.

This song signifies the many situations that may develop in a marriage and is a warning advice to the new bride who is about to enter marriage. Some of the *Geetharines* themselves have told me how their husbands brought along a second wife to cohabit in the same house with them.

□

23

The Jhumar Songs

Jhumar

The Jhumar is a much awaited item in the whole *Geet Gawai* session. The *Geet Gawai Jhumar* style of singing is performed at various regional, national and international levels. Competitions with attractive prizes incite more *Geet Gawai* groups to be formed and more individuals to make an effort to learn the Bhojpuri Songs.

The vigorous *jhumar* is the climax of the evening singing session. Some of the songs are loaded with erotic sentiments. Melodious but also hilarious, they seek to make fun of the bride's or bridegroom's parties. The women dance in a circular motion, swinging their hips and hands. No menfolk are allowed. The women sometimes impersonate men and perform mock marriage rituals. Even the Bollywood Film: Ham Aap Ke Hein Kaun" featuring Salman Khan and Madhuri Dixit shows these folk customs in great details.. The *jhumar* depict the legends of Rama's and Sita's wedding, Krishna and Radha's romance, Krishna's playful moments known as *Lilas*, Nature in general (Singh 1979: 9-11), birds dress, ornaments and Hindu scriptural episodes. They also describe the Hindu women's fondness for jewellery and beautiful, colourful dresses. There are exquisite love lyrics.

The *Jhumar* is a vibrating, pulsating rhythmic spontaneous dance accompanied by the vigorous fast beat singing of the songs by the same name. Here besides the hip swinging and light footsteps of the group dancers, younger women and girls and other family members both male/female are coaxed to come and join in the performance. This is the moment everybody has been waiting for. The singing is sometimes halted. There is a small break *'chotta sa break'.* The ladies of the house serve hot *pakhoras– bhajias, samousas* and tea to the singers and the family members and friends.

The uninitiated try to join in here and there until they too would one day be adept at the singing. This is how the torch has been passed on. The beginning part of *Geet Gawai* is a slow moving singing in chorus without accompaniment. Younger generations are somewhat impatient however with the long repertoire of invocative songs and have no time to go the whole round of pre *jhumar* dance singing. They are eager to join in and dance. Due to the social demand and time factor many of the *Geet Gawai* groups reduce their repertoire to please the families where they are called upon to perform. But they say this breaks the spell and charm thus conjured by the gods and goddesses. The fast rhythmic *jhumar* song and dance items are originally, essentially a means to conjure auspiciousness and please the Goddess of Fertility to bless the new couple.

Ginger powder paste is also served. Formerly wrapped in leaves, then in newspaper pieces and nowadays lovely beautiful small plastic or carry bags are prepared. These are to soothe the throat especially of the performers.

Paan too (betel with lime – *chuna,* cloves and cardamom used to be served and still being served in some families. Generally it has been discontinued).

The whole performance ends with each one taking home a little handful of soaked black chickpeas in plastic minuscule bags. This is a symbol too of offerings and fertility. Modern science says that eating soaked pulses with new germinating roots is healthy and nutritious.

There is at least one *Geet Gawai* group in each village and town of the nine districts of Mauritius. Nowadays women from elite society too have manifested an interest to learn and practise the element, such as the urbanized professional women of the *Mauritius Alliance of Women* at Quatre Bornes Township and urban women of Rose Hill

The *Geet Gawai* practitioners have also performed in fusion with the Jazz Group of Paris. The *Dadi Unmole group* of Vallée des Prêtres, an extension of northern eastern suburb of Port Louis, who had never performed outside the four walls of a house with all its privacy, amazingly performed on huge public podiums of the Plaza Theatre at Rose Hill Town Hall, the Centre Culturel Français of the French Embassy and the Conservatoire de Musique François Mitterrand (a western classical Music Institution) based in Quatre Bornes to audiences not hitherto accustomed to such a style of singing: a marvelous fusion of traditional Bihari/ Bhojpuri singing, accompanied by the Jazz artists from Paris, France.

Jhumar Singing and the Traditional Odyssey of the Jazz Group of Paris

In September 1995 the Director of the *French Cultural Centre, Centre Cultured Français Charles Baudelaire* Mr. Patrick Pautonnier had contacted me to request for a *Geet Gawai* Bhojpuri singing group to perform on stage in a fusion with International Jazz Artists of Association Art Junction, Paris, France. It was a novelty. A new experience.

We arranged for a meeting with the *Geetharines* in the village of Vall*é*e des Prêtres. The Director of the French Cultural Centre recorded the *Jhumar* song of the group. After several rehearsals, they gave a public performance on stage in January 1996 at the prestigious Plaza Theatre, Rose Hill. It won huge acclaim.

The Jazz Group included Linley Marthe, Philippe Thomas, Gilles Renne and Philippe Sellam. They played the *Jhumar* tunes on the saxophone, Guitars, Trumpets and other Jazz Instruments and the *Geetharines* lent their voices to it!

At the request of the then Prime Minister Dr. Navin Ramgoolam, the performance was repeated again on 11, 12, 13 March, 1997 on the occasion of the 29th Independence Day Celebration of Mauritius, under the Ministry of Arts, Culture and Leisure in collaboration with the Ministry of Education, Science and Technology. Not only that! The French ladies danced to the melody of the *Jhumar* songs to the beat of the *dholak, lota* and *lakri taal* with the *Geetharines* of *Dadi Unmole!*

A Jhumar: Kehi Jala Hajipur

It is a very popular Jhumar here in Mauritius. It is also known to be sung Bombay, Calcutta, and Delhi and in the Bhojpuri belt of India. Mrs. Goonwantee Chummun aged 92 living at Cassis Road,

Port Louis, told me her brother in law who had been to Bombay in the 1940s knew this song personally. I heard it a decade or so ago (2009) from a singer Mrs. Mohun ICCR sponsored artist from Delhi who came to perform for the 2 November, 2008 at Aapravasi Ghat. I was astounded to hear her sing this song with the same wordings, word for word and in same tune at the official function. I ran to meet her after her performance to tell her that the song *Kehi jala Hazipur jhumar* is very much alive in Mauritius and sung by all *Geet Gawai* groups.

This is a *jhumar* song-dance. This song also gives a story of a woman whose brother, husband and father have all gone to work in Calcutta, Patna and Hazipur. The mention of these important urban areas as hubs of buzzing industrial activities and as important trade centres reflects the growing push and pull forces predominant during British India. Thousands left the far flung villages across the Gangetic Plains to search for work in big cities like Patna, Calcutta and Hazipur. In those days, Hazipur on the Sone River was a growing trading and ferry port as there was no road and railway connection, yet between the two banks of the Ganges. People from North Bihar used to take the ferry at Hazipur to come to Patna.

Amazing, that this song was brought to Mauritus and is still very popular here.

"Kehi jala Hazipur
Kehi jala Patna
Kehi jala Calcutta
Ke deshwa,
Kehi Jala –

Who goes to Hazipur?
Who goes to Patna?
Who goes to Calcutta?
The country of Calcutta

Baba jala Hazipur
Bhaiya jala Patna
Sainya jala Calcutta ke Deshwa
Sainya Jala

My Father has gone to Hazipur
My Brother has gone to Patna

My Husband has gone to Calcutta
Baba ane subah sari
Bhaiya ane kangana
Sainya ane more mathe
Ke sindurwa/bindiya

Father has brought for me a lovely sari
Brother has brought for me bangles
My Husband has brought for
Me the sindur (Vermilion) or tikuli/ bindiya

Phat gaili subah sari
Tut gaili kangana
Rahi gailli more
Mathe ke sindura/bindiya

The sari gets old, worn out and torn
The bangles are broken (glass)
The only thing that endures
Is the mid-hair parting vermilion.
Or the bindiya on my forehead

This *jhumar* also tells the nostalgic, lovelorn *purvi* sentiment of the village woman who is left behind while all her male relatives have moved to different areas in the East areas in search of work.

In the songs there are expressions of different types of love: Love of a Father, love of a brother and love of the husband. Stress is also laid on the fact that the gifts brought by Father and Brother will be torn or broken with time, but the love of the husband will be the enduring one. It reflects also an expression of romantic love for the husband which lurks in the heart of the lone pining woman left behind in the village by the cruel saga of immigration.

Many Jhumars have been composed in Mauritius too based on Mauritian scenes and social background, *Rose Hill ke bus stop wa par", "chirain kare chuk chuk, Mahal wa mein chor ba, Dewarwa bole chor ba", "Nakhon ke phuliya*

Gira ta ta gire de
Patli kamariya
Dola ta ta dole de".

Some of the original *Jhumars* from the Gangetic Plain too have been retained such as the well-known ***Kawana rang moongwa, kawan rang motiya***. The elderly *Geetharines* of Mauritius have this beautiful song in their repertoires. This *Jhumar* has also been interpreted in Bollywood films, which gave it further popularity.

Kawana Rang Moongwa

झूमर	Jhoomar
कवन रंग मुंगवा कवन रंग मोतिया।	Kawan ranga moongwa kawana ranga motiya
कवन रंग हो ननदो तोरे भैया (*बीरना*)।	Kawana ranga ho nanado tore bhaiya (*birana)* (2)
लाल रंग मुंगवा पियर रंग मोतिया।	Lal ranga moongwa piyar ranga motiya
समुझी रंग हो ननदो तोरे भैया (*बीरना*)।	Samujhi ranga ho nanado tore bhaiya (*birana*) (2)
टूट गैइल मुंगवा छितरा गइल मोतिया।	Toot gayil ho nanado tore bhaiya (*birana*)
खिसीया गइल हो ननदो तोरे भैया (*बीरना*)।	Khisiya gayil ho nanado tore bahiya (*birana*) (2)
चून लेली मुंगवा बटोर लेली मोतिया।	Choon leli moongwa bator leli motiya
मनाई लेली हो ननदो तोरे भैया (*बीरना*)।	Manayi leli ho nanado tore bhaiya (*birana*) (2)
कहाँ सोभे मुंगवा कहाँ सोभे मोतिया।	Kahan sobhe moongwa kahan sobhe motiya (2)
कहाँ सोभे हो ननदो तोरे भैया (*बीरना*)।	Kahan sobhe ho nanado tore bhaiya (*birana*)
गले सोभे मुंगवा गले सोभे मोतिया।	Gale sobhe moongwa gale sobhe motiya
बगल सोभेला हो ननदो तोरे भैया (*बीरना)*।	Bagal sobhela ho nando tore bhaiya (*birana*) (3)

*Note: In many places the word "*Birana*" is used.

पुरखों की जीती जागती परंपरा (भोजपुरी गीत गवाय), श्रीमती बीगय लक्ष्मी रामलोल लक्ष्मण 2019 फेमस प्रिंटिंग

□

24

The Relationships to Planets

Sukar Geet

This song was given to me by Mrs. Manty Ramodhin of Morcellement St André Village in the North of Mauritius. She is a veritable treasure house of ancient, undiluted Bhojpuri songs which she received from her mother and she in turn from her mother. Manty is one of the rare Bhojpuri Folklore tradition bearers whose accent and style of singing can be said to belong to the 19th and early 20th century. There is no Creole influence either in tone or style. Manty gave me this song earlier but when I read Chandramani Singh's account of this ancient idyll, I again contacted Manty on Friday 4th March, 2022 and she sang the whole song with explanations over the phone from 2:50 p.m. to 3:15 p.m.!

Exceptional

The story contained in this Bhojpuri song of *Geet Gawai* tallies with what Chandramani Singh has obtained in her childhood and retained in her book '*Marriage Songs from Bhojpuri Region*'. Mantee explains to me that this song is sung after the '*shadi ke geet*' at the boy's place. The boy's mother is counselled not to drink a drop of water on the day the *baraat* leaves until it comes back with the bride. She has to keep a *bhuk brat*- she has to keep a fast so that all goes well and her son comes back with his bride. Then only she breaks her fast.

Actually this is a legendary tale of the love affair between the planets Jupiter (*Brihaspati-Bifaya*) and Venus (*Sukra-Sukar*). The two planets never meet, however. Why? The explanation is found in the song.

Chandramani Singh says that the planets are parts of our environment and are ever present in the Bhojpuri songs. "Jupiter is a shy bride (*Brihaspati – Bifaya*) still waiting for her groom Venus (*Sukar – Sukar*) to come. He never turns up! The story of Shukra and Brihaspati is sung even today (my remarks – also in Mauritius!) – How Shukra forgets the wedding ornament (the circle box of vermilion the *'auwda sindur'*). He comes back to take it, when he finds his mother is drinking rice water behind closed doors. He asks why the mother is taking only rice water which is poor man's food. The mother answers that she is taking it because she does not know if Shukra's wife to be, who is someone else's daughter will give her rice water or not? Shukra says that if his mother is so worried about a thing like rice water, he would better remain unmarried, and does not go back to join the Wedding party."*

That is why, therefore, the bridegroom's mother maintains a fast on the day of the wedding. She only breaks her fast when the bridegroom comes along with his bride.

सुकर बिफया गीत (मानती राममुदिन)

भोजपुरी	Roman Translation	English Translation
1.कहंवा ही ए सुकर तोहरो जनमिया कहाँ वा ही रचे ला बियाह(2)	Kahanwa hi Eh Sukar Toharo janamiya Kahan wa hi Rache la biyah?	Where are you born O Sukar And where Are you going To get married?
2. नदिया के नीरे तीरे सुकर के जनमिया परबत पर रचे ला बियाह	Nadiya ke nire tirey Sukar ke Janamiya Parbat par rachey la biyah	Sukar is born On the banks of the River His marriage is fixed On the Mountain

* Marriage Songs from Bhojpuri Region, 1979, Kitab Mahal, Jaipur.

3. साजे देहू दादा/बाबा हो आजन बाजन अब सुकर जइहें बियाह साजे देहू चाचा हो आजन बाजन अब सुकर जइहें बियाह साजे देहु भइया हो आजन बाजन अब सुकर जईहें बियाह	Sajey dehu dada/ baba ho Aajan baajan Biyah Sajey dehu chacha ko Aajan baajan Ab Sukar jaihein Biyah Sajeh Dehu bhaiya ho Aajan baajan Ab Sukar jaihein Biyah	*Dada* has arranged all The musical entertainment And musicians. Sukar Is to proceed to get Married Chacha also Has made his Contribution So has the brother
4. साज देहू अम्मा हो दालऽ मौनिया अब सूकर जेहें बियाह	Saaj dehu amman ho Dala Mowniya Ab Sukar jeihein Biyah	Mother too has Contributed by supplying the *"mowni"* (basket) of *"neg"*
5. एक बन गईले दुई बन गईले छूटी गईले अवधा सेंदुर	Ek ban gaile Dui ban gaile Chutti gaile Auwdha seindur	After having crossed One forest and a Second one Sukar Realises he has Forgotten the box of Vermilion at home
6. बिरमाही आजन बिरमहू बाजन बिरमाही लोग बरियात छूटी गइले अवधा सेंदूर	Biramahi Aajan Birmahu Baajan Birmahi Log Bariyaat Chutti gaile audha seindur	Hold back, O you musicians Hold back Barat marriage party For I have left behind The box of vermilion!
7. हुवा से सुकर घरे घूमी अईले आके ही ओरी तरे थार थार भइली: खोलू खोलू अम्मा हो बजरा कांवरिया	Huwan se Sukar ghare Ghumi aile Aake hi ori Tare thaar Thaar bhaili: Kholu kholu Amma ho Bajara kanwariya	From there Sukar Turns back and Makes his way back home At home he halts under the *"Ori"*-the eaves of the roof. Standing there, he tells his Mother "Open the hard and sturdy gate O mother

छुटी गइली अवधा सेंदूर	Chutti gaile auwdha Seindur	I have forgotten the box Of *Seindur*
8. कैसे मैं खोलब बेटा बजरा कांवरिया हमहू बैसीला जेवनाई कैसे मैं खोलू बेटा बजरा कांवरिया	Kaisse mein Kholab beta Bajara kanwariya Hamhu baisila Jewanai Kaise mein Kholu beta Bajara kanwariya?	How will I open the sturdy gate oh my son(*beta*) I am seated to have My food How will I come to Open the gate?
9. अबही में अम्मा खोवा भात खइले अब ही बैसे जेवनार ?	Ab hi mein Amma Khowa bhaat khaile Ab hi baisse Jewanar?	Mother, just before going We enjoyed the Khowa bhaat (*khir*) Now why you are again Having food?
10. आवत होवे बेटा पर के हो धीयवा जुल्म होवे दुधवा के भात जुलम होवे (दुलुम) मरवा के भात (माड़)	Aawat howe beta Par ke ho dhiyawa Julum (dulum) howe Dudhwa ke bhaat Julum howe Marwa ke bhaat!	O my son, is coming to this house somebody else's daughter I do not know how she will treat me, will she give me *kheer* or *mar*?(rice+water) to eat?
11. जेहू तोरे अम्मा हो जुलम होईये (दुलुम) मरवा भात भलू सुकर रहिए कुमार	Jehu tore amma ho Julum (dulum) hoiye Marwa bhaat Bhalu Sukar Rahiye kumar(kuwar)	O Mother if you Apprehend a maltreatment And being fed the rice water (By the bride) in that case I better remain unmarried!
12. फिरी जाहू आजन फिरी जाहू बाजन फिरी जाहू लोग बरियात अब सुकर रहिये कुवार (2)	Phiri jahu aajan Phiri jahu baajan Phiri jahu log Bariyaat Ab Sukar Rahiye kuwar(2)	Go back Musicians Go back Marriage party Now Sukar will Remain a Bachelor (2)!

□

25

Mandar Puja

The *Kathaka Samhita* (xxii. 1) says that eight women whose husbands are alive should feed the priests and sing appropriate songs to the tune of the drum, *veena* (lute) known as *vana* etc and four women may also dance. *Manava Grihya Sutra* (1.9.29) says that four women whose husbands are alive should play on the *Nadi (Nad i.e. the drum)*.

Before the actual singing session starts, a little ritual is performed. The ceremony called *Nad Puja* or *Madar (mandar) Puja,* that is, worship of sound is performed. The lady of the house or daughter-in-law is asked to religiously cover her head and make a *puja* of the *dholak* (drum) which will be used to give the rhythmic beats to the songs throughout the singing session.

This practice of drum beating takes its roots in the Rig Vedic Period when the bride herself was asked to play on musical instruments such as the drum or the *veena* to the tune of a popular folk song, the *gatha* to keep the Goddess of fertility, *Indrani* pleased. The instrument was invoked as follows:

"Speak Auspicious One,
Hail hither, O Drum"

She said this to the *'dundubhi'*, big drum. To the small drum, she said:

"O Gomukha, may the ladies play in joy,
In auspicious mood along with Indrani".

The bride's mother is asked to have her hair oiled, and *sindur* (vermilion) applied in her mid-hair parting. She is symbolically given all her *shringar* (adornment) and *suhag,* proper for a married woman whose husband is alive. A little mustard oil is equally applied symbolically to the hair of other married women present. Likewise, *sindur* is applied to their hair parting. Then they ceremoniously comb their hair. The lady of the house is asked by the elders to cover her head. She is then asked to apply *sindur* at seven spots on the *dholak* with her right thumb. The *dholokiya* from the *Geet Gawai* group holds the *dholak* on her lap and the lady of the house does the '*tike*' or smearing of the *dholak* with *sindur* (vermilion) at seven different spots and light a lamp to manifest her reverence for *nad,* the cosmic sound, represented by the *damru* of Lord Shiva. A little rice, *hardi* piece, and *supari* (betel nut) on a betel leaf is offered to the *dholak.* A camphor placed on a betel leaf is lit on it. By this gesture she manifests her reverence for the *nad.* Some token money is offered and this money is taken by the drummer. In the past the *dholak* was played by particular caste women.

Nowadays, anybody from among the singing group plays the drum. The lady of the house then takes the whole lot of offering in her *anchal* without touching it with her hand. The drummer beats on two sides of the *dholak* and shakes the offerings to the lady's *anchal* (end of her sari). It is performed three times. This is a significant ritual. As simple as folk culture can be, it is highly philosophical and metaphysical and takes its roots in ancient traditions. *Nad* is the primal cosmic sound. And *Nad* is the symbol of *Nataraja,* the Cosmic king of Dance. Shiva, in his *Nataraja* form danced the *Tandav* or Cosmic dance to the accompaniment of his *'damru'.* By first offering a dedication to the sound, symbolized here by the *dholak,* the women singers pay homage to *Nataraja* who is the 'patron' of their singing and dance session!

In the *Dholak Puja* or *mandar (madar) Puja,* the *dholak* symbolizes the energy of sound to the beat of which the performers will dance throughout the night.

A *Mandar Geet* is sung to accompany this ceremony and the *dholokiya* then gives a few beats on the dholak.

Mandar Puja

Song sung at the Time of the Ceremony of Worship of the Dholak

Song obtained from Mrs. Manty Ramodhin

भोजपुरी	Roman Script	English Translation
1) केही जे मानदर गढ़ावेला केही पूजन करे दादा मोरे मानदर गढ़ावे ला दादी पूजन करे	1) Kehi je mandar gadhawe la Kehi pujan kare Dada more mandar Gadhawe la Dadi pujan kare	1) Who is making the *dholak*? Who will do its *puja*? Dada will make the *Dholak* Dadi will do its *Puja*
2) केही जे मानदर गढ़ावेला केही पूजन करे बाबा मोरे मानदर गढ़ावे ला अम्मा पूजन करे	2) Kehi je mandar gadhawe la Kehi pujan kare Baba more mandar Gadhawe la Amma pujan kare	2) Who is making the *dholak*? Who will do its *puja*? Father will do the construction Of the *dholak* Mother will do the *puja* (offering)
3) केही जे मानदर गढ़ावेला केही पूजन करे चाचा मोरे मानदर गढ़ावे ला चाची पूजन करे	3) Kehi je mandar gadhawe la Kehi pujan kare Chacha more mandar Gadhawe la Chachi pujan kare	3) Who will do the construction Of the *dholak*? My *Chacha*, Father's brother Will make the *dholak* My *Chachi* will do the puja of the *dholak*
4) केही जे मानदर गढ़ावे ला केही पूजन करे भैया मोरे मानदर गढ़ावे ला भौजी पूजन करे	4) Kehi je mandar gadhawe la Kehin pujan kare Bhaiya more mandar Gadhawe la Bhowji pujan kare	4) Who will build the *mandar* Who will do its veneration *puja*? My brother will make the *dholak* My sister-in-law will do its *puja*

माँदर पूजा/ झूमर गीत
Mandar Puja/ Jhumar Geet
(Provided by Mrs. Manty Ramodhin)

भोजपुरी	Roman Script	English Translation
दादा मोरे गढ़े ला माँदर वा दादी गावे ला नया गीत धमक्की माँदर बाजा गइलल गे	Dada More gadhe la Mandar wa Dadi gawe la Naya geet Dhammakki Mandar baja Gailal ge	Dada has made A *mandar* (drum) Dadi is singing A new song (to accompany) The drum's beats are resonant
बाबा मोरे गढ़े ला माँदर वा अम्मा गावे ला नया गीत धमक्की माँदर बाजा गइलल गे	Baba more gadhe la Mandar wa Amma gawe la Naya geet Dhammakki Mandar baja Gailal ho	Father has made A *mandar* (drum) Mother is singing A new song (to accompany) The drum's Beats are resonant
चाचा मोरे गढ़े ला माँदर वा चाची गावे ला नया गीत माँदर बाजा गइलल गे	Chacha more gadhe la Mandar wa Chachi gawe la Naya geet Mandar baja Gailal ge	Father's brother (uncle) Has made a drum Aunty (*chachi*) is Singing new song to accompany The drum's beats Are resonant
भैया मोरे गढ़े ला माँदर वा भौजी गावे ला नया गीत माँदर बाजा गइलल गे	Bhaiya more gadhe la Mandar wa Bhowji gawe la Naya geet Mandar baja Gailal ge	Brother has made A *mandar* (drum) Sister-in-law is singing a New song to accompany The drum's beats Are resonant

□

26

Dharti Bandhal Geet: Digbandhana

The *dharti bandhal* is a performance or custom that entails an invocation to Mother Earth, to request Mother Earth to give her *ashirvaad* her blessings so as to ward off any negative thoughts that may have been sent to prevent the dancers from giving a good dance performance. Songs accompany *dharti – bandhal.*

"Tar bandha
Dharti bandha
Bandha asmanke
Mein ghumi Phiri bandhi la
Devasthan ke mein "

The Dharti Bandhal Geet

The *Dharti Bandhal* geet is a Digbandhana and has great mystical link with ancient spiritual traditions and practices. It reflects the need for human beings to constantly protect themselves from natural or malefic powers. In this respect there are many protective spells, mantras in all religious beliefs that are chanted to ward off evil from causing harm to men, animals and material possessions. Nowadays, we have affirmations written by several motivators. One such well-known ancient mantra chanting is the *Durga Kavach* (The Armour of the Goddess).

In the beginning opening invocation of the *Durga Kavach* from the *Chandi Paath* or *Durga Saptasati* of the Markandeya Purana, the *Digbandhana* factor is invoked, so as to terminate all disturbances in the three Worlds.

Swami Satyananda Saraswati of Rishikesh says in a Foreword

to the Chandi Paath's (Motilal Banarsidass Publisher, 1995) translation which he did in English, "Daily reciting the verses, we offer to Mother all our troubles, afflictions, all manners of thought and perturbations – even the very Ego itself *"One by one she cuts them down and purifies them with the vibrations of her mantras".*

As we have mentioned earlier, the tradition bearers have sometimes merged lines unconsciously. If one singer has heard a song from an elderly person and may have forgotten some lines, therefore she may freely insert some words approximately, from remembrance which may fail her. Then the original song sung by an old tradition bearer may thus have got distorted over several generations of *Geetharines* singing it and it being spread from one village to another, from one tradition bearer to another. It may be also that a girl has been going to *Geet Gawai* at weddings with her mother, *Phouphou, Dadi or Nani* or other elders and neighbours as from a tender age of five and having grown up with it she came to memorise the songs from an early age.

She may have got married at an early age into a faraway village. She would integrate in the new society and when occasion would present itself may be after several years when she would have reached an age to be able to go to *Geet Gawai* without escort or being reprimanded by males and elders in the family. By that time, she may have forgotten some lines. She would thus add her own to the best of her memory's capacity to retain and her own abillty. Incredible wealth of knowledge has thus been passed on.

According to the Kannada-English dictionary, *digbandhana* is qualified as a binding of mystical power, preventing evil from causing harm to men, animals or materials.

The *Hindupedia* – the Hindu Encyclopaedia says that *Digbandhana* literally means 'shutting out the evil spirits'. In the Marathi English Shabdkosh *Digbandhana* means- *charming* the quarters or regions. Shutting out the evil spirits from all the directions. The *Ashta-Dik-Bandhana* is a powerful Sanskrit shloka representing *Anima, Mahima, Garima. "Ashta* means eight and *bandhana* means tying or fixing.

Therefore, *Digbandhana* was an *ancient* practice and has been handed down in several linguistic parts of India. The Shlokas to ward off evils spirits are daily recited. In the modern science, psychologists talk of warding off negativities or negative thoughts.

When the Indian Indentured Immigrants crossed the *Kala Pani* and braved the ferocious waves of the Indian Ocean they brought along these practices with them. Which are manifested also in their folk songs. The *Dharti Bandhal* is one such example.

After the invocation to all the gods and goddesses has been made in the *Geet Gawai* Session, and the Mandar (dholak) puja has been performed, now it is the turn for *Geetharines* to take the floor and dance the *Jhumars*. To the tunes of lilting rhythmic songs known by the same name. But before they start dancing, they have to do '*Digbandhana*' which in their simple language has been translated as '*dharti bandhal'*. The dance space has to be cleared of negativities and evil spirits or spells cast by other competing dancers. Even in the old days there used to be rival groups and as the fame of one *Jhumar dancer* would reach the ears of other villages, it aroused jealousy and envy too! Hence, the need to guard or ward off such evil intentions.

One *geetharine* told me that '*ham ke kar de lan sa*' 'हम के कर देलन सऽ'. 'They cast evil spells on me'. Since then she said her beautiful voice was lost and her voice remained hoarse since. I have heard her singing nonetheless in that 'hoarse voice'. Has it not been said that somebody gave Lata Mangeskar, the Nightingale of India, slow poison allegedly put in her food by one of her very own kitchen staff? It took her three months to recover and she had lost her voice completely. Such things happen. Finally after three months of being in doors, she recovered and started singing again.

At several points in the wedding ceremony, *geometric designs* are drawn, such as at the '*do mela*' or at the *vedi* the altar where the marriage ceremony will take place. These geometric designs are but the 'form pattern' of Sri Chakra, whose sound body is the Sri Vidya.* The *Sri Chakra* represented by the *Yantra* – the geometric designs is 'the basis', the foundation and continent of all the other Chakras mentioned in the Tantra". Says Shankara Narayan. It is

---

* The Ten Great Cosmic Powers– 'Das Mahavidyas's. Shankara Narayanan, 1996- Samata Books and Sri Mira Trust, Chennai.

'most auspicious and does the utmost good to the worshipper'. It is reputed as the abode of Goddess, the abode of all her myriad powers, Personalities and emanations"

Likewise, the *Geetharines* do their '*dharti bandhal*' before they start to perform the Cosmic Dance by involving the Mother Goddess, the Stars, the Sky, the Mother Earth and even the *smasan* or *masan* – a place where the dead bodies are burnt. The cremation ground–शमशान. Smasham-becoming 'मसान' *masan* in Bhojpuri. Has it not been said that the *masan* is the favourite spot of *Mahadeo* (Shiva)?

Even when the Gayatri mantra is recited, it begins first with the very powerful 'Om Bhur, Bhuva, Swah' the first addendum to the Gayatri invocation. It is first made to all the quarters so that the *Mantra* itself can be potent, so that the mind is freed from invading negative thoughts and desires. Likewise the *Mahamrityunjai Tryambakam* mantra is a powerful incantation to ward off evil spirits.

During festivals such as in the *Onam* of South India, geometric patterns are drawn with agricultural products such as rice, pulses and flowers and nowadays artificial colours are used. These artistic decorations are but the derivation of *Yantras*, drawn infront of homes or temple yards to ward off spells and with an intention to protect the space through '*digbandhana*'.

Swami Ved Bharati, disciple of the great Swami Rama of the Himalayan Institute and Sadhna Mandir Trust, Rishikesh and famous Bhojpuri Scholar who did his Ph.D. at the University of *Leiden Utreicht* in Holland in 1971, based on the Bhojpuri songs of Suriname prior to taking up Sanyasa, says in '*My Meditation Hut*":

"I have built myself a meditation hut, far from the traffic of planets and their satellites, where even the thoughts from the minds of the dwellers of various worlds cannot reach me. At a curve of the vast space beyond, where three space-flowing energy rivers converge, there in a place called 'tri-kuti Prayaga'. The trikuti is not only the meeting place of three sacred rivers but also the triangular centre in the upper half of the forehead, commonly known as the Third Eye.

Swami Ved Bharati adds, 'To ward off the invasion of

intruding thoughts of the world dwellers I have done many '*dig bandhanas*' by reciting '*Bhur, Bhuvah, Swah*'. When one sits to eat, one sprinkles water around the plate of food, to ward off evil designs. It is also performed when one is doing the Vedic Hawan.

At the time of meditation too, 'the first act one may perform is this '*dig bandhana to ward off all intruding thoughts*' Meditators are familiar with the word '*Digbandhanas*' which means tying up the directions, tying up the ten quarters around one'.

In the '*dharti bandhal*' *geet* too, the *Geetharines* tie up the directions and the ten quarters, before they perform the *Jhumar dances.*

I have tried to show that there is a strong relay and connectivity between the Shastric Literature and folk Oral Literature. Simple village folks express their feelings through village practices which are deeply linked to learned scholarly spiritual practices as in this case of *dig bandhana.*

Dharti Bandhal Geet-Version 1

Mrs. Manty Ramodhin 78 years old tradition bearer sang it for the purpose of this work on telephone on Wednesday 16 February, 2022 to the author.

धरती बांधल	Dharti Bandhal	English
1) **तार* बांधे, धरती ऊपर आसमान गे मायी बित्ता भर जगिया माता हमरो के दान दे मायी माई घूमी फिरी बांधिला देवा अस्थान गे माई	Tar bandhe Dharti, Uppar Asman Ge Mayi Bitta bhar Jagiya Mata Hamro ke daan de Mayi Mayi ghumi Phiri bandhila Deva Asthan Ge Mayi	I am tying the stars (And) The Earth (And) above the sky O Mother (Give) me a hand span of Space O Mother Give me O Mother I am turning round to tie The God's space O Mother

2) घरवा में बांधिला देवा अस्थान में बहारा में बांधिला चलते मसान गे माई	Gharwa Mein bandhila Dewa asthan Main bahara Mein bandhila Chalte masan Ge mayi	I am tying The house (I am tying)also The God's (altar) I am tying (also) the Cemetery (Cremation Ground) O Mother
3) केही तोरे गुरुवा केही तोरे चेलवा केकर भरोसे बांधे अस्थन के में ?	Kehi tore guruwa Kehi tore chelawa? Kekar bharose Bandhe asthan ke main?	who is your Guru? Who is the disciple? On whose authority Am I tying the Space?
4) राम मोरे गुरुवा भरत मोरे चेलवा ओकरे भरोसे बांधी ला अस्थान के मैं	Ram more Guruwa Bharat more chelawa Okare bharose Bandhi la asthan Ke main	My Guru is Ram And Bharat is the disciple I am tying the space On his Authority
5) राम गईला ससुरलिया भरत गइले ननिहाल चलते मसान हम बांधी ला अकेल मैं। ओकरे भरोसे हम बांधी ला अकेल माई	Ram gaila Sasuraliya (banwa?) Bharat gaile Nanihal Chalte masan Ham bandhi la akel mein Okre bharose Ham bandhi la akel mayi	Ram has gone to his Father-in-law's place (to forest) Bharat has gone to his Nani's place I am tying the moving spirits Alone (by myself) On his authority I am tying the space Alone

Note: **तार*- from *तराइन* = Stars/Constellations (Sanskrit)

Dharti Bandhal Geet- Version 2
Tying of Earth Song

धरती बांधल गीत

तार बांधी धरती	Taar bandhi dharti	I tied the Stars
ऊपर अस्मान गे	Upar asman ge	And above the Sky
मायी	Mayi	O Mother
घूमी फिरी	Ghumi phiri	I turn around
बांधी ला	Bandhi la	And tie the
देव अस्थान	Deo asthan	God's space
गे मायी	Ge mayi	O Mother
बीच भर	Bich Bhar	I have the
जगहिया	Jagahiya	space in the middle
हमरो के	Hamro ke	as a place to dance
दान दे मायी	Dan de Mayi	(Donate) Give it to me O Mother
चारों ही कोना	Charon hi kona	(In) All 4 corners
मैया	Maiya	O Mother
गोर तोहर लागीला	Gor tohar lagila	I bow and touch your feet
घूमी फिरी बंधीला ला	Ghumi Phiri bandhila	I turn round
देव अस्थान गे मायी	Deo asthan ke mayi	And tie the
बीच भर जगहियां	Bich bhar jagahiya	God's altar, O Mother
हमरो के दान	Hamro ke dan	Give me the central place
दे मायी	De mayi	O Mother
केही होवे गुरुवा	Kehi howe guruwa	Who is your Guru?
केही भैले चेलवा	Kehi bhaile chelawa	Who is your disciple?
राम हवे गुरुवा	Ram howe guruwa	Ram is the Guru
भरत भैले चेलवा	Bharat bhaile Chelawa	Bharat is the Disciple
राम के भरोसे	Ram ke bharose	So on Ram's authority
चल ले अकेल गे मायी	Chalale Akel ge mayi	I am going alone

राम गइले बनवा	Ram gaile banawa	Ram has been banished to the Forests
बिछड़ गइले भारत (वा)	Bichar gaile Bharat wa	Bharat is separated from him
जंगिया भरोसे	Janghiya bharose	I have but the force of my legs and (therefore)
हम चलले अकेल गे मायी	Ham chaal le Akel ge mayi	I go alone O mother!

(From Smt. Beegaylutchmee Ramloll Luchmun)
(Translation in English by Dr. Sarita Boodho)

There are several versions to this song. Another version goes thus from:

Taar bandhi dharti oupar asthan ge Maiyi
Ghumi phiri bandhi la
Deo asthan ge maiyi
Bich bhar jagahiya
Hamro ke daan de maiyi
Charon hi kona
Maiya gor tohar lagila
Ghumi phiri bandhi la
Deo asthan ge maiya
Bich bhar jagihiya
Hamro ke daan de maiya

Kehi howe guruwa
Kehi bhaile chelawa

Ram Howe guruwa
Bharat bhaile chelawa
Ram ke bharose
Chalale akel ge maiya

Ram gaile banwa
Bichar gaile Bharat (2)
Janghiya bharose
Ham chalale

Akel ge Mayi (2)
Ram gaila
Sasuraliya
Bharat gaila
Nanihal
Chalte Masan
Ham bandhi la
Akel
Okre bharose
Ham bandhi la akel
Akel ge mayi

According to Lilo Mathur, *geetharine* tradition bearer from Bambous, Black River District in West of Mauritius, she said:

"धरती के सकी कोई बंधे ?
धरती के, ओकर–पूजा होला।
आगे बहुत डाइन रहल।
ओहि खातिर ओझवा के बंधीला सऽ।
मारिया मसान के···औरु चलते बमत गे···"
बंगालिन लोग बोलत रहलन सऽ···जैसे
डी सायेरबा···ओसने ही बमत बा···"

"Dharti ke saki koi bandhe?"
Dharti ke okar puja hola.
Agey bahut daine rahal.
Oh khatir ojhawa
Ke bandhila sa,
Mariya masan ke auroo chalte bamat ge
Bengalines log bolat rahal
Jeisse Di, Sayer ba
Oisne hi bamat ba…
"Can anyone tie the Earth ?
We pray and do Veneration of (Mother) Earth.
Formerly there were many *daines* (Witches).
That is why we tied the Ojha
The *Mariya-Churail*-Witch and…

The cemetery...and also the walking *bamat*- a spirit.
This was known to the
Bengalis who came here first.
Just as we have spirits like
Di, Sayer so also the *Bamat*.

Note: *Mariya* is from *Mariamen* the Tamil equivalent of Kalimayi. During the immigration period each Sugar Estate Camp had a *Kovil* (Tamil Temple) and *Mariamen* was a prominent Goddess. It could also be interpreted as the मारी or महामारी (*mari/ mahamari*).

Dharti Bandhal Geet- Version 3

Lilo Mathur of Bambous (West of Mauritius) gave me an extraordinary version of the *Dharti Bandhal Geet* on Thursday 17 February, 2022 morning over the telephone. I had never heard of this song. Over the decades I had heard of the first two versions with some little variations but this third version holds a completely different variant in its bosom. She also took the pains to explain the esoteric meaning behind it and *'the natural and powerful forces which...belong to lesser known 'Folk cults'.**

1. तार बांधो धरती ऊपर असमान के घूमी फिरी बांधीला में घूमी फिरी बंधीला देवी अस्थान के मैं	Taar bandho dharti uppar asman ke ghumi phiri bandhi la main ghumi phiri bandhi la Devi asthan ke mein	I am tying the area Below and The sky above I turn round and Tie...I turn around and Tie the Devi's space
2. ओझावा के बांधीला मरिया मसान के डाइन के मैं बांधी ला चलते बमत गे मैं	Ojhawa ke bandhila Mariya Masan ke Daine ke main bandhi la Chaltey Bamat ke main	I tie the Ojha(exorcist) (The caster of spells, Charms) I tie the *mari*(spirit) The cemetery And I tie the walking Spirit

* Lopumudra Maitra Bajpai, Purbasa, East Meets West, 2019.

3. के तोरे गुरु वा के तोरे चेलवा केकर भरोसे चलते अकेल में	Ke tore guruwa Ke tore chelawa Kekar bharose Chalte akel main	Who is your Guru? Who is your disciple? By whose Authority I walk alone
4. राम होवे गुरुवा भरत होवें चेलवा उनकर भरोसे चलले अकेल मैं	Ram howe guruwa Bharat howein chelawa Ounkar bharose Chalale akel main	Ram is the Guru Bharat is the disciple I walk alone by Their Authority
5. छिति छिति कौली खोईचा बांधी लिहली गोद में बालक वा चलले अकेल गे मैं	Chitti Chitti Kowli Khoicha bandhi lihali Goad mein balak wa Chalale akel ge main	I take morsels of rice Tied in my kerchief (Khoincha) I have a child in my arms And I walk alone
6. हंसी हंसी पूछे ला सहर वा के लोग वा किया छोटा भाई किया हो छोटा देवर	Hansi hansi puche la Saharwa ke log wa Kiya chota bhai ho kiya ho chota dewar	Teasingly the city's folk ask me: Is it your brother (who is accompanying you) Or it is your *Dewar?* (husband's younger brother)
7. नाहीं छोटा भाई हो नाहीं हो छोटा देवरा करम के लिखल स्वामी हो हमार(2)	Nahin chota bhai ho Nahin ho chota dewara Karam ke likhal Swami ho hamaar(2)	Neither is he my younger brother Neither is he my *dewar* (husband's brother) It is my destiny That he is my Lord (husband)

The Explanative Underlying Substance of the 3rd Version of Dharti Bandhal Geet

Lilo Mathur has a different explanation to give of the *Dharti Bandhal Geet.* Even her song departs from what I have been hearing so far.

In her song which she obtained as a young girl from going around in *Geet Gawai* sessions with her *nanis, dadis, phouphous, gaon ke chachis,* she takes us to the netherworld which is included in the other two songs but not so explicity!

In '*tar bandha uppar asman ge*' she explains *tar* as *tare (*below*),* that is the *earth* over which the women would be dancing. She told me that in the old days there were many *daines* and therefore *ojhas* also were needed to exorcize people, So affected by the *daines*. She said to me that sometimes one would come across a '*teen konia' focal point of three roads* or *charkonia road (cross roads*) center of four road crossings, there would be at that spot offerings of broken coconuts, and a child's figure would be made with flour paste. '*okar kareja mein sat go soui bhokhat jat rahal'.* On the heart of the child thus made then with the flour paste – seven iron needles would be pierced and theses shady doings had evil purports. And if in the darkness of the night one were by mistake to walk over them, one would imbibe those evil vibrations and fall ill or should expect the worst of catastrophes in one's life. Till the 1970s I have myself witnessed such practices on the crossroads as I would be driving round the country in my youth movement *Seva Shivir* activities all over the island at night or at dawn. And one should avoid crossing over these substances. I do not see these, however nowadays!

She told me that the *Geetharines* on their *outings* on *Geet Gawai* singing sessions would sing such songs as to ward off any evil thoughts or Spirits. She told me even today when the *Geetharines* go to sing, they tie up a small bunch of *Sarso* – mustard seeds in a handkerchief and tuck it in their '*kamar*'- waist – '*kamar mein khons la' it* provides a protection. Once they are ready to dance after all the preliminary invocative songs are sung, the *Geetharines* then who used to sit on *chattai* – (mats) would turn the edge inside to make space for the dancers in the middle of the group.

As I have mentioned earlier, in the early days, the *Geetharines* would leave their huts/homes to come and sing, they are alone outside on the road in the night and need the protection of the Guru. Who is the Guru? Ram. The welfare of the lone *Geetharine* is left in the hands of Ram- the Guru. He is the all knowing protector. Here it is important to note that the *Ramayana Satsang* has been an important cultural trait of the *Girmitiyas.* The impact of Ramayana singing is felt on the *Geet Gawai* – just as the 'Var' the bridegroom is venerated as Ram, likewise one's protector too is Ram. So his brother *Bharat* is the disciple of Ram. A Guru needs a disciple. Bharat too is also involved. Ram has the Guru's *gyan*, knowledge, and he needs a follower. In this case, the disciple is Bharat. He assists Ram in his protecting measures.

Now if the *Geetharine* has neither the Protection of Ram nor his disciple she then musters her courage to go all alone to *Geet Gawai* singing. She thus does all her protecting mantras, before coming out of her house.

Another interesting aspect to this song is that, sometimes some lines were added by some ingenious *Geetharines*. The stories of Shakuntala, Nal Damyanti are very popular in Mauritius. Now in this song Shakuntala the legendary dutiful wife of Nal is taken as example! 'She' is going to sing...she carries a few grains of rice in her kerchief as a protection and '*khonso*' it, tuck it in her midriff, and carries her tender baby on one upper hip.

The town folk see her being accompanied by a young man shorter than her in height. They wonder: Who is accompanying her? Is it your younger brother or is it your husband's brother? Her reply is that it is neither her younger brother nor her younger brother-in-law *(dewar)*: She says it is my husband. It is my fate that I am taller than him!

Now such interpolations are known throughout the world's famous literature. Even in Tulsidas's Ram Charit Manas interpolations have been noted. Such additions are still more common in Oral traditions where new lines or words keep being added by new singers. In order to give the song more literary or scriptural coatings, such additions have been made.

From these simple observations made by village women who preserved these songs for generations and across the oceans, one can trace their origin to the Rig Veda, where praises are made of the Ratri Sukta or the Night of Duality. The Chandi Paath or Durga Saptasati, or Devi Mahatmya the Markandya Purana itself places its origin from the Rig Veda. Dispelling darkness in its manifold dimensions has been the preoccupation of mankind since the hoary past.

"एवं दश दिशो रक्षेच्चामुंडा शववाहना।
जया में चाग्रत: पातु विजया पातु पृठत: ।।"

"And all the ten directions may be protected by the Slayer of Passion and Anger, mounted upon the corpse of inert consciousness. In front may Victory protect me, and may Conquest protect me in the rear."

Man is always seeking protection from fear of the unknown.

From Devya Kavacham: (Vevses 49 & 51)

"अभिचारिणि सर्वाणि मंत्रयंत्राणि भूतले

(49) भूचरा: खेचराश्चैव जलजाश्चोपदेशिका: ।।

Abhicarani sarvani mantra yantrani bhutale

Bhucarah khecaras caiva jalajasaco padesikah"

All spells, mantras, amulets in existence, or those who move on the earth, or those who move in the air, or those born in water, or those counselled by others,

From Durgakavach:

"ग्रह भूत पिशाचाश्य यक्षगंधरवराक्षसा:

(51) ब्रह्मराक्षसवेताला: कूष्माण्डा भैरवादय: ।।

Graha bhuta pisacas yaksa gandharva raksasah

Brahma raksasa vetalah kusmanda bhairavadayah"

Or spirits of the planets, heavenly nymphs, celestial minstrels, demons, these proud of learning, goblins, demons causing disease, terrifying ones...

What the *Dharti Bandhal Geet* expressed in simple Bhojpuri lines, by *Geetharines* who want to protect themselves from all unforeseen misfortunes caused by supernatural forces, caused by an order of existence, beliefs or practices beyond the visible has been expressed before them in Shaastric texts recited by scholars and Pandits. The *Geetharines* have followed but the *Parampara,* the tradition- the concept of Oral tradition of yore.

The *Geet Gawai* songs form part of an important understandable units of the Indian Socio-Cultural experience dating back to the ancient times.

Dharti is exemplified as Mother. The protectress, the sacred female force who placates all forms of fear.

The Yajurvaveda Mantra:

विश्वानी देव सवितर्दूरितानी परासुव।

यदभद्रमतन्न आसुव।।

Vishwani deva savitarduritani paraasuva

Yad bhadramtann aasuva.

Is but an invocation to the Deva Savitar– the All creating

Divinity to 'keep far from us all evils and let us attain whatever be beneficial to us'.*

And again in the Atharva Veda:

अभयम नः करत्यंतरिक्ष्माभयम
धावापृथ्वी उभे इमे।
अभयम पश्चादभयम पुरसतादुततरा
दधरादभयं नो अस्तु।।

Abhayam nah karatyantarikshmabhayam
Ddyava prithivi oubhey imeh.
Abhayam paschadabhayam
Purastaduttara
Dadhara dabhayam no astu.

May the atmosphere give us peace and safety and may both these heaven and the earth be secure for us, may we be free from danger, from west and east and may there be no fear for us from north and south".

Finally from the Atharva Veda also:

अभयम मित्रादभयममित्रादभयं ज्ञातादभयं पुरोक्ष्यः।
अभयम नक्तमभयम दिवा नः सर्वा आशा मम मित्रम भवनतु।।

Abhayam mitradabhayam mitra dabhayam
Jyatadabhayam puroksha.
Abhayam naktamabhayam diva nah
Sarva asha mama mitram bhavantu.

"May we be fearless of our friends and even those who are unfriendly to us, may we never fall in dread of those whom we know and even of those whom we do not know, and may we remain free from any apprehension by night and in the day time. And may all the quarters be friendly to us."

Each era, each clime has its own songs whether Shaastric or folk or profane and mundane.

These *Geet Gawai* songs are mankind's Intangible Cultural Heritage. In today's world what Heritage are we to hand over to the future generations! What songs are we to create? If today's folk or bards are to create songs for posterity, certainly they would implore the powers that be to protect us from bio-chemistry

* Havana Mantras– Acharya Vaidyanath Shastri. Sarvadeshik Arya Pratinidhi Sabha, Delhi, 1982.

weapons and their nuclear destructive effects on mankind, may be from drones and social media's misuse-which are devised to harm.

What to say of the greatest Pandemic Mankind has known the Covid-19 which has upset the whole world and claimed millions in more than two years.

In the old days, the Immigrants and people in general prayed to Shitala Mata against '*Mahamari*' – epidemic such as small pox and measles. But Covid-19 defies the Goddesses! And it is still luring and producing several variants. What songs are we to compose for posterity to protect us from these deadly, dreadful manmade enemies?

□

27

Durga Kalimai–(Kalimayi)

"Nimiya Karwai nimiya
Shital beyar bahe
Tahi tare khar bhaile
Devi Maiya
Nimiya aahaar Kare"

(Given to me by Reeta Poonith, Head of *Geet Gawai* Schools)
(Wednesday 27 March, 2019)

"The leaves of the Neem tree are sour indeed
But they give cool breeze
Under the shade of that Neem tree
Stands the Devi Mother,
And enjoys the freshness of the neem leaves"

As Devi is the Goddess, protectress against small pox, measles etc., the neem leaves are used in bath water to cure affected persons or children.

The Mother Cult in the *Geet Gawai*

Mother Cult in the *Geet Gawai* is a very strong element. Before starting their singing and dancing session, the younger *Geetharines* touch the feet of the elders in the group and take their blessings.

Durga Worship – The Feminine Element

Worship of the Mother Energy is part of the *Geet Gawai* singing. The goddesses are invoked in many Bhojpuri songs.

Gawri's name and that of her epithets as well: the Sato Bahani, Sitala Mata and Durga, Kali is taken with much reverence. Mother worship is an ancient practice in not only the Hindu fold but many civilizations across the globe dating back to the hoary past.*

In fact the UNESCO gave recognition to the ancient Vietnamese tradition of worshipping Mother Goddesses in the same year they gave acceptance to the inscription of the Bhojpuri folk songs – *Geet Gawai* of Mauritius in December 2016 at Addis Ababa, Ethiopia. As per the Vietnamese traditions, a ritual is dedicated to the Mother Goddesses of Forests where 36 spirits are incarnated through dance, songs and offerings.

"The practice of shared values and strong belief in the compassion and grace of the Mother Goddesses provide a basis for social relations, connecting members of participating communities," said Mr. Nguyen Thu Hung, Head of the Vietnamese Department of Cultural Heritage at the UNESCO. This is an echo to a similar current in the Mauritian *Geet Gawai* singing. He added. "*Worship of the Mother Goddesses also contributes to the appreciation of women and their role in society*". Likewise the *Geet Gawai* Singing Session gives recognition to the role of the *Geetharines* in society.

The women *Geetharines* identify instantaneously very intuitively to the goddesses, as they share their joys and sorrows. They hold their *'anchra'* in both hands to make a supplication to the Mother.

When the *girmitiyas* landed in Mauritius it was a vast forested land with deep woods and forests which they cleaned to make way for sugarcane cultivation. As they would go to the fields walking long distances they would smear a stone here and there with vermilion to ward off evil and fear. A streak of vermilion (*sindur*) sanctified the stone and ensured protection to those passing by. The songs also mention that Debi's favourite site is under a *peepal* or *neem* tree. Thus at the end of each Bhojpuri village was found a little *Kalimai (kalimayi)* shrine which today has taken the shape of a temple.

Sitala mata would ward off diseases. In those days epidemics such as small pox, came ever so often and children and adults alike were not spared. There were many types of epidemic that

* Lopamudra Maitra Bajpai – Purbasa: East meets East 2019:194, 195.

would claim lives. Against all these the *Kalimai* was a deity who protected them and the village.*

"Nimiya ke daal maiya
Daleli hindolva
Maiya jhooli jhooli na
Maiya gave ni gitiya
Ke jhuli jhuli na"

(Provided to me by Padmashri Malini Awasthi from her album)

This is a very popular song sung by great Bhojpuri singers/ artists today in India who popularized the village *geet,* such as Manoj Tiwari now MP, *Padmashri* Malini Awasthi herself, Bharat Vyas and others. In Mauritius too there are several versions of this song that are retained.

Therefore to sing five songs in honour of *Sandhya,* Dusk also a feminine deity is very essential followed by other *Debi geets.*

Durga is one of the most formidable goddesses of the Hindu Sacred Space.

The month of Ashvin (September–October) marks the arrival of the Goddess Durga when she comes down from the Mount

* Dr. Sarita Boodhoo, Kanya Dan The Whys of Hindu Marriage Rituals: Mauritius Bhojpuri Institute, 1993.

Kailash in the Himalayas, the abode of her husband Lord Shiva. Durga Puja is more than a ritual. It invests the lives of everyone with a new consciousness for the nine days she is among us known as Navratri, the nine nights. There is an inexplicable fervour on the community around this time.

Durga is one of the most impressive and formidable goddesses of the Hindu Sacred Space. And no doubt one of the most popular. The term Durga itself signifies in Sanskrit a fortress referring to one who protects but who is also unassailable.

From the hoary past, Durga has epitomized Shakti, riding invincible on her vehicle, the fierce lion, and king of the forest. It is in the context of a cosmic crisis caused by a demon the *Mahisa* who could not be subdued by the gods that Durga came into being. Most unsubmissive, not even to the male deity, Durga rules mighty and alone. She is not given to fulfill household duties. She is a warrior. She can hold against any male on the battlefield. Unlike the normal role attributed to women, Durga stands outside the normal societal code. She stands on her own. It is at the inability of the gods to tackle *Mahisa,* who was granted a boon through his austerities that he would be invincible, except by a woman, that Durga was conceived. And thus the desperate gods created Durga out of a great cosmic light. She was so resplendent that her splendour spread throughout the universe.

Durga is empowered with all the Cosmic Energy. All her companions who manifest as different forms of her own self are female like her. She deludes the demon. She is beautiful and seductive in appearance. With this beauty she entices her victims who seek to be her lovers, the demons into a fatal encounter whom she tears to pieces. The female elements who support her are among others the ferocious Kali, and the group powerful deities known as the *Sapta Matrikas* – the seven mothers. They are as wild and fierce as she is. She is equally the most benign protectress of the Universe and humanity.

However the gods empower Durga with their weapons. Shiva gives her his trident, Vishnu gives her his *chakra* – the discus. Vayu – the Wind God gives her his bow and arrows. Durga holds all the weapons that can uphold Dharma, including her own weapons: the conch, sword, javelin, shield, and a noose.

Actually man lives by his imagination and myths and stories. When man first appeared on earth he was faced with the vast cosmos and its terrible climatic phenomena. He was awed by the cosmogony of the universe which puzzled and intrigued him. Over millennia, he developed myths and legends that followed him into his cave dwellings, into the forests, the fertile plains, the mountains, the deserts and the oceans. In this vast evolution of the universe, he too went on evolving, battling against all the hazards of nature and his own species, *Homo sapiens*. He needed a Father and a Mother to take care of him, to listen to his pleas and supplications and who would love him, protect him and console him.

Thus our ancient ancestors developed tales and lores that have passed on from several thousands of years into oral and then written literature.

And so began the story of the Devi Mahatmya, one of the most beautiful Sanskrit religious texts. The story existed much before it was actually composed. "Throughout the Eurasian land-mass as far back as Paleolithic times, women and men observed the female's awesome capacity to create new life and identified that power with divinity." (Devi Mahatmya - David Nelson 2003). The pre-Harappan cultures existing thousands of years before the Devi Mahatmya appeared worshipped the Mother Goddess/goddesses as did their counterparts in other civilizations in the Neolithic Near East.

The notion of one supreme Goddess is formulated in a Rig Vedic hymn known as *Devisukta* (Hymn to the Goddess Rig Veda V 10.125). Other goddesses too such as Vak, Saraswati, and Aditi etc. are mentioned. In these verses of the Devisukta the Devi reveals her might and glory. "She is the shining consciousness...in her, all lives who see and breathe and hear what is said." She is the mother of all. She rules and upholds the universe. Her greatness pervades heaven and earth. She is transcendental. It is therefore widely held by scholars and the learned that the *Devisukta* of Rig Veda holds the origin of the Devimahatmya.

It is much later that a story told and retold took shape

around the fifth or sixth century AD within the Puranic scriptures. Some however argue that the Devi Mahatmya originates several centuries before Christ. This marks indeed a defining moment in Hindu religious history of several millennia. The Devi Mahatmya also known as Devi Saptasati has united diverse strands of Indian mythology, practices, beliefs and philosophy, ultimately producing the one great magnificent divine poem glorifying the great Goddess Durga.

The three Durga Dhyana *Argala–Stotra*, *Kilaka Stotra* and *Devi-Kavaca* (all salutations to Candika) are the gateways to the unfolding of the splendour of Goddess Durga.

Believed to be developed from the Northwest of India in Kashmir, the Devi Mahatmya spread in quick strides into Bengal where it became known as *Chandi.* And the rest of India. When the outmigration of the *Girmitiya* Indentured labour took place from this Bhojpuri-Bengali-Awadhi-Oria- belt as from 1834 the people carried with them also the Devi story. That is why every village or hamlet of Mauritius had a *Kalimai* under a *Neem* tree, who guarded the village and protected the displaced Indian in an alien environment. The Ramakrishna Mission in Vacoas has been the precursor of Durga worship on a large scale in Mauritius and has for decades celebrated the Durga Puja as the much revered Ramakrishna was a *Bhakta par excellence* of the great Mother.

The Durga Puja gained greater prominence and popularity among all Hindus in India and the Indian diaspora with the advent of Bollywood and its magnificent devotional powerful soul stirring songs sung by equally powerful nightingales such as Lata Mangeshwar and Anuradha Paudwal, and others.

In 1975 the advent of the film *Jai Santoshi Ma* (Mother Satisfaction/Contentment) gave another boost to the worship of the Goddess and created a new wave in Mother worship.

But the picturing of Ma Durga in several Bollywood films with accompanying poignant Devi songs have given a new vibrancy to the worship of Durga and her other female companions like Kali. Greater academic research and studies by scholars in the West and E-technology have also helped in the impact of the Female Energy manifested through Durga Devi. In Mauritius during the Durga Puja festivals professional and working women worship the

Durga in their homes early morning before they set out to work. It goes without saying that this period is strictly a vegetarian regime for one and all in the family.

A myth is not a mere fiction, just because it does not describe a historical occurrence, say the authorities. Synesius of Cyrene said *"Myths are things that never happened, but always are."* Truths which elude us normally in our mundane life and difficult to explain or grasp in our own conventional ways, are grasped through myths told and retold orally, touching deeply at the root of the human psyche. The great mythologist Joseph Campbell defines myths as:

- Inspiring a sense of awe
- Explaining the origin and nature of cosmos
- Supporting the social and moral order
- Awakening individuals to discover their own Inner Self.

As is done definitely in the *Devi Mahatmya.*

The Devi Mahatmya or Sapta Sati also known as Chandi is divided into 13 chapters of seven hundred *mantras*. Three aspects of the Durga – Divine Mother are depicted (1) Mahakali (2) Mahalakshmi (3) Mahasaraswati.

During the *Durga Puja*, *kathas* or *Durga* Paath are conducted in all temples or improvised beautifully decorated pavilions. The many legends and other stories showing the victory of the invicible Durga are recited together with *upkathas.* Veritable cities of the Goddess are created. With sounds, symbols and other manifestations, *Bhakti* – devotion is aroused in the public. Truly the Devi significantly manifests herself to ardent devotees. Three characters are central to the Devi Mahatmya: the virtuous king Surath disowned by his own after the loss of his kingdom; the Merchant Samadhi equally dispossessed of his wealth and thrown out by his greedy family including wife and sons. The third character is the *Seer – Medha* in his hermitage in the beautiful peaceful forest abode. The *Sutradhara* – Markandeya relates the story. The Seer relates to them the story of Mahamaya–disillusion and how they can come out of it through surrender to the Mother Goddess.

Science and Maths too make use of symbols to reach a certain truth. Likewise the ancient people used lores, myths and symbols to take the restless mind of man especially the general folk to the Higher Consciousness or Truth.

"Goddess worship occupies an important segment of Indian socio-cultural phenomenon from very ancient times...the goddess is a primordial being who was believed in and worshipped by people for several thousands of years. She is often variously referred to as a source of life, and many examples can be found in caves... and in several manuscripts... as well as in numerous oral traditions and folklore.*

Nimiya ke daar: Swing on Neem Tree

1. **Nimiya ke daar maiya**
Lawelou Hindolwa ki jhuli jhuli Na,
Sato bahini gaweli gitti ki jhuli jhuli Na
Jhulte jhulat maiya
Lageli piyasiya
Ki chali bhaili
Malahoriya awase ki chali bhaili

O mother on the branch of a
Neem tree you have built a swing
On which you are enjoying the swing
The seven sisters are singing while enjoying the swing
While swinging, the Mother feels thirsty
She makes her way to the Gardener's house

2. ***Sutal howe je***
Maline jagal baaru
Ki boondwe mohi
Mohi paniya piyaye ki
Boondwe moh

Are you sleeping or
Are you awake, a drop of water
Give me a drop of water
Give me a drop of water to drink

* Lopamudra Maitra Bajpai – Purbasa: East meets East 2019:194, 195.

3. ***Kaisse ka paniyan***
Piyayi ho maiya
Ki godiye more
Howe sewaka tohar
Ki more gode
How can I give you water to drink,
O Mother
I hold your child on my lap.

4. ***Sone ke hindolwa***
Maline balaka sutawaho
Ki boondwe mohi
Pani piyaye
Ho ki boondwe mohi

O garderner's wife put your child to sleep on the
Golden cot, a drop of water,
O gardener's wife give me a drop of water to drink.

5. ***Sone ke hindolwa je***
Devi balaka sutaiba
Ki i dhurijai ho
Balakwa rawri bhueeyan
Ho ki loti jayi ho
If I put my child to sleep
O Devi in the golden cot
The child will fall
From the golden cot
To the floor.

6. ***Dhiya jaihe naihar***
Patohiya jaihe sasural
Ki boond we mohin paniya
Piyaya ho ki boondwe mohi

My daughter has gone to her mother's place
My daughter-in-law to her in-laws'

(Here the lines seem to have been mixed by the tradition bearer)
O Give me a drop of water
O Gardener's wife

7. ***Ek hath le le maline***
Dawana maruwa ho (flower fragrant)
Dahine haathe ho ki
Paniya piyaye ho ki
Dahine haathe...

O Mother, I pour water for you
From my right hand
And offer you flowers of **dawna** (sweet scented)
And **maruwa** *from the other.*
Quench your thirst, O drink Mother.

8. ***Jaissé ki maline***
Mohi jurawlou ki oissé
Tor patohiya jurayi
Maline oissé
Tor dhiyawa jurai ho
Ki oissé

Just as you quenched my thirst, O Gardener's wife
And comforted me,
In the same way
Your daughter-in-law will be happy and blessed
In the same way
Your daughter will be blessed in her home

In other versions the last verse goes like this:
The gardener's wife says
"***Dhiya baardhé sasurar***
Patohiya baarhe naihar
Kekra maiya dihal asish ho ki kekra"

My daughter is at her in-law
My daughter-in-law has gone to her parents' house
To whom are you giving your blessings?
O Mother?

The Goddess answers:

"Dhiya jurahiyein aapan
Sasurarwa ge maline
Tohre patohiya lowti
Aihein sasurarwa
Sanjhé diyara barihein
Devi khijamti karihein"

O Gardener's wife
Your daughter will be happy
And blessed at her in-law's place
And your daughter-in-law
Will come back to her (in-laws')
Your house
And she will light the lamp in honour of ***sanjha*** *(Dusk)**

The Village Kalimai

'Nimiya Ke Daar', Debi hymn.

Folk songs dedicated to the Mother Goddess are deeply entrenched in Mauritius as well as in the Bhojpuri belt of India. As it moved from the thousands of villages in Bihar and Eastern Up in the throats of the *girmitiyas* to Mauritius, likewise it also moved from the villages to the urban areas of Patna, Varanasi, Delhi, Kolkata and Mumbai, wherever the eastern people migrated.

* 1. Marriage Songs from Bhojpuri Region
Chandramani Singh Champa Lal Ranka and Co Published by Kitab Mahal, Jaipur. 1979. P. 42 – 43

2. निमिया के डाढ़ि मईया लवली हिंडोलवा
भोजपुरी संस्कार गीत संपादक : हंसकुमार तिवारी राघावल्लभ शर्मा बिहार-राष्ट्रभाषा-परिषद, पटना-1977, पृ. 182-183 मइया गीत

The *Nimiya ke daar* Bhojpuri song has been further made popular through its rendering by internationally known Bhojpuri singers.

The Debi likes to take her seat under the *Neem* tree, dear to her. The song depicts a story relating a dialogue between the Debi and the *'Maline'*, the gardener's wife. It is the *maline* who used to make the first offerings to her taking her choicest flower especially the red *'ulhur'*. So while enjoying the swing in midday on the *Neem* tree, the Goddess feeling thirsty goes to the *maline's* house to ask for 'a drop of water'. The *maline* is putting to sleep her baby in her lap.

The *maline* replied that how she can give the Goddess water, when the baby is in her lap, fast asleep. So the *Debi* answers that you put the baby on my golden *'khatolwa'*- a small cot. The *maline* replies that the cot will be broken and my baby will fall on the earth. The *Debi* then replies that I will grant you grace when you satisfy my thirst. The *maline* further tests the *Debi* that my daughter is married away in her *sasural* and my daughter-in-law is at her *naihar* (parents' place). To which the *Debi* replies that she will shower her blessings on her married daughter and her daughter-in-law will come back to her and lead a happy life. The *Debi* is close to the village woman who unfolds her heart to her about her social and family life. To the *maline* the baby in her lap has the first priority. It only illustrates the mother's love for her baby and the women folk in her house.

The *Debi* is referred to also as *Durga* and the *sato bahanis,* her epithets. In different variations to this song found in India and in Mauritius she is sometimes referred to as *Shitala Mata. Shitala* is the protectress against small pox. The epidemic of small pox used to cause havoc in pre-Health prevention days whether in the Gangetic belt or in Mauritius. And now we are facing the ravage of the Covid 19 Pandemic!

In the collection of Bhojpuri folk songs of Bihar published by *Rastra Bhasha Parishad* available at Bhojpuri Academy of Bihar, (Bhojpuri *Sanskar Geet* P 182 -183) the editors say that the *'Nimiya ki daar'* song is sung prior to the *Tilak vidhi*. In this the bride groom's mother gives water to *Shitala Mata* to appease her thirst so that she gets her blessings for her daughter-in-law to be.

Late Pandit Dr. Kuber Mishra former Founder Principal of Mahatma Gandhi Post Graduate College of Maltari, Azamgarh was the first one to make a deep research on the Bhojpuri folk songs of Mauritius as a PhD research scholar in 1977-1978 and toured the whole island meeting and listening to Bhojpuri women folk singers. He brought out a book entitled *Mauritius ke Bhojpuri Lokgeetan ka Vivechnatmak Adhyayan* based on his scholarly work. Among the Bhojpuri songs collection he came across the *Debi geet 'Nimiya ke Daar'* almost as sung in the Bhojpuri belt of India, with some variations which is a normal phenomenon of folk songs and especially after a long separation from the Mother Country in time and space. He has given a comparison with one variety of the same song found in Pandit Krishna Deo Upadhyaya's book *Bhojpuri Folk lore* from Varanasi. The similarity is indeed remarkable.

One also finds *'Nimiya ke Daar'* song in Dr. Suchita Ramdin's book *'Sanskar Manjari'* which was published by the Mahatma Gandhi Institute in 1989 (P210-211). Dr. Suchita Ramdin went round interviewing Bhojpuri folk singers all around the island in the 1980s as Head of the Department of Bhojpuri, Folk lore and Oral Traditions of the Mahatma Gandhi Institute. The song bears a remarkable resemblance to the one collected by Dr. Kuber Mishra in 1977-78 with slight variations, as well as to the other *'Nimiya ke daar'* songs still prevalent in India till date as sung by Manoj Tiwari, Malini Awasthi, Bharat Sharma and other well-known popular Bhojpuri Singers.

In Dr. Chandramani Singh's *'Marriage Songs from Bhojpur Region',*[*] again in the *'Nimiya ke Daar'* song reference is made to the same dialogue between the *Debi (Shitala)* and the *Maline* (gardener). Fantastic journey of a folk tale song.

Nimiya Ke Daar

I personally collected one version from Chhapra on 11 April, 2013 at Prof Lal Babu Yadav's place and another one from Shanti

---

* Published by Kitab Mahal Jaipur in 1979, P. 42 –43.

Devi, wife of Bhojpuri Writer, Publisher Nagendra Prasad Singh at that time residing in Patna (31 March, 2013).

Some slight variations occur here and there but the gist and essence are the same, with the same tune and the same theme of a dialogue between the *debi (Shitala)* and the *(malahoriya)* gardener's wife.*

□

* **Dr. Kuber Mishra: Nimiya ke Daar**

Dr. Krishnadev Upadhyaya – Bhojpuri Lokgeet, P. -154-55; 2 Edition, Prayag

(a) *Smt. Prabhavati Singh– Lokgitika, P. 52-1969*

(b) *Durgaprasad Singh– Bhojpuri Lokgiton mein karuna ras, P. 458*

(c) *Ramnaresh Tripathi– Kavita Kaumudi 3rd Part Gram geet, P. 699, 2 Edition, 1955, Bombay*

28

The Fire Worship: Homa Bhaile

Agni the Fire Worship

The *Geet Gawai* performers sing songs for every stage of the Hindu marriage ceremony, such as at the time of the welcoming of the bridegroom and his party by bride's parents and people, at the giving away of the daughter ceremony known as *Kanya Dan,* the lighting of the sacred fire – the *'Agni'* on the *Vedi* or marriage altar, around which the *dulha* and *dulhan* move four times to take the marriage vow, the *sindur dan* ceremony or application of the vermilion powder on the brides' mid – hair parting by the bridegroom. For the Hindu ceremonies, the lighting of the sacrificial fire plays a primordial role. The Fire is considered as the sacred central cultural witness and in fact is a symbol of the fire of life, from the time a child is conceived to the end of human being's life, when the body is ultimately consumed by fire.

The *Geet Gawai* performers sing to accompany the lighting of the sacred Fire.

"Homa bhaile jap bhaile
Dhumwa akas gaile
Baba ke dev sab anand bhaile
Aaju ghar wa jug bhaile
Sorahi gaye ke ghiv howein
Aam ke lakariya howein
Amwa ke pallawa bipre homa kaile
Aaju gharwa jug bhaile"

"With the lighting of the sacrificial fire,
And the chanting of the Sacred Mantras (verses)
The family gods are pleased,

As the smoke rises heavenwards.
Father's gods and deities are blissful and pleased, that they have been thus honoured. And shower their blessings on the house.
The environment is purified and exudes fragrance.
The sacrificial fire is lit with the purest of clarified butter.
The butter has been obtained from the milk of the best of cows.
The choicest of mango twigs has been selected for the sacrifice
(Mango is one of the nine sacred woods used for the sacrificial Fire)
The tender mango leaf/leaves are used by the priest to offer the oblation.
The house is blessed as the smoke rises from the sacrificial fire. Thus exhorted it spreads a sweet fragrance
In the house and atmosphere."

Fire is a means to eliminate, to burn the impurities. As the *dulha* and *dulhan* together pour the offerings in the sacred fire, they also burn their own impurities and come together burning their own ego. Thus, they pledge themselves in front of this Great Witness to unite as one to face the responsibilities of a new life together.

□

29

Other Types of Bhojpuri Songs

Many other varieties which have been preserved comprise *lalnas or sohar* – birth songs. People when celebrating the 6th day of bath – the *Chathi* or the *barhi* (twelve days bath of the mother and child) after child birth invite friends and family members to a ceremony with feasts where the *Geetharines* sing *lalnas* and *sohar*. Other songs such as *sabad* are sung principally by the *kabir panthi* traditionally to accompany the funeral procession to the funeral pyre ready for cremation. They are also known as *'nirguna'*, and based on the *dohas* of Kabir, a Bhojpuri poet saint of the Middle Ages. It should be remembered that many of the Indentured Labour immigrants came from this vast Gangetic Plain that was crossed by Kabir, two centuries prior to the immigration and his disciples who continued his message, left their impact on the migrating people's consciousness.

Harparawri Songs

Tradition bearers also sing songs to implore the Rain God, Indra to give rain during the drought period. The *harparawri songs* are sung to invoke Lord *Indra* – to give rain in times of drought. These songs are still found in the repertoire of the *Geet Gawai* women and are known as *harparawri* or rain giving songs. An ancient custom in India in times of drought it has been adopted to Mauritius too. It gives the village women folk also an opportunity to participate in the welfare of the economy of the country. For there is nothing worse than drought for an agricultural community. They also sang the *jantsar* or stone mill song as they laboriously crushed the pulses on the *'djanta'*, grinding stones. These songs are still known and sung in Mauritius as they tell the pathetic plight of the daughter-in-law at the hand of the all-powering mother-in-law in an orthodox joint family system.*

ओम् इन्द्राय स्वाहा।
इदमिन्द्राय इदन्न मम।।
"Om Indraye Swaha
Idan Indraye Idan Mama"

Yajur Veda

Indra in the Vedas

Indra in the *Vedas* is the paramount *God.* In the *Puranas,* he has been relegated to a subordinate position (to *Vishnu* and *Shiva*).

But to the Vedic seers, *Indra* is higher than all the cosmos:

'Vishwamat Indra Uttarah'

He *(Indra)* is the overload of our triple existence of

Matter
Life and
Spirit

And master of *swarg* which is the luminous world of the *Divine Mind.*

In the words of Shri Aurobindo:

"He comes down into the world.
As the Hero with the shining
Horses and slays darkness
And division with his
Lightings, pours down the life-giving heavenly waters."

हरपरवरी गीत	Harparawri Song (Roman)	Harparawri Song (English Translation)
आला सुख गईल	Al(a) sukh gail	• The whole area is parched
पाला सुख गईल	Pal(a) sukh gail	• The dam is dried up

* *'Leisure and the Indian Migrants in Mauritius and Reunion'*
—Dr. Sarita Boodhoo, 1995

सुख गईल दादा के धान, हो !	Sukh gail Dada ke dhaan, ho!	• Dried up is the rice field of Dada
बरस बरस	Baras baras	• Give us Rain-2
इन्द्र देबता	Innar debta	• Innar (Indar) Deota (God)
पनिया के पड़ल बा अकाल हो ! बरस बरस बरस बरस	Paniya ke Padhal ba Akal ho ! Baras baras Baras baras	• There is scarcity of water • Come give us Rain, Give us Rain • Give us Rain. Give us Rain

Note:
हर – Har - Plough
परव – Parav - Festival
हरपरवरी – Harparawri – The Festival of Ploughing the Field

Jantsar

To ease their hard work, the suppressed daughters-in-law gave vent to their pent – up feelings in singing the *jantsar* pathetic songs. Meeting at the village tap or well to collect water was also a moment of respite where they sang songs such as *'Cheingan Maingan Pani Bhare Pani Nai Ba'* They organised themselves in groups for washing clothes at the local riverbanks or to collect fire wood for the house *chulha* or walk for long distances with their *hanswa* (Sickle) on their shoulders to fetch bundles of fodder on their head. While doing all this, they brought out numerous oral songs stored in their repertoire or memory. These today form the basis of the *Geet Gawai* in Mauritius. Unknowingly, the *Geet Gawai* women have been as tradition bearers and practitioners, the repository of a long *civilizational ethos* that dates back to the Rig Vedic period.

Jantsar (Jatsar)

The *Jantsar* songs are a collection of Bhojpuri songs sung by women while turning round by hand the flour mill stone or the *djanta (chakki*). In the old days pulses, rice, wheat etc. had to be pounded by these hand driven flour mill stones, once the harvest done on local lands. Two three women used to sit around to turn the wheel while pouring in the pulses to be grounded. It was very hard work and while doing this tedious work women sang pathetic songs of woe and distress. These songs are very touching and heart rending. The daughter-in-law sang about the dominance and overbearing reprove of the Mother-in-law. The bride's brother who would come to visit his sister after a long period would be shocked to see the maltreatment of his sister and the poor conditions in which she would be living. Sometimes he would be treated with disrespect at his brother-in-law's place. Sometimes unable to bear the harsh conditions subjected by the in-laws, the young bride would throw herself in the village well. All these affronts and afflictions have been woven into beautiful lyrics sung by generations of women in the Gangetic belt. These sad songs tell many stories replete with mercy, pity, pain and sympathy. The tunes of the songs help to create that sort of languorous melody that touches the heart of both singer and listener with grief, bringing tears to eyes. When the Indian immigrant women-the *Girmitiyas* came to Mauritius, they brought along with them these songs and refrains and maintained them for generations while doing the same job of turning the *djanta* here on Mauritian soil in a new alien environment. The songs used to be part of a reality until came the new revolution of electric electronic kitchen gadgets. But these songs are a veritable gem of intangible Cultural Heritage of Humanity and need to be preserved for future generations as a rich compendium of human experience.

In Mauritius, every Indian home had a *djanta*. Today they have become tangible historical relics that speak of a gone by age of woe and are kept as museum pieces in homes and institutes such as at the Mahatma Gandhi Institute's Indian Immigration Museum or the Bikramsing Ramlallah Interpretation Centre of the Aapravasi Ghat Trust Fund in Port Louis at the former Indian Immigration Depot.

जांतसार

मचिये बैठल होवे सासु हो बढ़ईतीन,	Machiya baithal howe Sasu ho badhaitine (as a mother-in-law)	The Mother-in-law in all her Glory or distinguished position (as a mother in law) is sitting relaxed on the Raised platform the *machan* (A sort of a bench)
काई होयें आजू के भोजन वा हो राम भइया मोरे अईलऽ पहुना वा हो राम काई होयें आजू के भोजन अहलऽ पहल बहूआ भूंजी भाजी उपरे लहरिया के दलिया हो दीहिये राम	Kai hoyein aaju Ke bhojan wa Ho Ram Bhaiya more aila pahun wa Ho Ram Kai hoyein aaju Ke bhojan? Ahal pahal bahuwa Bhunji bhaji Upare lahariya ke daliya ho dihiya Ram	O mother, asks the daughter- in-law what do we cook for today Ho Ram My brother will be coming as our guest Ho Ram What shall we prepare For lunch? O daughter-in-law, whatever is Available such as leafy vegetables You may cook and serve the ***Arhar dal* soup over and above. O Ram
एही होइए आजू के भोजन हो राम स्वामी मोरे बैसे ला जेवनारी	Ehi hoiyein aaju ke Bhojan ho Ram Swami more baisse la Jewanari	This will be today's meal Oh Ram My husband and my brother sat down (on the mat) to have their Their meal
भैया मोरे बइसल जेवनारी हो राम बहनोइया बैठल बा जेवनारी सार हो भोजन जब बैसे हो राम	Bhaiya more baisse la Jewanari IIo Ram Bahanoiya baithal ba Jewanari Sar ho bhojan jab baisse Ho Ram	Both the *behnoi* (brother in law) and his *sar* (wife's brother) are sitting for the meal
भैया ही बैसे ला जेवनारी नैना धरे हो लोर वा हो राम	Bhaiya hi baisse la Jewanari Naina dhare (bhai ke ankh) ho lor wa Ho Ram	As my brother sat to have his food, his eyes were filled with tears.
चाँद सूरज ऐसन बहिनी बीहली बहिन बसे ला ससुरलिया हो राम दोनों नैना भरे लोर वा	Chand suraj eissan Bahini bihali Bahin bassey la sasuraliya Ho Ram Donon naina bhare lor wa	***(He was reflecting to himself That my sister who has been)*** Brought up with so much care and love and who looked as bright as the sun and beautiful as the moon now look at her situation at her in laws! His two eyes were filled with tears

साजी देबू धनिया ढाल तलवार हम जैबो मधुबन अब सिकरवा हो राम	Saaji debou dhaniya Dhal talwar Ham jaibon madhuban Sikarwa ho Ram	(after the meal) The husband tells his wife O wife give me my Shield and sword we are going for a Hunting session in the forest Ho Ram
धार झरोखा चढ़ी बहिनी नीरखे बहिनिया झरोखा पर चहर स्वामी मोरे मारे खेले ला सीकरिया हो राम जब मोरे स्वामी गइलन मधुबन भइया जी के मारे तलवार खेले लन सीकार मधुबन स्वामी मारे लन भइवा धार तलवार भइया मोरे मारे चटकनिया से	Dhar jharokha chadhi Bahini nirekhe Bahiniya jharokha Par chahar Swami more mare khele la Sikariya Ho Ram Jab more Swami gailan madhuban Bhaiya ji ke mare talwar Khele lan sikar madhuban Swami mare lan bhaiya dhar talwar Bhaiya more mare Chatkaniya se	When they left, the sister climbed on the small window of the house to look beyond at what was happening! My husband took out his sword O Ram When my husband went to the forest he removed his sword from the sheath and he attacked my brother with his sword This was his game O Ram! But my brother was unarmed and defenceless and he defended himself with his hands
बेल तरे मरलन बबूर (बबूल) तरे ओढ़ईले बा बबूर तिक्ति के पत्ता होरयले बा	Bel tare marlan Babul tare Odhaile ba babur Tikti ke paata horaile ba	My husband (thus) killed my brother and put his body to rest under the foliage of the *Bel* creeper And buried his Body under The Babul (the gum-arabic Tree-*Acacia Arabica*) He covered the body with The leaves of the Babul And the leaves of the (*tiktika* /Sanskrit) The bitter gourd leaves *(Momordica charantia)*
आजी राती गईले पहर राती गईले स्वामी मोरा अइलन खोलू मोरा धनिया बजरा कंवरिया	Aaji rati gaile Pahar rati gaile Swami mora ailan Kholu mora dhaniya Bajara kanwariya	My husband came back after two nights and said: O Wife open the sturdy steel framed gate
कहंवा ही भीजेलऽ ढाल तलवरवा हो रहिया चलत हौवें बाग हो सियार वा होवें मोहे भिंजेली पेली हो मोरे तलवरवा हम लहूआ	Kahanwa hi bhinjela Talwar wa ho Rahiya chalet howe Bag ho siyar wa Howein mohe bhinjeli peli ho More talwarwa ham lahuwa	(Asked the wife?) How and Where did your shield get Soaked (with blood)? There were tigers and jackals on the wayfare, this is how My shield and sword got soaked in blood This is how my horse too got covered with blood

कैसे में भिंजल स्वामी पाँव वा तोहर हो बहुत घंसवा सीतला में भीजल गोर मोरे (पाँवा) रहिया में हौए धनिया बहुते ही धसवा हुवों मोरे भिंजल मोरे पाँवा	Kaisse mein bhinjal Swami Paaw wa tohar ho? Bahut ghanse wa Sitala mein bhinjal Gor more (panwa) Rahiya mein Howe dhaniya Bahute hi ghanswa Honwe more bhinjal More panwa	But O husband how did your feet got soaked in blood? There was a lot of dew in the grass O wife, it was foggy and my feet got wet O Wife There was a lot of grass on the thoroughfare This is how my feet got wet O Wife
झूठे नाही बोलऽ स्वामी साचे साचे बोल कहाँ हमार भाई ? हमार भाई के कहाँ सुतइला तोहरा ही छोड़ स्वामी कोई के नाही होइबऽ	Jhuthe nahin bola swami Sacche Sacche bola kahan Hamar bhai? Hamar bhai ke kahan sutaila? Tohra hi chhor Swami Koyi ke nahin hoyib	Do not lie O husband Tell me the truth Where is my brother ? Where have you laid Down his body? I have no one besides you O my husband
सच्चे सच्चे हमरो बतावऽ हो राम तोरहा ही छोड़ स्वामी कोई का नाही होइब बेल तरे मरली बबूल तरे सुतइली तिक्ति के पत्ता होरईले हो राम	Sacche sacche hamro Batawa Ho Ram Tohra hi Chhor Swami Koyi ka nahin hoyib Bel tare marli Babul tare sutaili Tikti (tiktika) ke patta Horaile ho Ram !	Tell me the truth where did you kill my brother and where did you lay his body to rest? I have only you in my life I struck him under *Bel* creeper And laid him to rest under the *Babul* (Acacia Arabica) And covered the body with The leaves of *tikti* (Sanskrit) (Bitter Gourd).
तोहर छोरी स्वामी हम कोई के नई होवब	Tohar chhori Swami ham koyi Ke nai howab	Besides you O my hu Husband, I will never give myself To another one!
चलू (2) भइया के बतावऽ हम देखब भैया के सुरतिया	Chalu (2) bhaiya ke batawa Ham dekhab bhaiya ke suratiya	Come, come show me where you have laid Down my brother I want to see his face
जावू (2) स्वामी हो खोजी लकरिया	Jawu (2) Swami ho Khoji lakariya	O my husband Go fetch the woods
भैया जी के अंतिम करावब हो राम	Bhaiyaji ke antim karawab ho Ram !	So we can do the last Funeral rites of my Brother!

गोदिया जंगिया में सुरतिया ही लिहली भैया जी के सिर वा दूनों नैना लोर धरतऽ	Godiya jangiya mein Suratiya hi lihali bhaiyaji ke sir wa Dounon naina lor dharal	She took her brother's Head and placed him on Her lap and her eyes Were filled with tears.
सतवा के होइबे हमरो मोरे भैया धरती से अगनी धनकाव हो राम! जरी जई हें भाई बहिनिया	Saṭwa ke hoyi be Hamro more bhaiya Dharti se agni dhankawa ho Ram ! Jari jayihein bhai baheniya	If you belong to the Righteous path O Brother let the fire emerge From the Earth. Both Brother and sister were in This way consumed by The flames.
नाही हम जनली धनिया बुदधी मोरे हरा (धरा) गैल ज्ञान मोरे हरा गईले हो राम!	Nahin ham janli dhaniya Buddhi more hara (dhara) gayil Gyan more hara gayil Ho Ram !	Had I known my wife I would not have done so! I lost my senses. I lost control of my mind. O Ram !

** Note-The *arhar* (lahar) is the pigeon pea, formerly obtained in every compound. The plants yielding these peas used to form a sort of hedge. The woody plant which yield these seeds, with pods and foliage are also used as fodder. In Mauritius, the *arhar* is known as *Embrevade* which in Mauritian Bhojpuri has become and is pronounced as '*barbat*'. Both the terms *arhar* (*lahar*) and *barbat* are used locally. One can see that it is very common ordinary pulse that grows wild and that nothing special was cooked for the daughter-in-law's brother!

The Suhag Geet

The ***suhag*** means the auspicious marriage. Gods and goddesses are invoked by their names to see that all goes well for the bride and bridegroom coming together.

सुहाग
सादी के गीत के बाद सुमिरन धरती के गीत होवे ला तब सुहाग गीत होवे ला—मानती राममुडीन

नदी तरे मालीन लोढ़े फूल हुवाँ में हो राम	Nadi tare Maline lodhe phul Huwan mein ho Ram	By the river bank The gardener's wife is Plucking flowers O Ram The bridegroom is standing

दूल्हा थारी रही (दादी पुछतह) हंसी हंसी पूछे ला दादी दूल्हा के	Dulha thari rahi (Dadi puchatah) Hansi hansi puchela laa Dadi dulha ke	By the roadside and is watching The *dulha's dadi* (paternal grandmother) is teasingly Asking him: "O grandson What attributes"
दादी: "नाती बहूआ कवन गुण के आगर (आगार) बा"	Dadi: "Nati bahuwa kawan Gun ke aagar (aagaar) ba?"	And merit does your Bride possess?
जवाब: दादी बहूआ के इतना सुहाग एहजी इतना सोहाग उंकर सेंदुर वा पर निर्मल मोही देले बा	Dadi, bahuwa ke Etna suhag Ehji etna sohag Unkar sindur wa Par nirmal mohi Dele ba	O *dadi* (grandmother) Your granddaughter- in-law has so much merits and Ornaments. She possesses lots of jewellery that her *seindur* is so attractive and bestows a glow on her face
अम्मा: हँसी हँसी पूछे ला दूल्हा के अम्मा बेटा बहुवा कवन गुण के आगर (आगार)	Amma: Hansi hansi puche la Dulha ke amma: "Beta bahuwa kawan gun ke aagar (aagaar)	The dulha'mother is teasingly asking her son: "O son tell me what are the qualities or merits your bride is bringing along with her?"
बेटा : "अम्मा बहूआ के इतना सोहाग उनकर बिंदुरी पर निर्मल मोहे रहे"	Bahuwa ke etna suhag unkar binduri par Nirmal mohe rahe	Son: "O mother your Daughter-in-law is Possessed of such Merit and ornaments O mother she is the Repository of such Beautiful Ornaments That her Binduri shines without Fault on her forehead"
चाची : हँसी हँसी पूछे ला दूल्हा के चाची "बेटा बहूआ कवन गुण के आगर (आगार) बा	Chachi hansi hansi puche la Dulha ke chachi: "Beta bahuwa kawan Gun ke aagar(aagaar) ba?"	The bridegroom's Paternal aunt asks him: "O son what qualities does your bride possess?"

दूल्हा : "चाची बहूआ के एतना सोहाग उंकर झुमका निर्मल मोहे रहे"	Dulha: "Chachi bahuwa ke etna sohag unkar jhumka Nirmal mohe rahe"	Nephew (Dulha):"O aunty your daughter in-law is possesed of such great qualities That her *jhumka* Hanging from her ear Is resplentent."
बहिन : हँसी हँसी पूछे ला दूल्हा के बहिन "भैया भौजी कवन गुण के आगर (आगार) बा ?"	Bahin: hansi hansi puche la Dulha ke bahin "Bhaiya bhowji kawan Gun ke aagar (aagaar) ba?"	The dulha'sister is Teasingly asking him O brother tell me What qualities does my sister-in-law have?
जवाब : "बहिन भौजी के एतना सोहाग उंकर हार वा पर निर्मल मोहे रहे"	"bahine bhowji ke etna sohag unkar har ba Par nirmal mohe rahe"	O sister she is so full of auspicious qualities that her necklace Shines resplendently
भौजी : हँसी हँसी पूछे ला दूल्हा के भौजी "बाबू बहूआ कवन गुण के आगर (आगार) बा ?"	Bhowji: "Hansi hansi puche la Dulha ke bhowji "Babu bahuwa kawan does your bride have? Gun ke aagar (aagaar) ba?"	The dulha's bhowji (Sister-in-law) Babu, what qualities Dulha: O my Sister-in- law
देवर : "भौजी बहूआ के एतना सोहाग उंकर कंगन पर निर्मल मोहे रहे"	Devar: "bhowji bahuwa ke etna sohag Unkar kangan par Nirmal mohe rahe"	she is posssed with great qualities such that her bangles shine glowingly
फूफू : हँसी हँसी पूछे ला दूल्हा के फूफू "बेटा बहूआ कवन गुण के आगर (आगार) बा ?"	Phouphou hansi hansi puche la Dulha ke phouphou "Beta bahuwa kawan Gun ke aagar (aagaar) ba?"	Dulha's father's sister the dulha's *phouphou* teasingly asks him: "O nephew what qualities does your bride have?
बेटा : "एतना सोहाग उंकर पैजन पर निरमाल मोहे ला"	Beta: "Etna sohag Unkar paijan par Nirmal mohe la"	Dulha: "O *phouphou*, She brings such merit That her tinkling anklets Leave a melodious sound When she walks!"

Another type of rare song which was prevalent in Mauritius at the time of Immigration is the ***Jhus Geet.***

झूस गीत Jhus Geet

This song was given to me by Late Dadi Unmole on 26th September, 1995 at her residence at Vallée des Prêtres, on the eastern outskirt of Port Louis.

She told me this is a very old song she obtained from some tribal *girmitiyas* of the early Immigration Period during her childhood. The song is known as *Jhus* and sung by these women accompanied by a tribal dance where 4-5 women meet each other from two sides and they lace or intertwine their hands around each other's waist.

भोजपुरी	Roman Script	English Translation
घर पिछुवरिया हो लीला (नीलवा) के गाँछिया मोरे बलमवा हो लीले (नील) रंग चुनरी हो रंगाई (3)	Ghar pichuwariya Ho lila (Nila) ke ganchiya More balamwa ho Lil (Nil) rang chunari Ho rangayi (3)	Behind my house Is a (lila) nil "indigo" tree O my husband Do dye my sari in The blue colour (3)
चुन्दरी रंगावत मोहे बहिया मुरुक गइल मोरे बलमवा हो सहर से हो बैधवा मंगाई (3)	Chundari rangawat mohe Bahiya muruk gail (3) More balam wa ho Sahar se ho baidhwa mangayi	While dying the sari My arm got sprained O my husband Do call the *Baidh* (doctor) From the town (3)
बैध जे माँगे ला साठ हो रुपैया (3)	Baidh je mange la Sath ho rupaiya ho (3)	The *Baidh* (doctor) asked for 60 rupees for his treatment
मोरे बलमवा हो गलवा के मोहर भंजायी (3) मोहरा भंजावत हो मोरे अंखियां उलट गईल मेहरी भैले जीव के जंजाल (3)	More balamwa ho Galawa ke mohar bhanjayi (3) Mohara bhanjawat ho More ankhiyan oulat gaile Mehari bhaile Jiva ke janjal (3)	O my husband Do change my golden ***guirneas*** (coin necklace) (3) into cash While changing the golden coin necklace My eyes rolled in dismay. I was exasperated. Wife is indeed a nuisance for one's peace of mind!

□

30

Protest Songs

Over the years and decades, local history, political figures and environment too have found their place in the Mauritian Bhojpuri songs. Some of the songs talk of the sugar factory of *Mr. Manes* the French estate owner, which has caught fire. It contains within its lines the harsh treatment meted out to the sugarcane workers and labourers and the back breaking jobs they had to do for long hours in sun, rain or periodic cyclonic weather. Whether the sugar factory caught fire or was set to fire, one does not know, but the song reflects the jubilation of the women singers as they dance to the rhythmic *jhumar* and jeer at *Mr. Manes,* the notorious sugar factory owner. It is a protest song.

Known as *Chansons engagées* in creole, they express the protest inherent in their hearts and minds. For example:

"Mousse Manes
Ke mulwa jargaile
Agal bagal cane
Bich mein kaptan
Sahib ke mulwa
Jargaile
Mousse Manes
Ke Mulwa
Jargai, jargai, jargaile".

Mr. Manes is a sugar baron of the time. His sugar mill has caught fire. The *Sirdar* or overseer – the *'Captan'* is standing between the two lines of sugarcane crops. The boss's mill is on fire. Mr. Manes mill is on fire. Oh, it is burning, it is burning.*

* Dr. Sarita Boodhoo, 1993; P. 151.

Mulwa is a Mauritian Bhojpuri word derived from French *moulin* meaning mill.

This song throws light on the agitation that was taking place on the sugar plantations during the 1930s and 1940s. There was an uprise among sugarcane workers. There was unrest.

Mousse Manes

Moussé manes ke mulwa
Jari gaile ho

The sugarcane field of Mr. Manes
Has caught fire

Moussé manes ke mulwa
Mulla mein aag lagal
Damkal na pani

The factory has caught fire
No sign of fire extinguisher nor water.

Sara mulla jari gail
Lachiminiyan re nisani

The whole factory is burnt down
Only thing left as a souvenir
Is the chimney

Jari gaile ho, jari gaile ho
Dari dari kane planté
Mirai mein makaye

The whole sugarcane field is burnt down
Sow the sugarcane plants
Row by row
And sow the maize on
The walls (also the mound of stones known as '*mel*' from Bhojpuri word '*medh*'.

Kaphir sala bolat bate
Jaldi re tarvaye

The *kaphir* (maybe Sidar, overseer) the merciless
Sala (gali in Bhojpuri) – term of abuse towards men
Is saying
Hurry up in your work

Jari gaile ho
Moussé manes ke mulwa

Mr. Manes's factory has caught fire!

Agal bagal kane lagal ba
Bich mein kaptan

Here and there (everywhere sugarcane has been planted)
The overseer too (kaptan – captain)
Is in the middle

Sonse karo bhasma ho gail
Jari gaile kaptan
Jari gaile ho

The whole plot (square) of
Sugarcane field is burnt down
The overseer too is burnt in it

Jari gaile ho
Moussé Manes ke mulwa

O the factory of Mr. Manes
Is burnt down

The repression suffered by the sugarcane labourers, was so harsh that when a planter's factory and field caught fire, there was jubilation among the workers. Sometimes, fire is set criminally too and sometimes by accident especially in summer.

Moussé Manes – French/ Creole terminologies incorporated in Mauritian Bhojpuri

Manes – the mill owner

Mulwa – factory – *mulla* from *moulin* French factory

Mulwa Bhojpuriased

Lachiminiya – from French *La Cheminée* – Chimney

Kane – sugarcane

From canne – French – cane

Planté – to sow

Planter – French

Miraille mein – मेंड़ – mel

Border

Muraille – wall

French – Mur

Tarvaye – from French travaille – work

Bhojpuriased form

Sonsé – complete

Karo – from French

Carreau – square

The sugar fields were divided into square plots to facilitate allotment of work. *Carreau* has been bhojpuriased.

Moussée – from French Monsieur, English Mr. (Mister)

Boundary – wall between two fields or beds, field ridge hedging.

Pani Nai Ba- Protest Song

चेंगन मैंगन पानी भरे पानी नई बा	Cheingan meingan Pani bhare Pani Nai ba	Children have gone to the Village tap, to fill water There's no water
भला बांबु में डिग्री डाले भला पानी नई बा	Bhala Bambous mein degree dale Bhala pani nai ba	Oh, In Bambous, the technician is testing the water level there's no water.

भला सेंत क्रवा में डिग्री डाले पानी नई बा	Bhala St. Croix mein degree dale Pani nai ba	Oh, in St. Croix, the technician is testing the water level there's no water.
हो भला चेंगन मैंगन पानी भरे पानी नय बा	Ho bhala cheingan meingan pani bhare Pani nai ba	There's no water. Children have gone to the Village tap, to fill water.
भला बॉन तेर में डिग्री डाले पानी नई बा	Bhala Bonne Terre mein degree dale Pani nai ba	Oh, in Bonne Terre the technician is testing the water level
हो भला चेंगन मैंगन पानी भरे पानी नय बा	Ho bhala cheingan meingan pani bhare Pani nai ba	There's no water. Children have Gone to the village tap To fill water There's no water.
भला सीते में डिग्री डाले पानी नई बा	Bhala Cite mein degree dale Pani nai ba	Oh, in the Cité the technician is testing the water level. There's no water.
हो भला चेंगन मेंगन पानी भरे पानी नय बा	Ho bhala cheingan meingan pani bhare Pani nai ba	There's no water. Children have gone To the village tap to Fill water. There's no water.

Pani Nai Ba
Bhojpuri Protest Folk Song

'Pani Nai Ba' has developed as a protest song. It depicts the great social problem caused by drought and the difficulty of getting drinking water. Women and children are queuing up at the village tap to fill their buckets with water. And there is no water. Water cuts during drought periods have been a constant social problem facing the common man, then and now and the whole world over! Today the government is coming up with various financial aids and schemes to help people purchase water tanks. And storage of rain water is being encouraged for cleaning, gardening and washing of cars.

Protest songs are current in oral tradition and folk singing. Several versions of the same song may be available. This song is a Mauritian Compostion which has been sung by several generations of women.

In September 1982, while working on the ballet '*Parbatia*', saga of Indian Indentured Immigrants for the Mauritius Bhojpuri Institute, I collected this song from the same village of *Geet Gawai* group of Richelieu, on the western outskirt of Port Louis. I utilised the song in the ballet with enactment of children filling water by the village tap, and dancing to the tune. With my team of young artists and musicians, we recreated and recomposed the *Geet Gawai* song of **Pani Nai Ba** and put it to music. It became an instant hit and made the round of not only the local TV channel and radio but schools, colleges and other NGOs where it was played and adapted for various functions and events. Generations have grown up with it including Ministers and other Personalities.

It is still very popular and has been translated and adapted by famous Mauritian Sega singer Alain Ramanisum of International fame and also taken up by ABAIM, a children's NGO and even translated into Tamil Language.

□

31

The Evolution and Research Work by Scholars

Awakening On the Mauritian Scene

By 1901 political and social awakening was taking place in Mauritius.

Gandhiji's Arrival in 1901 had set the tone for a '*prise de conscience*' by the suppressed *Girmitiya* Community. Later on his name would be taken in Bhojpuri folk songs both in Mauritius and in India such as in the *Champaran Satyagraha Movement*. The arrival of Mohan Das Karamchand Gandhi not yet a Mahatma in October 1901 in Mauritius was the beginning of the wind of change for the *Girmitiyas*. Appalled by their conditions of living and work and the squalor to which they were subjected to, he addressed them at huge gatherings at several places and exhorted them to educate their children and join politics. He sent Manilal Doctor a French knowing barrister in 1907 to take up their cudgels and plead for the Indian planters and labourers in court and elsewhere. Both Mahatma Gandhiji's and Manilal Doctor's names have been taken in Bhojpuri folk songs of Mauritius.

In the first few decades of the 20th century many *sirdars* rose in social and economic mobility. Their family life style had a great impact on the rest of the community. *Geet Gawai* women going to sing at their fastidiously lavish weddings were encouraged and given handsome '*negs*'. With the advent of Indian Cinema, names of dancers such as *Zarina* stuck to some well-known *Geet Gawai Geetharines*. Going to sing at the residence of the Sirdars and Job Contractors for a ceremony was a great honour for them.

With the rise in popularity of '*Ramayana Satsang*' in *baithkas* and private residences and in the masses, *Rama Charit Manas* of Goswami Tulsidasji Maharaj too exerted an influence on the *Geet Gawai* singers.

"Hai sumiran karle mere mana
Bitijala umar"
"Tulsidas bhalu asa charan ke
Hari charan chit lagi"

These refrains have been added towards the end of many songs by the *Geetharines* as they were impacted by the weekly home based *Ramayana Satsang* where verses – *chawpai* and *dohas* were read and sung from *Ram Charit Manas.* They added these lines to give a lustre to their *Geet Gawai.* Adding a line mentioning *Tulsidas* at the end of their songs, gave a certain *Shastric tone* or lift to their songs considered *ganwar.*

Arya Samaj's Crusading Movement
Mrs. Bhagyawati Devi Makhansingh Gayasingh

The Arya Samaj was set up in Port Louis in 1909 unofficially. Set up firmly on 15 December, 1910 at Prince Regent Street in Port Louis at a gathering of well-meaning and thinking people of the Hindu Community, it was then known as *Arya Paropkarini Sabha.*

By 1910, the Arya Samaj was firmly established. In 1912, the hereby named people – Pandit Khemlall President, Guruprasad Daljeetlall, Mananiya Pandit Gayasingh, Shri Bahadoor Ramjeelall, Kersingh, Durgabhagatji, J. Gopal, met under the chairmanship of Barrister Manilal Doctor – at the house of Bahadoor Ramjeelall at Prince Regent Street in Port Louis to discuss the way forward.

They condemned the '*pardah system*' of women and formulated that women should come out of '*pardah*'. Bhagyawati Devi Makhansingh was invited to give talks. At first she was completely terrified to speak in public, she writes. But encouraged by the menfolk she set forth to make her first speech. In November 1912 she set up a '*Stree Mandali*' which is the basis of today's sprawling network of *Arya Mahila Samaj* in Mauritius. The president of this first *Arya Stree Mandali* was Smt. Dulari Devi, the wife of Shri Bahadoor Ramjeelall, the Secretary was Smt. Sita Devi, the wife of Shri Narayan Diljore and Smt. Bhagyawati Makhan Singh Gayasingh was herself the Treasurer. At the same time they collected 400 rupees – in the name of the *Stree Mandali* – and which was sent to Poona, India to help those Indians imprisoned in Natal, South Africa in Gandhiji's movement.

With the setting up of '*the Stree Mandali*' came the movement for the education of women.

In a preface to her book *'Vivah Mangal'* Bhagyawati Devi Makhan Singh writes that she had the opportunity to go to the distant villages of the island accompanying Smt. Sumangali Devi wife of Dr. Chiranjiv Bhardwaj the veteran Arya Samaj intellectual, a doctor by profession and who was invited to Mauritius to give lectues to mobilise the masses. He was at the time in Rangoon, Burma. He came on 15 December, 1911 – and stayed at the house of Guruprasad Daljeetlall. On those occasions, Bhagyawati went to several districts of Mauritius. At the *Arya Paropkarini Sabha* – She was a voluntary preacher. 'अवैतनिक उपदेशिका' for eight years (she toured the different zones and preached relentlessly for the uplift of Mauritian women.

She attended several marriages. During those occasions she was upset to see the many malpractices and the raillery that were directed towards the men folk.

"पुरुषों के समक्ष, अश्लील शब्दों में विवाह गान करते जरा भी उन्हें शर्म नहीं आती।" –She adds:

"उतने समय में मैंने देखा कि प्रांतों की बहनों ने विवाह में शुभ मंगल के अवसर पर अश्लील शब्दों से गायन करती थीं। इस कारण मुझे इस पुस्तक को लिखना पड़ा है।" —भाग्यवती धर्मपत्नी गयासिंह

Many new songs were thus recomposed by Mrs. Bhagyawati Devi Makhansingh Gayasingh. Mrs. Bhagyawati campaigned against those '*ashlil*' Bhojpuri '*gali*' songs sungs by women in weddings infront of the menfolk and considered offensive by her.

"कि विवाह तथा जन्म के अवसर पर जिस रूढ़ी और अश्लील शब्दों से माता बहनें दुषित होती है, वह बहुत सुधार हो सकता है।"

Thus she brought out a book entitled: *Vivah Mangal,* comprising new songs based on the old Bhojpuri songs, between 1909 and 1918 year in which she died. The *Vivah Mangal* comprises of 55 marriage songs including *dadra, aarti* and *bhajans* also. It was first published in 1925 in *Mauritius Mitra* newspaper. The songs were finally published in book form as *Vivah Mangal* in 1936. Mrs. Bhagyawati Makhansingh Gayasingh then set out to recompose these marriage songs. She also composed songs inspired by other good "models from other books".

This paragraph from Pandit Atmaram Vishwanath's book 'Hindu Mauritius' (1936) (translation: 2012 Edited by Pahlad Ramsurrun) corroborates the words of Smt. Bhagyawati Devi in so far as collection of fund for the Indentured Women Satyagrahis of South Africa is concerned. Secondly it gives testimony to the activities of Smt. Bhagyawati Devi Makhansingh Gayasingh carried out at the time.

"It would not be out of place to give a brief description of the activities of the women at that time. At the end of 1912 the Satyagraha campaign of Mahatma Gandhi in South Africa was at its peak. The most respectable and great leader of India, the late Shri Gopal Krishna Gokhale had appealed to the Indians in the colonies and in India to come forward with financial help for the Satyagrahis and Rs. 1,500 were collected at a public meeting, organized by the writer in the Port Louis theater in the city. Smt. Dulari Devi, the wife of Sri Ramlall, Smt. Bhagyawati Devi, the first wife of Babu Gaya-Singh and Smt. Sita Devi, the wife of Shri Narayan Diljor, helped in collecting Rs. 150 from the womenfolk. All this money was remitted to Shri Gopal Krishna Gokhale in India. Bhagyawati Devi and Dulari Devi had participated in the work of publicizing. The example of the wife of Dr. Bhardwaj was there before them."*

***Note:** *Mrs. Bhagyawati writes in the "Vivah Mangal's preface, that they had collected 400 Rupees.*

The *Vivah Mangal* was finally published as a book on 15 September, 1936 by Pandit Gayasingh after his wife's demise. Residing at 26 St Denis, Street Port Louis, Pandit Gayasingh, was a progressive minded former police officer and he was one of the founder members of the Arya Samaj in Mauritius. He found *that* the songs composed by his wife published at first in *Mauritius Mitra* Newspaper in 1925, to contain many proof mistakes and he took the decision to bring the collection in the form of a book.

Bissoondoyal Movement–Jan Andolan

Followed thereafter in the 1940s the *Jan Andolan* movement of Prof Basdeo Bissoondoyal who had arrived from Calcutta following his MA at Calcutta University and other studies at undergraduate Level at Lahore University in Undivided India.

New Bhojpuri songs were created– *"Outho mahabharat ke beti"*

With the movement of Pandit Basdeo Bissoondoyal in the 1940s for the uplift of the community, there came a new awakening again among the Indo-Mauritian community. This no doubt had its impact on the *Geet Gawai Geetharines*. They were quick to incorporate these new waves in their songs just as in India too the *jhumars* focused on *Veer Kunwar Singh*, Gandhiji and the Independence movement of India.

"Outho Mahabharat ke beti
Hanthon mein jhanda leke
Desh mein prachar ba
Sahar mein updesh ba
Outho Mahabharat ke beti
Hanthon mein jhanda leke..."

*"Socio-economic and political conditions also form a subject for these songs, especially in dance songs – jhumar. These are composed by youth girls and therefore based on the then contemporary subjects, for example many of these songs depict the episode of Kunwar Singh or the Second World War, Mahatma Gandhi, Jawaharlal Nehru, scarcity of grains, or a flood in the Ganga or other rivers in this area".**

The Revolt against The Oligarchy

In the 1940s, there was a rise in revolt among the masses against their no more bearable suppression and exploitation on the sugar estates. These protests led to the creation of many local Bhojpuri songs which are sung by the *Geetharines*. I have already given an example of protest songs. (Chapter on Protest Songs)

* Chandramani Singh writes: In her book Marriage Songs from Bhojpuri Region P. 12.

भोजपुरी	Roman Script	English Translation
"अंगाजे रहल भइया, अंगाजे रहल भइया।	*Engagé* rahal bhaiyya *Engagé* rahal bhaiyya	It was the era of *engagé* O brother! It was the era of *engagé*
एक महिनवा में पाँच रुपैया हो	Ek mahinwa mein Panch rupaiyya ho	We received Five Rupees in one Month
अंगाजे रहल भइया।	Engagé rahal bhaiyya (2)	It was the era of *Engagé* O brother!
खाइ के मोटका चाउर रहल खुबे लाल, कोको के तेल आउर खेसारी के दाल	Khayi ke mottka chawoor rahal Khube lal, koko ke tel awoor Khesari ke dal	We had but the coarse (thind grade) rice It was red (the worst type) We had Coconut oil and the *Khesari* dal for food
ओढ़े के गोनी और सुते के चटइया,	Oudhey ke goni awroo Sutey ke chatayi	But a *goni* to cover ourselves And slept on *chattayi* (mats)
अंगाजे रहल भइया।"	*Engagé* rahal bhaiyya (2)	It was the era of *Engagé* O brother!

Note: **Engagé–** term in Mauritian Kreol and Mauritian Bhojpuri as well signifying *girmit* or *Indentured Labour.*

Note: **Khesari–** (Indian pea or grass pea commonly grown for livestock feed in Asia and East Africa. *Lathyrus Odaratus* – a hardy pulse crop (India prohibited the sale since 1961 because it contains a toxin that produces lathyrism a condition that could lead to paralysis of lower limbs).

Independence Movement

Dr. Seewoosagur Ramgoolam on his return from London after his medical studies in 1936 started a wide spread *'mass movement'*. He toured the *baithkas* in the villages and made rousing speeches in the evenings of weekdays and in weekends to awaken the masses towards the Independence of Mauritius. Mauritius won Independence on 12 March, 1968. This inspired many Bhojpuri songs to be composed which were taken up by the *Geetharines* of *Geet Gawai* too. These led to the Independence Movement.

Creation of New Songs

New creations are being made. In August 2017 the Bhojpuri Speaking Union organised a Theatre Workshop and invited Shri Mahendra Prasad Singh, Director Founder of *Rangashree,* New Delhi to conduct short courses for the benefit of various Bhojpuri theatre groups as well as the Petit Raffray *Geet Gawai* tradition bearers. The theme was the 100th anniversary of Gandhiji's *Champaran Satyagraha.* As quite a few *girmitiyas* of Bihari origin hail from *Champaran,* it was befitting to bring the link with Mauritius, especially as *Gandhiji* had set foot in Mauritius first in October 1901. The script included many songs based on local Bhojpuri tunes such as *sohar* and *jhumar.* One such *jhumar* very succinctly incorporated by the *Geet Gawai* group enacting it was—

"Gandhiji ailan
Gandhiji ailan
Moris ke deshwa
Mein Gandhiji
Ailan"

Second Gandhi Song

It was produced as part of the workshop organised by *Bhojpuri Speaking Union* on Gandhiji's *Champaran Satyagraha* in collaboration with Shri Mahendra Prasad Singh.

The song was based on the Bhojpuri *Sohar* Style and composed by Shri M.P. Singh who also did the English translation—

नेपथ्य से गाना उभरता है—राग-सोहर
"मोहनदास करमचंद गांधी पच्छिम देश से देसे आईले
हो रामा छोड़ी दिहले आपन बलिस्तरी फिटिनिया छोड़ी मुइयाँ चलें
हो रामा संगे चललें राज कुमार सुकूल अउरी रजिनदर बाबू
हो चंपारण के साजन लोग संगे चलस दुखवा-दरद बाँटे
हो रामा
छोड़ी चलले हाँथी हथिसरवा त दुखवा-दरद बाँटे"

"Mohandas Karamchand Gandhi came back from the Western country, leaving his Legal Profession and his Chariot and is walking from one village to another. Raj Kumar Shukla, Rajendra Babu and gentlemen of Champaran leaving their elephants are accompanying

him on foot to share the miseries of the people."

This was a historic occasion that linked the grassroots with the patriotism required to appeal to a wider audience.

Note: *Dr. Rajendra Prasad – Later First President of India.

Research Work by Scholars on *Geet Gawai*

- **Dr. Kuber Mishra Book—**Late Pandit Kuber Mishra from Azamgarh, UP was the first one to make an in-depth study of the *Geet Gawai* songs in 1977-1978 after the passing visit of Prof Usher Budh Arya from University of Leiden, Netherlands (later he abandoned this field as he took to *Sanyas* and became Swami Ved Bharati). Pandit Kuber Mishra came twice to Mauritius to undertake his survey and research and went round the island meeting the *Geetharines* assembled in Social Welfare Centres or at private residences. They sang soulfully for him. Later he compiled these songs in a book entitled: मॉरीशस के भोजपुरी लोकगीतों का विवेचनात्मक अध्ययन (*Mauritius Ke Bhojpuri Lokgeeton Ka Vivechanatmak Adhyayan).* Dr. Kuber Mishra's collection and detailed interpretation was presented by him in his Thesis for a PhD at the Benaras Hindu University. Later he became Principal of a Post Graduate College in a village, Maltari, Azamgarh which is known by the name of Mahatma Gandhi PG College and is affiliated to Jaunpur University. Dr. Kuber Mishra was an Educationist, a Sanskrit Scholar and a fine Linguist who easily grasped the Mauritian Bhojpuri and Creole words in the language with the perfect pronunciation. He has given these in detail in his book, published on the basis of his PhD research. The book was twice revised and the third edition was published in 2011. Panditji was closely linked to Mauritius and made several visits thereafter.
- **Dr. Suchita Ramdin—**As Head of the Department of Bhojpuri, Oral Traditions and Folklore of the Mahatma Gandhi Institute, Ms. Suchita Ramdin, collected a vast amount of *Geet Gawai* songs and compiled some 400 of them with detailed notes in her book संस्कार मंजरी — मॉरीशस के भोजपुरी संस्कार गीत *Sanskar Manjari* – Collection of Sanskar Geet, published by the Mahatma Gandhi Institute in 1989. She also made an LP, *'The Swarna Chakra'* based on a selection of particular wedding songs such as

Hardi, Tilak and *Parchawan*. Some of these *Geet Gawai* songs have been used at wedding ceremonies, for decades. Later Ms. Suchita Ramdin researched for a PhD at the University of Mauritius on the theme of Patriotism in the Bhojpuri folk songs of Mauritius.

- **Shri Madhukar Bhagat**—A versatile Hindi-Bhojpuri poet of Mauritius, known as *'Mauritius Ke Rashtra Kavi'*, Shri Brajendra Kumar Madhukar Bhagat compiled the traditional Bhojpuri *Geet Gawai* songs in his Book: **मॉरीशस के राष्ट्रकवि ब्रजेंद्र कुमार भगत 'मधुकर', काव्य रचनावली, संपादक—डॉ. कमल किशोर गोयनका नटराज प्रकाशन, 2003** Brajendra Kumar Bhagat 'Madhukar' Kavya Rachnavali (Collection of Poetic Works of the National Poet of Mauritius Brajendra Kumar Bhagat Madhukar) Edited by Dr. Kamal Kishore Goyanka, Published by Natraj Prakashan in 2003.

In the book *Madhulika* the poet gives a set of Bhojpuri *geet*, some based on traditional Bhojpuri folk songs which he has readapted such as 'सरजू नहाई के' *Sarju nahaye ke*–on P. 336 of this Collection. However many are his own creation of *Jhumar, Sohar, Birha*. His other Bhojpuri Poetry compilations include '*MadhuKalash*' and '*Madhu Bahar*'. Some of the Bhojpuri songs are of patriotic nature too, composed in the context of the Independence Movement of Mauritius.

- **Shri Pahlad Ramsurrun**—Pahlad Ramsurrunji has published a book entiltled भोजपुरी लोकगीतिका–सुंदरी रामशरण/*Bhojpuri folk songs by Smt. Soondree Ramsurrun* with an introduction by Dr. Kuber Mishra, published in 2009 by Atmaram And Sons New Delhi. Shri Pahlad Ramsurrun renowned Mauritian writer with over 70 books to his credit, has published these *Sanskar Geets* Sung by his Mother Soonderi Devi.

- **Mrs. Beegay Lutchmee Luchmun**—A more recent publication 'पुरखों की जीती–जागती परंपरा भोजपुरी गीत गवाई' *Purkhon Ki Jiti Jagti Parampara Bhojpuri Geet Gawai* has been collected by Smt. Beegaylutchmee Ramloll Luchmun in 2019 published by '*Famous Printing*'. Mrs. Beegaylutchmee pays homage in the book to her Mother Smt. Lekhrani Kalicharan from whom she learnt *Geet Gawai* Singing.

Mrs. Beegaylutchmee Ramloll Luchmun's book *Purkhon*

ki Jiti Jagti Parampara was launched by the *Bhojpuri Speaking Union* on the 1 December, 2019 at the Indira Gandhi Centre for Indian Culture (IGCIC) Phoenix. It was on the occasion of the third Commemorative Anniversary Celebration of the Inscription of *Geet Gawai* as Intangible Cultural Heritage of Humanity at UNESCO.

The launching ceremony was performed by the newly appointed Minster of Arts and Cultural Heritage, Honourable Shri Avinash Teeluck, the High Commissioner of India Shri Tanmay Lalji and Dr. Sarita Boodhoo Chairperson of the Bhojpuri Speaking Union.

- **Mrs. Indira Padaruth**—Mrs. Indira Padaruth former Head of Department of Performing Arts of Mahatma Gandhi Institute took up a study of Bhojpuri folk songs of Mauritius for her Dissertation for MA in Vocal Hindustani Music in (1983-1985) under the able guidance of Dr. A.S. Paintal at the Music Faculty, Delhi University. Later she also followed a course in Thumri Singing and Devotional Music under the guidance of Savita Devi Maharaj.

- **Dr. Pittiviraj Joyram**—Dr. Pittiviraj Joyram, currently, Senior Corruption Prevention Officer with Independent Commission Against Corruption (ICAC), interviewed several groups of *Geetharines* in the year 1990s towards his PhD doctoral work in 1994. His thesis is entitled *"A Study of Music Prevalent in the Mauritian People of Indian Origin with a Special Reference to Indian Migration of Indentured Labourers"* submitted at Indira Kala Sangit Vishwa Vidhyalay, Khairagarh, Madhya Pradesh. The work will shortly be published in Book form. These songs are now secured at the Archives and Research Centres for Ethnomusicology, American Institute of Indian Studies, Haryana, India.

Dr. Pittiviraj Joyram also submitted a Project entiltled:

"Safeguarding and Transmission of the folk songs of the Bhojpuri Speaking people in Mauritius."

To the Indian Council of Cultural Relations (I.C.C.R), Ministry of External Affairs, India.

- **Dr. Varsharanee Bissessur-Doolooa**—"A study of Bhojpuri culture and change in Mauritius, with a focus on wed ding songs".

She submitted her Thesis to the *Open University of Mauritius (UOM)* in 2020 and earned thereupon her Ph.D.

• **Dr. Oodayenarain Gangoo,** Arya Neta—Dr. Oodayenarain Gangoo, renowned Educationist and prominent Leader of the Arya Sabha, Mauritius while lecturing at the Mahatma Gandhi Institute and working in the team headed by Dr. Suchita Ramdin in the Collection of Bhojpuri Sanskar Geet and Bhojpuri vocabulary towards the preparation of a Bhojpuri Dictionary, later was inspired to do his PhD on these Bhojpuri folk songs. These were published in book form in Hindi: 'मॉरीशस का भोजपुरी लोक साहित्य एवं भारतीय संस्कृति' *Mauritius Ka Bhojpuri Lok Sahitya Ewam Bharatiya Sanskriti,* in 1992 by Mahatma Gandhi Institute. Dr. Oodayenarain Gangoo received a good number of the songs from his mother.

• **Dr. (Mrs.) Sarita Boodhoo**—This author has given in her book *Kanya Dan – The Why's of Hindu Marriage Rituals* over 100 Bhojpuri songs in illustration at various stages of the wedding ceremony and why the songs are sung on such occasions (1993). She has also given some Bhojpuri songs in other books such as *'Bhojpuri Bola', 'Mauritius Ki Bhojpuri Paramparaein', and Bhojpuri Traditions of Mauritius.* She has also presented a good number of Research Papers on these songs at national and International Seminars, Conferences, Online Conferences and Webinars and published her well-documented papers in various Research Journals.

• **Smt. Priyamvada Jeebaun**—Smt. Priyamvada Jeebaun has also written about *Geet Gawai* in her book: मेरा जीवन और मेरा भरा पूरा परिवार Mera Jeevan Aur Mera Bhara Pura Parivar published by Star Publications New Delhi in 2014. She has dedicated one whole chapter – chapter 25 to the *Geet Gawai* songs as well as the life sketch of her sister-in-law (*nanad*) from whom she compiled the songs. 'सुमती जीबन का जीवन एवं उनके द्वारा गाए जाने वाले भोजपुरी गीत! Soumattee Jeebaun ka Jeewan Ewam Gayey Janey Waley Bhojpuri Geet. I had also interviewed Soumattee Jeebaun in May 2014 at her residence at Petite Rivière and have included one of her Mahadeo Songs in this book. Soumattee Jeebaun is the doyen of *Geetharines* in Mauritius. She is 94 as at date born (21 April, 1928).

• **Shri Dim Lalah Mohit**—Shri Dim Lalah Mohit in his book *Heera Moti* (part VII - Vol. II) has given a wide collection of Bhojpuri riddles and songs and published by author in June 2010 - Bel Air, Rivière Sèche. He collected these songs from his mother and published some of the songs in his books used as text books at the. Professor Basdeo Bissoondoyal College, Flacq. This pioneering work was commissioned by late Shri Ramnath Jeetah to encourage the learning of Bhojpuri as a classroom activity. Shri Dimlalah Mohit has also compiled Riddles, Proverbs, Idioms and Bhojpuri folk songs in prior publications.

• **Professor Helen Myers**—Professor Helen Myers, American musicologist has written immensely about the Bhojpuri Songs of Felicity Village in Trinidad which she studied for over 20 years and published in her voluminous book *'Music of Hindu Trinidad'* which speaks also of *'The Marich des Phenomena'.* She came to Mauritius in 1999 and carried out a similar work on the Bhojpuri folk songs of Mauritius by interviewing Smt. Manty Ramodhin of whom I have mentioned in this book. Manty's songs rendered in her melodious voice are given at various points in this book.

• **Catherine Servan Schreiber (Champion)**—Dr. Catherine Servan Shreiber (Champion) eminent Bhojpuri Scholar and Literateur at the prestigious Sorbonne University in France and later at the Centre D'Etudes de L'Inde et de L'Asie du Sud has done immense work on the Bhojpuri folk songs and folk stories of the Gangetic Plain under the tutelage of renowned folklorist Dr. Krishna Deo Upadhayaya in Vanarasi, under whom she studied for four years. She later published these studies in her book: *Traditions Orales dans le Monde Indien (Oral Traditions in South Asia) by Catherine Champion Servan Shreiber (Editions de l'Ecole des Hautes Etudes en Sciences Sociales, Centre D'Etudes de L'Inde et de L'Asie du Sud) 1996.*

Her book: *"Histoire d'une musique metise à L'île Maurice: Chutney Indien et Sega Bollywood,* Riveneuve Editions-2010 is an outstanding collection of Mauritian Bhojpuri folk songs.

□

32

Transmission to Younger Generations: UNESCO Declarations

UNESCO

That the UNESCO took the decision to protect the Intangible Cultural Heritage of the world under the Declaration of 2003 has given the opportunity to all State Parties to make the effort at national and international levels to protect the Intangible Cultural Heritage within their territory. Armed with this assurance, the *Bhojpuri folk songs in Mauritius – Geet Gawai* are vested with a new impetus and claim for *raison d'être*. The immense impact of the inscription at UNESCO has given *Bhojpuri folk songs in Mauritius – Geet Gawai* a new sphere of action of great emotional, socio-cultural and political reach.

Youth and *Geet Gawai*

One interesting development is that of passing on this intangible cultural heritage to the younger generation which is more prone to globalised western music culture or Bollywood. UNESCO encourages the transmission of Intangible Cultural Heritage to the youths. It is one of the safeguarding measures. It is indeed amazing to see the interest taken by children and youth who are quick to link with the past and heritage through their smart phones, tablets and You Tube. The Chinmaya Mission conducted a Workshop at Beau Bassin, Mauritius in 2017 to induct children mostly from elite families in *Geet Gawai* Intangible Cultural Heritage it was a resounding success. Children enacted scenes of Ramayana such as *Sabri*, the forest woman tasting the '*Ber*' before offering them to Lord Rama, while the *Geetharines* sang in chorus a '*Geet Gawai*' on this subject. The content was not only potent. But it had a lesson for the children of the *Bal Vikas* group of Chinmaya Mission to learn from the humility of Lord Rama. Moreover, they came to realise the importance of Intangible Cultural Heritage as well. They were familiarised with the *Geetharines* and what is *Geet Gawai*.

It has not always been easy for the *Geetharines* to learn the Bhojpuri *sanskar geets.* In the old days, they were very much frowned upon. Some ladies talk of their youth days. As girls and daughters-in-law they suffered repression, were scolded by the husband and brothers. They were even beaten. But they persisted. The urge to learn the songs was so deep seated, they would run away with their elders and their groups in the darkness of night carrying an earthen lamp, away from the sight of the reprimanding male in the family.

A happy development has been noticed with the opening of a Heritage Music Museum at the Conservatoire de Musique François Mitterrand in Quatre Bornes, Mauritius where teaching classical western music is carried out. Here, along with other elements from Mauritius such as *Sega Tipik* and *Sega Tambour of Rodrigues and Sega Chagos* (all three also UNESCO inscribed) *Geet Gawai* traditional musical instruments are also exhibited. At a ceremony in 2019, a *'Lota'*, ceremonial musical symbol, a must in *Geet Gawai* Singing, was presented by the Chairperson of the Bhojpuri Speaking Union to Mrs. Claudie Ricaud, the Director of the Conservatoire National de Musique François-Mitterrand Trust Fund.

Raising awareness of the need to preserve world's intangible cultural heritage was first signaled by Bolivia in 1973 at a UNESCO meeting. In 2003, UNESCO adopted a Convention for the safeguarding of Intangible Heritage of Humanity of which Mauritius is a signatory. The 2003 Convention is the first legally – binding instrument devoted to the preservation of the Intangible Cultural Heritage of the world. In fact Mauritius was among the first State Parties to sign the Convention. UNESCO organised a workshop in Mauritius in 2011 to acquaint parties concerned of the necessity of conducting inventories of the country's Tangible as well as Intangible Cultural Heritage.

Thereafter, Mauritius through the National Heritage Fund (NHF) embarked upon a comprehensive Inventory of the country's Tangible and Intangible Cultural Heritage. With this Inventory vetted and endorsed by UNESCO, Mauritius entered *Sega Tipik, and Mauritius Bhojpuri folk songs—Geet Gawai* to be considered for Inscription as world Patrimony.

□

33

Conclusion

Geet Gawai: A Vehicle of Human Experiences

The *Bhojpuri folk songs in Mauritius- Geet Gawai* – as a Mauritian Intangible Cultural Heritage and of humanity at large after its inscription at UNESCO provides a medium of cultural expression as a common denominator through its songs, music and dance in a pluri-ethnic, pluri-cultural, pluri-lingual Mauritian society. It has earned respect as a vibrant performing art and reflects the cultural diversity of the country. As a creative performing art form, it encompasses the family unit, the community at large to assume the role of transmitter of national values.

One of the five criterias on which the *Geet Gawai* was inscribed as a world Patrimony at the UNESCO was*: "The file indicated that inscription of the element would contribute to enhancing the visibility of Intangible Cultural Heritage in general and to promoting awareness of the importance of oral traditions and relevant social practices as part of the cultural identity of communities. Geet Gawai originates in Immigrants'experiences against the background of a history of Indentured Labour: inscription would foster cohesive multicultural communities while promoting respect for cultural diversity. Geet Gawai is also a dynamic performing art, experimenting with new techniques and creating new lyrics: its inscription would also contribute to an enhanced appreciation for human creativity".*

Another important criteria-(Criteria number 5) on which the Nomination Dossier of *Geet Gawai* was accepted at UNESCO is that: *"The element was first included in the National Inventory of Intangible Cultural Heritage of the Republic of Mauritius in 2011 and updated in 2012, 2014 and 2015. The file indicates that the inventory was carried out with the participation of practitioners, bearers and community representatives".*

It also reflects not only a medium of singing and expression of myths, based on scriptural texts and epics, legends and popular stories such as the Puranas but also awareness of Environment Nature and Climate Change; values such as sentiments and emotions and sharing and caring. Since the 1970s *Geet Gawai* has led to a consolidation of society.

With its inscription at UNESCO, it contributes and consolidates to the recognition of the Aapravasi Ghat also as a landing place of ***Girmitiyas*** at the harbour of Port Louis and a world recognized heritage site of UNESCO where they brought with them their cultural heritage, practices of rites and rituals, performing arts and beliefs through the element of the Bhojpuri language. The flexible nature of the Bhojpuri language increased its capacity to adapt in alien surroundings and in succeeding historical and political stages of the country leading to its voyage through Independence from a mono crop sugar economy to an upper middle income economy and globalized ICT networking of the 21st century. *Geet Gawai* is verily through its hundreds of lively songs a veritable vehicle of human experiences. I am giving an A to Z of Recommendations of the imperative need to protect the *Geet Gawai* as a Heritage by the State Party and how it can enhance the image of Mauritius on the World Cultural Platform. (Please see Appendix)

The *Geetharines'* Hall of Fame

The *Geetharines* mastered their destinies. They had and have strength and verve. Their songs carry with them, the intensity of a lasting effect.

The words of the songs carry the might and weight, the force of tradition and of society. They are compelling and compulsive.

It is this compulsion behind the songs that have channelled the *Geetharines* to the Hall of Fame and Recognition.

Through the *Geet Gawai,* the *Geetharines* have orchestrated the dance of the universe and choreographed a unique style that has enriched not only the Mauritian cultural landscape but gifted the World patrimony with a remarkable Intangible Cultural Heritage.

The parallel between the journeys of—

1. The *Girmityas*
2. The Women tradition Bearers- *The Geetharines and*
3. *The Geet Gawai Songs*

is indeed a remarkable phenomenon of history.

As the *Geetharine* tradition bearers climbed the 16 steps of the Aapravasi Ghat in Port Louis descending from the "*coolie ship*" after a long journey of several weeks on the rough and turbulent Indian Ocean, in a cramped condition from far flung villages across Bihar and other states of the Presidency of Oudh, Bihar, Bengal and Orissa from 1834 till 1924, (the end of the Indenture Period) did they realise that they were carrying in their throats and collective consciousness the strains of an oral literature that would endure across time to become a permanent legacy of Mauritius and humanity as a whole?

We give below a list of 50 Bhojpuri *Sanskar Geet* preserved in Mauritius which accompany every ceremony of wedding rituals.

□

34

Sequence of 50 Bhojpuri Folk Songs Associated with Marriage

We give below a list of 50 Bhojpuri ***Sanskar Geet*** preserved in Mauritius which accompany every ceremony or wedding ritual.

Sequence of the Bhojpuri folk songs sung during the different stages from pre-wedding to the main marriage ceremony and post marriage.

1. Neota Song – Dharti bhi neowatila
2. Dharti Pujan – (i) Thaali bhara chandan, (ii) Apan Ganga Maiya
3. Lagan kholai – Humro laganiya le le
4. Lagan Geet (Pre-wedding song) – Awa awa saguni, saguna wa ho le le awa
5. Saanjha – Saanjh bhailé saanjha, gharé gharé ghumé
6. Devi Devta ke Geet – Nimiyaa karouwaiyn nimiyaan, sheetal beyar bahé
7. Pinda Geet (Homage to Ancestors) – Dada je chalélan Benaras Gaya pinda paarab ho
8. Arti Geet – Ghar mein se nikalelan Dadi suhagin, ordha ke pitambar, kawan bar ké arti utarab, kawan bara sundar ho
9. Devi Devta Geet - Lota bhar paani - Lota bhara paniya ho, thaali bhara chandana, lipila dharam duwarji
10. Mahadeo Geet – (i) Gaii ke gobar angana lipay ke, (ii) Purain pata par sutaili Gaura Dei, sapna dekhi ek ajgot
11. Tilak ke Geet – Kahawan se bipra awelan, aho bipra awelan

12. Haldi Geet – (i) Girl's Haldi – Soné ke katoriya mein pissal haradiya ho, (ii) Boy's Haldi - Kehi je hardi upjawé la, kehi besawé la ho, (iii) Another Haldi song – koirine koirine – kahuwan ke hardi ho, kehi upjawela.
13. Shaadi Geet (i) (For the boy) – Angana mein thara hoké, rowela Dulha "Himanshu" (any Dulha's name)
    Shaadi Geet (ii) (For the girl) – Chaaro hi kona dada, chaaro hi khamba ho, biché biché bindiya bandhayo ji
14. Suhaag Geet – Dada pichuwariya sohagwa ke jariya Koriya ho Sohag ke jariya
15. Ram ke Shaadi Geet – Chitthiya je likhila, vibhishan bhanchi
    Sunawé Raghunandan, Ram Janakpur biyakar ailé
16. Sumiran – Hai Sumiran karle, mere manna
17. Mandar/Madar Puja (Dholak Puja) – Rumaki Jhumki mandar bajé, Kanhaiyya Lal
18. Dharti Bandhal – Gorwa tohar lagila, dharti ho maiyya, taar bandhi, dharti upar asmaan, ghumi Phiri bandhela deva asthan (Homage to Mother Earth)
19. Chutney Geet – (i) Najar laagi la Raja tor bangle par, (ii) Dil leke bhaga, daga deke bhaga, (iii) Phulori bin chutney kaisse bani (From Trinidad)
20. Sukaar Geet (at the Boy's place) – Kahanwahi eh Sukar Tohar janamiya
    Kahanwahi Raché la Biya ho
21. Bhagwan ke Araj – Bich mein phailawé mohar mala
22. Jhumar – There are several Jhumar Songs:
    (i) Kawano rangana moungawa, kawana rangana motiya, (ii) Rose-Hill ke bistopwa par, (iii) Kalkutta se chutal jahaj (History Song), (iv) Paani nai baa Song (Protest Song), (v) Nakhon ke phuliya girat ta giré de, (vi) Jhumar Song till late night reaching climax – Kehi jala Hajipur, Kehi jala Patna, kehi jala Kalkutta ke deswa
23. Lota Geet – (Teasing song towards the climax of Jhumar dancing) – Dada ke paisa
    Chuha lele jala, dede nachaniya ke daan, Gamat wa hoi be kari Shaadi (Wedding Day)

24. Maro Chawaiyn – Bans wa katayi ke, khambawa garhayi ke Chaaro konowa khamba garhayi, biché-biché bediya bandhayi
25. Peetar Neota Parati Song – Hota parat maiyya jagelan, karra Ganga Snan Ji.
26. Khir Khawai Song (At the Boy's and Girl's place) – "Chapet lele dulha, tanko na chorle" – A khelawni (A game teasing the Dulha)
27. Pokhra Geet – Keouje Pokhra Khanawela, ghat banhawela Kekar bharle kahar, Ta Ram (Bridegroom) nahawele
28. Khunwar pat – (Dulha ho ya Dulhan) – Khunwar pat uttaral? Haan uttaral!
29. Nahané ke Geet (after the bath of the Boy or the Girl, a custom is done to cast away evil eyes – Jeera jawaiyn dadi oinché dekhiya ho koyi najar na lagé
30. Imli Ghontai Geet- Arabe se ayha bhaiyya, darab se awe bahini imli ghontai
31. Dulha jaike parchawan Geet – Prem se arti utaare ji, bar biyahan jaye
32. Dhan kholai Geet – Humro laganiya lele koyalrala, ghumle koyalrala
    Kehi mohe lagana sonchaya ji
33. Mati korayi (Matkor) Geet – Uthu uthu matiya ho, iyari se pyari ho, tohar binu kaisan biyah.
34. Dwaar Puja (When the groom arrives) – Dasuruth ji utare, Janakji ke dware
35. Another Dwaar Puja Geet – Desh hi desh mein neota, kar dihar pujari ji
36. Dulha aiy ke Parchawan Geet – Gawahu mangal chaarji, awa dulha biya rachane
37. Haris Geet – Dhawa ho, nawa ho, dhawa ho, bariya,
    Dhaayi Ayodhya mein jayi
38. Puja Geet – Kahuwan se awe la, Bramha oh Bisun
39. Homa Geet – Homa bhaile, jaap bhaile
40. Ghurathi – (i) Bipraje par le ho, par le veda ke mantra ho, tat, paath, path mori, auru haruwa saungad ho, (ii) Jab Raghuvansi marua chal ailan, mor lipan jaani, dhanji ailan

41. Bhanwar Ghume Geet- Going around the sacred fire song – Madhowa mein bipra mantra ucchare la, var-vadhu bhanwar ghumé
42. Kanya Dan Geet – Jhiri- jhiri nadiya ho Dada
Ki bahela ho sewar
43. 'Lawa Geet' – when brothers give lawa (roasted) rice to Sister – Pehle bhanwar jab Ram hi ghuméla, Sita ghuméla Bhaiyya hi lawa milawé la
44. Sindur Bahoraw Geet – when Sindur is applied to bride's hair-parting by bridegroom- Dada dada pukari la, dada nahi bolela
Dada ke barh joriya, sindur barh dalela
45. Kohbar Geet – Kaanch pitar ke ihi bar Kohbar
46. Samdhi (Boy's Father) meets Samdhi (Girl's Father) at Girl's place - Gopal Gaari: Kahwa ke raja rachi mahal outhawe, kahwa ke howe Rajwa, galh Mahal uthaye Kahan ke Raja, Patisaruwa garha
47. Bidayi Geet: (i) Khudiya hi chuni chuni, dhiya hamar posli Sehun lele jaala, dulaar bagiya, (ii) Aho loto jaide sasurji ke angna (Mauritian Composition)

Other songs which are sung by the Geet Gawai ladies include Sohar, Lalna and janeo songs.

SOHAR/LALNA

48. SOHAR/LALNA Geet (Intangible Cultural Heritage) –
    (i) Chait ke tithi ta, Naomi, nowbat baje la ho, aho lalna...
    (ii) Eh lalna ghumri ghumri mohe lagela, kekra se bolab hum

    Beet gayi ek mass, duyi mass, eh lalna
    Khatta meetha mann karela, kekar se boli
    JANEO GEET (Thread giving Ceremony Song)
49. Janeo Geet – (i) Awadha ke Rishi Munni Ved ke mantra uccharen ho, (ii) Pehle main pujila ho, dharti ho maiyya
Awarila puji akash, aju ghar nati ke Janeo
50. Harparawri Geet - Holé-holé barasa ho Inder Dewa, paani ke barsawat ho.

□

35

Bibliography

References

1. Maitra Bajpai Lopamudra – The Force of the Divine Femininity, p. 29 – in Purbasa – East meets East, Lalit Mansingh, Anup Kumar Mudgal, Udai Bhanu Singh (Ed.), Pentagon Press Ltd., 2019
2. Maitra Bajpai Lopamudra – Intangible Cultural Heritage: Connectivity Across Traditions of South and South – East Asia in Purbasa – East meets East, Lalit Mansingh, Anup Kumar Mudgal, Udai Bhanu Singh (Ed.), Pentagon Press Ltd., 2019
3. Catherine Servan – Schreiber – Chanteurs Itinérants en Inde du Nord – La Tradition orale Bhojpuri – L'Harmattan, Paris, 1999
4. Carter Marina – Across the Kalapani – The Bihari Presence in Mauritius – Crios, 2000
5. Boodhoo Sarita – Religious and Cultural Traditions of Biharis in Mauritius in Across the Kalapani – The Biharis Presence in Mauritius CRIOS Carter Marina, 2000
6. Carter Marina and V. Govinden. The Recreation of Tradition 'Marriage and the Family under Indenture in Across the Kalapani – The Bihari Presence in Mauritius – (Ed.) Marina Carter CRIOS, 2000
7. Deerpal Singh Saloni, Marina Carter and V. Govinden – The Making of a New Community – in Across the Kalapani – The Bihari Presence in Mauritius – Carter Marina (Ed.), CRIOS, 2000
8. Myers Helen – Music of Hindu Trinidad – Songs from the

India Diaspora – The University of Chicago Press, 1998

9. Servan – Schreiber Catherine Champion – Histoire d'une musique métisse à l'île Maurice Chutney Indien et séga Bollywood-Riveneuve Editions, 2010
10. Boodhoo Sarita – Bhojpuri folk songs in Mauritius – *Geet Gawai* – Ministry of Arts and Culture, Bhojpuri Speaking Union, 2016
11. Jain Jasbir – Films, Literature and Culture – Rawat Publications – Institute for Research in Interdisciplinary Studies, Jaipur, 2017
12. Boodhoo Sarita – Bhojpuri Traditions in Mauritius, Mauritius Bhojpuri Institute, 1999, 2000
13. Chakraborty Gautam – Calcutta Port and the Hoogly River: A brief Historical overview, 2009
14. Chanda Dr. A.K, I.A.S – Bollards of Time – Published by Kolkata Port Trust – Maritime Archives and Heritage Centre, 2009
15. Boodhoo Sarita – Kanya Dan – The Whys of Hindu Marriage Rituals, Mauritius Bhojpuri Institute, Port Louis, Mauritius, 1993, 1994
16. Boodhoo Sarita – Mauritius ki Bhojpuri Paramparayein published by Prabhat Prakashan, New Delhi, 2000
17. Singh Chandramani – Marriage Songs from Bhojpuri Region – Kitab Mahal, Jaipur, 1979
18. Mrityunjay Singh– Ganga Ratan Bidesi (Bhojpuri Novel), Published by Bharatiya Jhanpith, New Delhi, 2018
19. Hugh Tinker – A New System of Slavery – The Export of Indian Labour Overseas, 1830–1920 – Oxford University Press, London, 1974
20. Dhuny Dharam Yash Deo – Chairman – Aapravasi Ghat World Heritage Site – Mauritius, Published by Aapravasi Ghat Trust Fund, 2016
21. Gopauloo Dr. Nagamah and George Easton – A Unique Place in Time and Space – A Pictorial Presentation of the Aapravasi Ghat World Heritage Site and the Indenture Experience in Mauritius, 1834–2014, Published by AGTF, 2014
22. Mudgal Anup Kumar – High Commissioner of India in

Mauritius September, 2014 in Preface in 'A Unique Place in Time and Space – A Pictorial Presentation of the Aapravasi Ghat World Heritage Site and the Indenture Experience in Mauritius, (1834–2014) 2014. In the Context of the 180th Anniversary of the Arrival of Indentured Labourers in Mauritius, October, 2014

23. Jeebaun Priyamvada – Mera Jeevan aur Mera Bhara Pura Parivar – Autobiography – Sumati Jeebaun Ka Jeewan ewan ounke dwara gaye jane wale Bhojpuri geet, p. 161– 216, Published by Star Publications, New Delhi, 2014
24. Dr. Gangoo Oodaye Narain M.A., Ph.D. – Mauritius Ka Bhojpuri Lok Sahitya ewam Bharatiya Sanskriti, Mahatma Gandhi Institute, 2002
25. Mishra Kuber Dr. – Mauritius Ke Bhojpuri Lokgeeton Ka Vivechnatmak Adhyayan, 1981, Sanjay Prakashan, Varanasi
26. Upadhyaya Krishna Dev Dr. – Bhojpuri Loksahitya, Vishwavidhyalaya Prakashan, 2nd Edition, 2008, Varanasi
27. Pandey Rajballi – Hindu Samskaras, Motilal Banarsidass, Delhi, 1987
28. Mangru Basdeo – The Elusive El Dorado, Essays on the Indian Experience in Guyana University Press of America Inc. Lanham, Maryland, USA, 2005
29. Ghosh Amitav – Sea of Poppies – Penguin/Viking, New Delhi, 2008
30. Edgard Sienaert, Meg Cowper – Lewis and Nigel Bell – Oral Tradition and its Transmission – The many forms of message. The Camp Bell Collections and Centre for Oral Studies. University of Natal Durban, 1994, (Papers given at the Fourth International Conference on Oral Tradition – University of Natal, Durban, 27–30 June, 1994
31. Boodhoo Sarita – The Bhojpuri Marriage Songs of Mauritius and their Message – Paper presented at the Fourth International Conference on Oral Tradition – University of Natal, Durban, 27–30 June, 1994 published in 'Oral Tradition and its Transmission – The many Forms of Message – Published by The Campbell Collections and Centre for Oral Studies, University of Natal, Durban, 1994

32. Brajendra Kumar Bhagat 'Madhukar' – Kavya Rachanavali (Collection of Poetic Works) – Edited by Dr. Kamal Kishore Goyanka – Published by Natraj Prakashan, New Delhi, 2003
33. Sinha Jyoti Dr. – Bhojpuri Lok Geeton Ke Vividh Ayaam – Omega Publications, New Delhi, 2013
34. Ramdin Suchita Dr. – Sanskar Manjari Mauritius ke Bhojpuri Sanskar Geet Mahatma Gandhi Institute, Moka Mauritius, 1989
35. Sharma Shri Radha Vallabh – Maithili Sanskar Geet (Edited by) Bihar Rashtrabhasha Parishad, Patna, Bihar, 1986
36. Hanskumar Tiwari and Radha Vallabh Sharma – Editors – Bhojpuri Sanskar Geet – Bihar Rashtrabhasha Parishad, Patna, 4 – Bihar, 1977
37. Sipahi Singh Shrimant – Tharuhat Ke Lok geet – Collection of folk songs of Bhojpuri Speaking Tharuhat – Shrimant Prakashan, Gopalganj, Bihar, 2002
38. Sarup Leela Gujadhur – India – East India Company Indentured Labour – A brief History Published by Aldrich International, Kolkata, 2011
39. Kim Knott and Sean McLoughlin – (Editors) Diasporas-Concepts, Intersections, Identities, Rawat Publications, 2010, 2011. First published in 2010 by Zed Book Ltd., London and New York
40. Mohit Dimlalah – Heera Moti – Riddles and Songs Part VII – Volume II, Bujhawal Ewan Geet, 2010, Published by author
41. Sone Chirainya – Paati Edited by Padmashri Mrs. Malini Awasthi, Published by Sone Chirainya Parivaar, Lucknow, UP, 2011
42. Pandit Atmaram Vishwanath – Hindu Mauritius (1936) Edited by Pahlad Ramsurrun (2012) Published by Star Publications Private Ltd., New Delhi
43. Satyendra Peerthum – 'They came to Mauritian Shores' the Life Stories and the History of the Indentured Labourers in Mauritius (1826-1937). Published by Aapravasi Ghat Trust Fund (AGTF) in 2018
44. Brij V. Lal, Mr. Tulsi's Store – A Fijian Journey Published by Pandanus Books, 2001, Australia

45. Catherine Champion Servan Shreiber *Traditions Orales dans le Monde Indien (Oral Traditions in South Asia) by (Editions de l'Ecole des Hautes Etudes en Sciences Sociales, Centre D'Etudes de L'Inde et de L'Asie du Sud)* 1996
46. Sunandan Roy Chowdhury – Sampark – Journal of Global Understanding No. 13 January, 2010. Mauritius Making home of a land. Published by, Calcutta
47. Dr. Krishna Deo Upadhyaya – Bhojpuri Log Geet- Published by Hindi Sahitya Sammellan, Prayag, 1953
48. Dr. Pittiviraj Joyram – Ph.D. Doctorate Thesis, 1995, 'A Study of Music Prevalent in the Mauritian People of Indian Origin with a Special Reference to Indian Migration of Indentured Labourers. Indira Kala Sangit Vishwa Vidhyalay, Khairagarh, Madhya Pradesh. (unpublished)
49. Bhojpuri Lok-Sahitya by Dr. Krishna Deo Upadhyaya, M.A., Ph.D., Vishwa Vidhyalaya Prakashan, Varanasi, 2nd Edition, 2008

□

Appendix-1

The Obligations of Mauritius as a State Party Following the Inscription of the Bhojpuri folk songs– Geet Gawai on the UNESCO Representative List of the Intangible Cultural Heritage of Humanity

1. The *Bhojpuri folk songs in Mauritius – Geet Gawai* were listed on 1 December, 2016 on the *UNESCO* Representative List of the Intangible Cultural Heritage of Humanity at the 11th Session of the *UNESCO* Intergovernmental Committee for the Safeguarding of the Intangible Cultural Heritage in Addis Ababa, Ethiopia.
2. Following the Inscription of *Bhojpuri folk songs- Geet Gawai* as a World Patrimony of Humanity, there is a definite commitment on the part of Mauritius to promote, preserve and transmit Bhojpuri Linguistic and Cultural Heritage.

   The obligation is legal as Mauritius is a State Party as well as a Member of the Intergovernmental Committee for the Safeguarding of the Intangible Cultural Heritage in line with the 2003 Convention of which Mauritius is one of the first signatories.
3. Mauritius as a State Party is bound to raise awareness, build up capacities and promote and take educational measures in the field of the Intangible Cultural Heritage on its territory – in this particular case – in the field of the *Bhojpuri folk songs – Geet Gawai.*
4. Following the inscription, Government should seek

international financial assistance namely from *UNESCO* and co-operation from other international and national bodies to encourage the *Geet Gawai* transmission and preservation.

5. The Mauritius State Party should ensure *recognition* of and *respect* for the *Bhojpuri folk songs – Geet Gawai* in society as an integral part of the intangible cultural heritage of the country, in particular through developing educational programmes both formal and informal.
6. Mauritius as a State Party should take safeguarding measures to enable the viability of the *Bhojpuri folk songs – Geet Gawai* through continued enactment, performance and transmission.
7. Definition of Intangible Cultural Heritage as per Convention-2003 of UNESCO
   a. The Convention 2003 defines Intangible Cultural Heritage as *'the practices, representations, expressions, knowledge and skills'*. As applied to the *Bhojpuri folk songs – Geet Gawai* the *Geetharines* and tradition bearers as groups of communities and as individual artists do recognize the above attributes as part of their intangible cultural heritage.
   b. They are in conformity with human rights and belong to one or more of the prescribed *'domains'* of the Intangible Cultural Heritage as stipulated in the Convention 2003.
   c. For the sense of identity and continuity of these communities and groups Government should provide all such facilities such as musical instruments. *Geet Gawai* Artists and performers should receive support for performing in national, international festivals and extravaganzas through the Artists' Assistance Scheme.
   d. The *Geet Gawai* should be promoted through the Cultural Exchange Programme with other State Parties.
   e. In line with UNESCO's safeguarding measures

Bhojpuri folk songs – Geet Gawai can benefit from International Development Grant Scheme.

8. Safeguarding Measures include:

i. Promotion of Bhojpuri language, oral literature and its Cultural Heritage in the Educational system both formal and informal – i.e. both in Educational Institutions under the Ministry of Education and Human Resources, Tertiary Education and Scientific Research as well as in informal institutions run by NGOs such as in *Baithkas* to ensure the preservation of the language and transmission as Bhojpuri is the vehicle of the *Bhojpuri folk songs – Geet Gawai.* Please *see the extract of UNESCO 2003 Convention.*

UNESCO's 2003 Convention for the Safeguarding of the Intangible Cultural Heritage Paragraph 1 proposes five broad 'domains' in which intangible cultural heritage is manifested:

- *Oral traditions and expressions, including language as a vehicle of the intangible cultural heritage;*
- *Performing arts;*
- *Social practices, rituals and festive events;*
- *Knowledge and practices concerning nature and the universe;*
- *Traditional craftsmanship.*

ii. Among these domains, it is paramount to note that the *Bhojpuri folk songs in Mauritius – Geet Gawai* as *'an oral tradition and expression'* are sung in *BHOJPURI* which is the medium of these expressions.

iii. As such it is important for Government to not only ensure the *Safeguarding of Bhojpuri folk songs- Geet Gawai* but also to preserve, promote and transmit – the vehicle of its expression – *the Bhojpuri Language.*

iv. Government should increase National Awards and Honours for outstanding contribution of *Bhojpuri folk songs – Geet Gawai* and other related genres by tradition bearers in the safeguarding and promotion of *Intangible Cultural Heritage.*

v. Government should harmonize policies involving Ministries such as Ministry of Arts & Culture, Ministry of Tourism, Ministry of Education and Human Resources, Tertiary Education and Scientific Research, Youth and Sports, Social Integration and Economic Development, Gender Equality, Child Development and Family Welfare and Social Security, National Solidarity and Reform Institutions to promote and safeguard the element.

vi. Government should establish a *'Living Treasures Scheme'* to recognize the best practitioners especially the elderly, thus contributing to better safeguarding of *Geet Gawai* and youth encouragement. Inventories to compile and catalogue their knowledge and songs should be conducted. For this, financial assistance is required.

9. The *Bhojpuri Folk Singers, Geet Gawai practitioners* and *tradition bearers* should get *financial assistance* through their associations and through project based training, workshops and seminars, as well as Awards and other incentives.

10. a. *The Bhojpuri Speaking Union* operating under the *Ministry of Arts and Cultural Heritage* is a body set up by an Act of Parliament with as *sole* mission and function to promote, propagate and ensure the transmission of Bhojpuri language and its related cultural heritage. It should be further given capacity building and financial support *(current budgetary grant is too minimal)* to enable it to carry on this mission and see to fruition the safeguarding measures of UNESCO. It must be given such financial, manpower and transport facilities that can enable it to implement the functions as enumerated in the *Act of Parliament of 2011.*

b. *Bhojpuri Speaking Union Geet Gawai Schools*

The *Bhojpuri Speaking Union* has set up so far a *Geet Gawai School* at Petit Raffray in 2013 and to date 52 branches of *Bhojpuri Speaking Union Geet Gawai Schools* have been opened throughout the country with more than 35 pending demands from the community and practitioners. The State Party should extend financial assistance for the running of these schools so far carried out on a voluntary basis.

c. There is an urgent need for Government to support the *Bhojpuri Speaking Union* in carrying on the inventory of the tradition bearers as the elders are a disappearing lot. The Government should consider this urgently as a menace and endangered group. The elders die with their *knowledge and skills.* They should be transmitted through recordings, CDs, videos and film documentaries and written and audio records using E-Technology for posterity.

d. University, College and School students and other interested parties should be involved in production of films and clips in Bhojpuri in collaboration with the Mauritius Film Development Corporation under the aegis of the Ministry of Arts and Cultural Heritage.

11. **Challenges Faced**

Challenges faced in terms of the ravages of modernity and dis-interestment of youth in heritage culture should be targeted, and debates, dialogues and organizations of competitions encouraged about how best to safeguard the *Bhojpuri folk songs – Geet Gawai* and ensure transmission to younger generations.

12. *Bhojpuri folk songs in Mauritius Geet Gawai in the Media*

The *Mauritius Broadcasting Corporation* (MBC TV) is a most powerful and viable partner with the Government to ensure visibility and audibility of the *Geet Gawai* and its vehicle the *Bhojpuri language.*

13. **The Ministry of Tourism**

The Ministry of Tourism as an integral part of the State should give promotion to *Bhojpuri folk songs in Mauritius – Geet Gawai* as part of its *cultural tourism* strategy. *Geet Gawai* Ladies should be enlisted to perform at the Airport and at Civic Receptions of State guests and other dignitaries and at hotels and other Cultural Extravaganzas and roadshows.

14. **The Mauritius Film Development Corporation**

The *Mauritius Film Development Corporation* should be encouraged to make feature films and documentaries on the Bhojpuri folk songs, the tradition bearers and their lives.

15. **National Bhojpuri Institute**

Finally, Government should set up a *National Bhojpuri Institute (Bhojpuri Speaking Union* parameters are limited with meager financial grants – (Rs. 1.2 million only annually including recurrent, other charges and activities).

16. **Periodical Reporting by State Party**

Mauritius as a State Party has to carry out periodical reporting to UNESCO every six years on the safeguarding measures that take place and the progress done in ensuring the promotion, preservation and transmission of *Bhojpuri folk songs – Geet Gawai* since its inscription on the Intangible Cultural Heritage List of Humanity.

—Dr. Sarita Boodhoo
Chairperson
Bhojpuri Speaking Union

□

Appendix-2

4th Draft on Nomination Dossier Bhojpuri folk songs inMauritius Geet Gawai on UNESCO Representative List of the Intangible Cultural Heritage of Humanity

Team Work: Dr. (Mrs.) Sarita Boodhoo Consultant on Consultative Committee of UOM

To Dr. Anwar Janoo.

As a Consultant on the Consultative Committee of University of Mauritius I helped to prepare the Nomination Dossier on Bhojpuri folk songs of Mauritius: Geet Gawai

I prepared these Obligations on second of January 2013.

We worked hard on the Nomination Dossier of *Geet Gawai* to UNESCO. On the eve of my departure scheduled for 4 January, 2013 for the *Pravasi Bharatiya Divas* held in Kochi Kerala Dr. Anwar Janoo, Senior Lecturer at the Department of History, Faculty of Social Studies and Humanities at the University of Mauritius, one of the responsible parties on the Consultative Committee in the preparation of the Nomination Dossier on *Geet Gawai*, phoned me in the morning of 2 January, 2013. It was a public holiday. He wanted me to give a paper urgently on the Obligations of the State Party Mauritius to show in what ways the Nomination of *Geet Gawai* at UNESCO would be beneficial.

I told Dr. Anwar Janoo that I have no computer at home that I would be traveling to India on the morning of 4th January. Dr. Anwar Janoo told me he would come to the Ministry of Arts and Culture at the seventh level at Renganaden Seeneevassen Building, Port Louis on 3rd January at 9 a.m. with his laptop and would type my proposals which had to be as per the exigencies of the UNESCO within 750 words. It was a New Year festive period. The family was meeting.

On that morning of the third, I woke up at 5 am and sat down from 6am to 8 a.m. to write down the Obligations. In a flow I wrote an A to Z proposals. Dr. Anwar Janoo typed them all as I dictated and we summarised it into 750 words. We worked till 4 p.m. Late Mr. Islam Bhagun, Culture Officer at the time had his office opened and we worked there on the Obligations. I had not even done my packing. I was leaving early next morning for India!

"Didi, I always believed in your dedication for the Bhojpuri language and music. I still recall the consultative meeting with the numerous practitioners and singers at the University although I do not speak Hindi. But with your guidance the approval of the recommendations was unanimous for preparing the dossier. I value these instance of work. Thank you." Dr. Anwar Janoo, Former Senior Lecturer at the Department of History of the Faculty of Social Studies Humanities (FSSH) University of Mauritius, Department of History currently, Member of the Aapravasi Ghat Trust Fund Board (AGTF). 25 April, 2022.

Safeguarding Measures Proposed. (750 Words)

What measures are proposed to help to ensure that the element's viability is not jeopardized in the future especially as an unintended result of inscription and the resulting visibility and public attention?

Proposal of Measures to safeguard the endangered genres so as to keep the naturalness and tradition of Geet Gawai:

a. As Bhojpuri, the language of *Geet Gawai* has been introduced in the School cursus, it should be accompanied by the curriculum developers as part of the syllabus in the form of games, songs, riddles, proverbs. Children in upper classes should be taught the meaning, the history and origin of the different aspects of the genre and the occasion on which they are performed. This will help them understand and appreciate the element as well as enjoy it while developing a sense of pride and a sense of responsibility towards its promotion and propagation as a valuable Intangible Heritage of Humanity, worthy to be classified in the World Patrimony.

b. There should be a scientific and Methodological collection and classification of all aspects of *Geet Gawai* by the Ministry of Arts and Culture through a collective work of its Para-statal bodies concerned such as the National Heritage Fund, the AGTF, the Bhojpuri Speaking Union, the Mahatma Gandhi Institute and other non-governmental bodies.

c. Continuous workshops with practitioners and tradition bearers should be held to safeguard the element and bring to them the necessity to preserve and maintain the *Geet Gawai* in its pure tradition in the face of modernity and exposure to public attention.

d. Every village or hamlet has loads of Bhojpuri Heritage in various aspects whether as artifacts or Intangible forms. It is proposed that *'village discovery projects'* be set up at Secondary and Tertiary levels, with interesting and attractive dazzling prizes to the best projects undertaken. Participants will therefore be compelled to research on UNESCO's aims and objectives of the need to preserve the Intangible Cultural Heritage of Humanity and familiarize with its conventions, laws governing these measures. They will thereby discover the need to promote and preserve these elements as future generations.

e. More academic and research work can be carried out at grassroots level by the University of Mauritius (UoM). Students of the primary, secondary and tertiary levels can embark on those projects of codifying, classifying and cataloging of different types of songs, rites and rituals with which they may be associated and other related aspects as well. This project can be undertaken jointly by University of Mauritius in collaboration with the Bhojpuri Speaking Union, the NHF, the AGTF, the MGI/RTI and other bodies.

f. In order to continue creating awareness in the public, the National Television and Radio (Public and Private) should give voice and visibility to the tradition bearers and practitioners and encourage the younger generation of the need to preserve and disseminate the Heritage of *Geet Gawai*.

g. Bhojpuri festivals should be more regularly organized to incorporate *Geet Gawai* and associated forms to give it a sense of importance in the eyes of younger generation.

h. Teams of young women singers should be prepared to sing the *Geet Gawai* and perform it in the traditional way. This work can be undertaken by the *Bhojpuri Speaking Union* under the aegis of the Ministry of Arts and Culture. Competition of young tradition bearers in the different genres should be organized on a regular basis and attractive prizes given so that they feel a sense of pride for the element as well as have respects for the elder generation of tradition bearers.

i. The elder generation of tradition bearers of *Geet Gawai* must be given their due recognition and made to have a sense of esteem for themselves for the immense contribution they have made in preserving the world's Intangible Cultural Heritage on their own. For generations and that too orally. They can be justly compensated as well as feel the urgency to pass it on to the young generation.

j. *The Geet Gawai* should be integrated in the programme of Cultural Tourism. Workers of the tourist industry (tourist guides) hotel managers, events managers of various Ministries and other bodies should be apprised of the background and importance of the element. Special booklets, pamphlets and brochures information with illustrations should be published and distributed to disseminate the knowledge amongst all concerned as well as for tourists and tourist guides.

k. A catalogue of the tradition bearers of *Geet Gawai* (past and present) should be published giving their discography, and a short history, biography and curriculum vitae of each tradition bearer, their village, from whom they learnt the songs, how they learnt the *Geet Gawai* and its associated genres.

l. The Government must consider the promotion and preservation of the Intangible Cultural Heritage of its Nation seriously. For this, legal measures should be taken or amended where needs be to preserve and safeguard the elements. The Ministry of Finance must realize that sustainable development does incorporate the Intangible Cultural Heritage of the country as well and must be made to release adequate funds towards the maintenance, safeguarding of the element of *Geet Gawai* through responsible and trained resource persons and be equipped with necessary scientific tools to collect and process data. This must be considered as a serious work.

m. Municipalities, District Councils, Village Councils and Community Centres should be involved in the promotion and propagation of the *Geet Gawai* as it is an invaluable tradition of their mandates. They should hold events bearing the philosophy of safeguarding the element in mind.

n. National and International Conferences of Bhojpuri Mahotsaw should be organized by the *Bhojpuri Speaking Union* to highlight the importance of *Geet Gawai*. World renowned Research scholars should be involved from the Indian Diaspora in general. These would involve oral historians, folk tradition research scholars, ethnographers, ethnologists, cultural anthropologists and musicologists of the world to debate and suggest means to preserve, promote, codify, catalogue, classify the *Geet Gawai* in various forms practised throughout the world.

o. The tradition bearers and other associated practitioners such as *gamat, latent* singers should be given good and sustainable support and incentives to continue producing as well as make CDs and DVDs of their performances.

The financial assistance currently offered by the Ministry of Arts and Culture should be adequately increased. The National Television should be able to give financial incentives to the tradition bearers whose elements it broadcasts. They should also be compensated in terms of being incorporated or attached to a production unit or Event Company for Sustainability.

p. A National Heritage music label based on the Takamba label of PRMA (Pole Regional des Musiques Actuelles) of Reunion Island can be undertaken by the Ministry of Arts and Culture in collaboration with the Indian Ocean Rim or C.O.I or Iles Vanilles.

q. The *Bhojpuri Geet Gawai* is part of the collective memory of humanity and therefore must be given all due necessary legal measures to protect it.

r. *Geet Gawai* groups or individual singers should be encouraged to share their rich treasure with the World especially the countries of the Indian Diaspora. They must have a group or team leader who is well versed and trained in the background of each aspects of *Geet Gawai* so that it can be produced and be understood by non-initiated audience. A collaborative framework to facilitate their travel, performance and financial implications, incentives should be prepared by the Ministry of Arts and Culture.

s. The *Bhojpuri Speaking Union* should be empowered to create an *Academy of Geet Gawai* for the dissemination of the element to the public in general and the younger generation. It should have a multipurpose centre where an archive of documents related to the elements and tradition bearers, Library of CDs, DVDs, Research Room, Library of books related to the elements, a performance hall with a museum to give photographic visibility of tradition bearers and practitioners, a recording room and sound and light projects.

   The artefacts associated with *Geet Gawai* also should be on show such as *Lota, dholak, chimta, lakri taal.* Demonstrations can also be given to visitors. Lectures should also be organized by trained personals on the history, origin and particular details of each aspect of *Geet Gawai*, thereby highlighting its importance as a World Heritage of Humanity.

t. *A Bhojpuri Geet Gawai Heritage Site* should be created with sound and light where fashion stars, Bhojpuri food and song fairs and period costumes jewellery exhibits could be held.

u. Children/students should be encouraged to trace their roots, the history of their ancestral village from elders and thereby be exposed to the historical background of *Geet Gawai*. The *Bhojpuri Speaking Union* under the aegis of the Ministry of Arts and Culture could conduct these in collaboration with the NHF, the AGTF, UOM, MGI and NGOS.

v. Life cycle programmes could be undertaken to valorize the songs of the *Geet Gawai*. These can be held under the umbrella of Bhojpuri Speaking Union.

w. An academic journal on *Geet Gawai* and related forms should be published on an annual basis where serious intellectual/academic treatment could be given to the element, thereby giving scope to intellectuals and scholarly debates and incite research among the younger generation of academicians and researchers.

x. More films and documentaries should be made on each aspect of the *Geet Gawai*. With adequate funding and training, commentaries on these should be precise and fully researched for a wide presentation in the public. These can be shown locally on the Bhojpuri Channel of the National Television, at various exposes, in the regional and international cultural fairs. The National Television should initiate more debates, literary talks, forums in *Bhojpuri* accompanied by performances of *Geet Gawai* with interviews of practitioners.

y. A vast campaign must be undertaken to free people from the inferiority complex associated with the element and its vehicle the Bhojpuri language. Adult Education and Leisure classes should be mounted for parents so that they encourage their children to speak *Bhojpuri* and sing the traditional songs as a cultural heritage thereby nurturing its preservation and continuity in the family environment.

z. Finally a sound Cultural Policy must be chalked out for the safeguarding and protection of the Intangible Heritage of *Geet Gawai* and *Bhojpuri culture*. Educational Policies must be formulated to give the *Geet Gawai* its rightful and legitimate place at all levels in education and in the cultural domain. The time has come for its proper and formal recognition at all levels of education, culture and government. A permanent network should be established involving all para-statal bodies concerned such as the *Bhojpuri Speaking Union*, the National Heritage Fund, the various Ministries of Education, Tertiary Education, the Ministry of Tourism, the Ministry of Arts and Culture, the Ministry of Finance, the AGTF, the NGF and other bodies.

3 January, 2013 **—Dr. Sarita Boodhoo**

□

Appendix-3

UNESCO inscribes Bhojpuri folk songs in Mauritius – Geet Gawai on the Representative List of the Intangible Cultural Heritage of Humanity on 1 December, 2016:

The Committee

"1. Takes note that Mauritius has nominated *Bhojpuri folk songs in Mauritius, Geet Gawai* (No. 01178) for inscription on the Representatives List of the Intangible Cultural Heritage of Humanity.

Geet Gawai is a pre-wedding ceremony that combines rituals, prayers, songs, music and dance. It is performed mainly by Bhojpuri Speaking communities in Mauritius of Indian descent. The traditional practice takes place at the home of the bride or bridegroom and involves female family members and neighbours. It begins with five married women sorting items (turmeric, rice, grass and money) in a piece of cloth while other participants sing songs that honour Hindu gods and goddesses. After the site has been sanctified, the mother of the bride or groom and the drummer honour musical instruments to be played during the ceremony, such as the dholak (a two-headed drum). Uplifting songs are then performed and everyone joins in and dances. *Geet Gawai* is an expression of community identity and collective cultural memory. The practice also provides participants with a sense of pride and contributes to greater social cohesion, breaking class and caste barriers. Knowledge about the practice and its associated skills are transmitted from older to younger generations on an informal and formal basis. This takes place via observation and participation by family's semi formal teaching, houses, community centres and academies. Nowadays the practice of *Geet Gawai* extends to public performances and men also participate.

2. Decides that, from the information included in the file, the nomination satisfies the following criteria:

R 1: The practice of *Geet Gawai*, through its participatory performances is shown to contribute to social cohesion, breaking free of class and caste barriers and to have become an expression of collective, cultural memory whilst strengthening a common identity. The wedding ceremony symbolizes the sustainability of individuals and community, while the public performances reinforce relations between groups. The file offers a clear description of the element's bearers and practitioners, whose knowledge and skills are transmitted to new generations through informal and formal means.

R 2: The file indicates that inscription of the element would contribute to enhancing the visibility of Intangible Cultural Heritage in general and to promoting awareness of the importance of Oral Traditions and relevant social practices as part of the Cultural identity of communities. *Geet Gawai* originates in immigrant experiences against the background of a history of indentured labourer: inscription would foster cohesive multicultural communities while promoting respect for cultural diversity. *Geet Gawai* is also a dynamic performing art, experimenting with new techniques and creating new lyrics: its inscription would also contribute to an enhanced appreciation for human creativity.

R 3: Current and future efforts to safeguard and promote the performance of *Geet Gawai* are elaborated in detail. The groups concerned have to date documented, researched and updated the element to ensure its viability, with State Support. The file demonstrates that local groups and stakeholders will continue their work to document and spread knowledge on the element. Threats that may occur as unintended results of inscription are recognized. The submitting State intends to contribute to safeguarding by funding national festivities and through documentation and inventorying projects:

R 4: The community concerned participated in the

preparation of the nomination through workshops and individual consultations between 2010 and 2015. Consent is shown through varied (written and oral) evidence, of a non standardized nature. Access to the knowledge and practice of *Geet Gawai* is open (with the exception of the Pre-wedding event):

R 5: The element was first included in the National Inventory of Intangible Cultural Heritage of the Republic of Mauritius in 2011 and updayed in 2012, 2014 and 2015. The file indicates that the inventory was carried out with the participation of practitioners, bearers and community representatives. The inventory is maintained by the National Heritage Fund/Ministry of Arts and Culture.

3. *Inscribes Bhojpuri folk songs in Mauritius, Geet Gawai* on the Representative List of the Intangible Cultural Heritage of Humanity:

4. Encourages the submitting State when promoting the element at the international level, to provide a translation of lyrics of the songs, particularly for the video, into widely spoken languages".

□

Appendix-4

Bhojpuri Speaking Union *Geet Gawai* Schools

No.	Bhojpuri Speaking Union *Geet Gawai* School	Teachers of Bhojpuri Tradition Bearers *(Geetharines)*	Day	Time of Class
1.	Petit Raffray, Social Welfare Centre (Headquarter)	Mrs. Dhundevi Poonuth (Rita Poonith) (Head)	Friday	9.00 am To noon
2.	Lalmatie	Mrs. Anita Taurah	Wdenesday	9.00 am To noon
3.	Lalmatie	Mrs. Anita Beejadur	Friday	9.00 am To noon
4.	Dagotiere	Mrs. Kamla Koonjal	Friday	9.00 am To noon
5.	Queen Victoria	Mrs. Jasswantee Duchwa	Thursday	9.00 am To noon
6.	Bonne Mere	Mrs. Makuna	Saturday	9.00 am To noon
7.	Piton	Mrs. Shobha Bundhoo	Wednesday	9.00 am To noon
8.	Plaines des Roches	Mrs. Amowtee Gunowree	Thursday	Noon to 2.00 pm
9.	Laventure	Mrs. Parmawtee Dhunoo	Tuesday	9.00 am To noon
10.	Plaines des Papayes	Mrs. Devimatee Mooruth	Thursday	Noon to 2.00 pm

11.	Creve Coeur	Mrs. Champa Lagooni	Tuesday	9.00 am To noon
12.	Quatre Bornes	Mrs. Bulliram	Friday	10.00 am To 12.30 pm
13.	Medine Camp De Masque	Mrs. Tribhuwan	Tuesday	12.30 – 2 p.m.
14.	Mare Goyaves Camp De Masque	Mrs. Anuradha Boodia	Thursday	12.30 – 2 p.m
15.	Poste De Flacq	Mrs. Indranee Khudisingh	Thursday	1 p.m. – 2.30 p.m.
16.	Deux Freres	Mrs. Madri Sidari	Tuesday	9 a.m. – 11 a.m.
17.	Castel	Mrs. Ratnabai Boodhoo	Depending/ Wednesday	4 p.m. – 5.30 p.m.
18.	Bon Acceuil	Mrs. Muneeram	Tuesday	9 a.m. – 10.30 a.m.
19.	Mahebourg	Mrs. Luchman	Thursday	10 – 11.30 a.m.
20.	Valton Montagne Longue	Mrs. Jhingree	Thursday	1 – 3 p.m.
21.	Quatre Soeur	Mrs. Mantee Girdharee	Thursday	12 – 2 p.m.
22.	Dagotiere	Mrs. Chandanee Bansee / Mrs. Lata Koonjal	Tuesday	10-12 noon
23.	Cottage	Mrs. Sooryawantee Hurnam	Tuesday	12.30 – 2 p.m.
24.	Triolet, 7th Mile	Mrs. Jharry	Thursday	12 – 2 p.m.
25.	Royal Road Ecroignard	Mrs. Aartee Ramtohul	Thursday	12 – 2 p.m.
26.	Deux Frères	Mrs. Sidary		
27.	Bel Air	Mrs. Coosmawty Beharry Or Mrs. Geeta Bunsy		
28.	Montagne Blanche	Mrs. Basanty Ramdany		
29.	Riche Mare	Mrs. Ratna Purgass		
30.	Hollywood Vacoas	Mrs. Sadna Ramjeet		
31.	Mare D'Albert	Mrs. Sangeeta Dhununjay		

32.	Rose-Hill	Mrs. Sheela Nuched		
33.	Le Hochet	Mrs. Mala		
34.	Belle Vue Maurel	Mrs. Vidhyamati Nunkoo		
35.	Grand Bay	(1) Mrs. Madvi Ragunatjh (2) Mrs. Sharmily Jummun		
36.	Bambous	Mrs. Lilo Mathur		
37.	Surinam	(1) Mrs. Gokool (2) Mrs. Rama		
38.	Roche Noires	Mrs. Aaraty Aukhajan		
39.	Camp Diable	(1) Mrs.Gianty Motee (2) Mrs. Saloni Bundhun		
40.	Mare la Chaux	(1) Mrs. Hema Madan (2) Mrs. Dhanwanty Ramchurn		
41.	Sebastopol	Mrs. Megoo		
42.	Petite Retraite Bois D'Oiseaux	Mrs. Shakuntalee Berjoo		
43.	Quatre Bornes La Louise	Mrs. Sita Ramyead		
44.	Bois Cheri	Mrs. Vasantee Mattan		
45.	Sottise	Mrs. Jusruth		
46.	Henrietta	Mrs. Ganga Mahadeo		
47.	L'Escalier	Mrs. Shanti Beedassy		
48.	Glen Park Vacoas	Mrs. Daby		
49.	St Pierre	Mrs. Anju Kissoon		
50.	Caroline Bel Air	Mrs. Sewlall		

The days and time may vary at times according to the availability of the Site and the Group of Geet Gawai of the respective areas.

Two More Schools have been set up after the Pandemic.

□

Acknowledgement

For writing *Geet Gawai–An Ode to Geetharines of Mauritius,* I owe a great debt first of all to the many *Geetharines*. They who have unhesitatingly shared their knowledge and skills with me and lovingly sang their *geet* for me, for the community and for the humanity at large. They have placed Mauritius on the forefront of the Nations/State Parties through the Intangible Cultural Heritage *Bhojpuri folk songs in Mauritius – Geet Gawai* with its inscription as a World Heritage of Humanity on 1 December, 2016.

In this context, my hearty thanks go to Mrs. Rita Poonith, Head of the Bhojpuri Speaking Union *Geet Gawai* Schools and to the *Guruwaines Geetharines* of our 52 *Geet Gawai* Schools of Mauritius, who have accompanied me on this *Geet Gawai* voyage.

I owe a great debt to UNESCO. Without UNESCO's 2003 Convention for the Safeguarding of the Intangible Cultural Heritage, the *Geet Gawai* would have been lost to the onslaught of modernity and ravages of commercialisation of culture. The *Geetharines* would have been dumped aside. They are custodians of Humanity's Heritage. Thank You UNESCO.

I should like to make mention of the many scholars, linguists, dictionarists whose names and books are mentioned in the book and in the Bibliography. Their works and thoughts have been a template for me to advance in this vast uncovered territory so far.

I must say a great 'Thank You' to Amitav Ghosh, one of the world's finest storytellers who placed Mauritius forcefully on the world map by making it the scenario for his rich saga "*Sea of Poppies*" in the unveiling of the *Girmitiya* movement and the voyage of the *Girmitiyas* across the *Kala Pani* stripping them of their dignity. Not only that, he brought to the forefront the resilience of the Bhojpuri people, their languages, traditions and folk songs. I am particularly indebted to him for making his heroine Deeti sing '*Sanjh bhaile sanjha*', a Mauritian preserved *Geet Gawai* song which he took from my book *Bhojpuri Traditions of Mauritius 1999* (p. 63), thus for ever immortalising and internationalising Mauritian Bhojpuri folk songs. Eight years before they became a World Heritage guarded by UNESCO (1 December, 2016).

I offer a sincere gratitude to the Diaspora Research and Resource Center (DRRC) of Antar Rashtriya Sahayog Parishad (ARSP) and its Directorate who commissioned me to write the book and for having taken charge of its publication. I should like to make special mention of Ambassador Shri Virendra Gupta, President of ARSP, Shri Shyam Parande Secretary General of ARSP, Prof. Gopal Arora, Secretary of ARSP, Shri Narayan Kumar, Honorary Director of ARSP and Dr. Ruchi Verma Research Fellow at DRRC for their patience, support and encouraging words.

I would like to offer my heartfelt thanks to Mrs. Rashedah Malleck Beebeejaun who went through the draft of a research paper on *Geet Gawai* and found it worthy to be put in book form.

I also have a special word for Dr. (Mrs.) Nalini Leela Devi Luckheenarain, former Permanent Secretary and Senior Executive Officer at the Ministry of Arts and Cultural Heritage for believing in my aims and objectives towards making *Geet Gawai* a treasured heritage of humanity. A word of special thanks to the current Permanent Secretay Mrs. Indira Padaruth Ruchaia for her words of encouragement and appreciation of my work. To late Mr. Islam Bhagun and late Mr. Gautam Soobarah, Former Directors of Culture who supported me during the preparation of *Geet Gawai* Nomination Dossier and Bhojpuri events. To Shri Arvind Boodhun, current Director of Culture a big 'thank you' for his encouragements. Also I would like to thank Mrs. Anupama Chummun Chaumoo, Deputy Director of Culture and Mrs. Mariella Annabelle Arekion, Principal Culture Officer. My sincerest gratitude to Ms. Preeti Bamma, Principal Culture Officer at the Ministry of Arts and Cultural Heritage for her constant support and encouragement and lovingly 'chiding' me to focus on my writings.

I would like to place on record my sincere thanks and gratitude to Sandhya Devi Seeruttun, Ayesha Dilchand Jeewooth,

Viveka Vidhi Gunness, Rucksika Seewoonarain, Soni Luchmee Chunnoo, Vashni Purushram for their great efforts in helping with the typing of the manuscript. In this context I should like to make a special mention for Kavita Boyjoo for her meticulous, patient and dexterous handling of the proofs and her long typing labours of both English and Bhojpuri Devanagari Script again and again until we reached finality.

In India where I am fondly known as *'International Didi',* I should like to place on record the many Bhojpuri professors, scholars, Bhojpuri lovers and intellectuals as well as the Media/TV people who arranged for my many lectures on the subject at the Benaras Hindu University; IGNOU; Jawaharlal Nehru University (JNU); the Jai Prakash University, Chhapra; Veer Kunwar Singh University, Bhojpur, Arrah; Delhi University New Delhi and other Institutions. I have made mention of them in the book.

I should like to place my sincerest gratitude to all those who opened the doors of their homes wide open to me at various places, in several districts and offered me loving hospitality from 1983 onwards, when I started to undertake my tour of the Bhojpuri belt beginning with Shri R.K. Sinha, former MP, Rajya Sabha and his loving wife Rita Sinha, Advocate; Shri Swayam Prakash in Patna, Head of Zee News Bihar and Jharkhand; Dr. Sadanand Shahi, former Head of Bhojpuri Adhyayan Kendra, Benaras Hindu University and currently Vice Chancellor of Shri Shankaracharya Professional University at Bhilai, Chhattisgarh. Ambassador Anup Kumar Mudgal and his loving wife Savita Mudgal and their family. To Mr. Mukesh Aggarwal, Vice President of the ARSP for putting at my disposal, not only a room at Palm d'Or Hotel, Paharganj, New Delhi but also his entire staff. I cannot forget my friends Dr. Nishi Gupta and Mr. Ambuj Gupta, Industrialist at Varanasi for their hospitality.

To late Dr. Kuber Mishra my guide and mentor and his entire family at Berkunda, Maltari and Karsauli village in Azamgarh for having made a home away from home for me for several months and over several decades and to his faithful student friend Shri Heera Sharma of Bilariaganj. In this context, the late Professor Krishna Deo Upadhyaya world renowned Folklorist and Bhojpuri Writer and scholar and his family also made me feel at home at

Durgakund, Benaras, and at Sarnath. These two scholars have helped me immensely in the collection and comparative studies of Bhojpuri songs of the Bhojpuri belt of India and Mauritius.

A special word for Media and TV personality, Manoj Bhavuk, in New Delhi and Kuldeep Shrivastava in Mumbai, Shivraj Singh, Secretary General of Purvanchal Ekta Manch in Dwarka, New Delhi.

I owe a special gratitude to the Indian High Commission in Mauritius. I should like to place on record my special thanks to the current Indian High Commissioner H.E. Smt. Nandini Singla, who readily acknowledges and supports unflinchingly my efforts in the promotion of Indian languages and the Indian ethos as brought by the *girmitiyas*. My thanks to Shri Janesh Kain, former Deputy Indian High Commissioner as well as to the Second Secretary for Culture, Education and Languages, Smt. Sunita Pahuja for their loving support. Facilities provided at Indira Gandhi Centre for Indian Culture (IGCIC) Phoenix have given great visibility to *Geet Gawai* and are kindly acknowledged.

I should like to place on record my sincerest gratitude to the Government of Mauritius for believing in me and my mission by appointing me as Chairperson of the Bhojpuri Speaking Union since its inception on 3 August, 2012 till date. This State support has enabled me to work continuously without a break not only for the sustainability of the Bhojpuri language but by giving visibility, audibility and acceptability to its tangible and intangible cultural heritage, including the *Geet Gawai*. In submitting the Nomination Dossier of *Geet Gawai* as an Intangible Cultural Heritage of Humanity at UNESCO the State has played a major role which is of capital importance. Mr. Pravind Kumar Jugnauth, Prime Minister and his wife Kobita Jugnauth have taken particular interest in giving the *Geet Gawai* and Bhojpuri language the desired esteem and endorsement. To them a special 'Thank you'. In the same breath, I have a special word for the Minister of Arts and Cultural Heritage, Shri Avinash Teeluck who has brought a fresh insight in ensuring that the *Geet Gawai's* viability is not jeopardized *"as an unintended result of inscription and the resulting visibility and public attention"*. I should also like to place on record the support given to me by the President of the Republic of Mauritius HE Shri

Prithvirajsingh Roopun and his wife Sayukta. HE the former Vice President of the Republic, Janab Raouf Bundhun, HE Paramasivam Pillay Barlen Vyapoory who always encouraged me in my efforts to take *Geet Gawai* towards its recognition.

A special word of endearment for Professor George Abungu, UNESCO Consultant for his appreciation of my relentless pursuits in giving *Geet Gawai* and the *Geetharines* a place of esteem. I would also like to make mention of Shri Rajkumar Ravi Sookun Minister Counsellor and Deputy High Commissioner at the Ministry of Foreign Affairs, Regional Integration and International Trade who has been a great support.

A special thanks to Mr. Anooj Ramssurrun, Director General of the National M.B.C. TV and his entire Production Unit headed by Shri Sanjay Ghoorah as well as Mr. Dharam Nanka of the Bhojpuri Channel for the visibility given to *Geetharines* and the element. A special word of thanks for Shri Bhimsen Conhydoss, Producer. In this vein, I would also like to make mention of Shri Bikram Sachin Jootun, Director General of the Mauritius Film Development Corporation (MFDC), Mr. Vinay Bacorisen, Senior Project Programme Officer at MFDC and their staff for their ever ready collaboration.

Last but not the least I owe a deep debt to my family especially my husband Harish Boodhoo who has given me the required latitude to carry on my mission. My father Suttaiburuth Makhan Singh and mother Sookea Chandrawati always instilled in me the search for Truth and Vedic knowledge. To them, I say fondly "Thank You Pitaji and Mataji". My Uncle Beekrumsing Ramlallah Mentor and guide and wife Chachi Champa encouraged me in all my socio cultural activities. Likewise, my family including my brothers and sisters and their family: Vijay Singh Makhan and wife Ouma and family, daughter Davina, and Son-in-law Stefan Leiderer, children Siara Sahana and son Tej Siddharth Shaan and Dr. Shyamant Singh Makhan; Devendra Singh Makhan, his wife Mila Makhan, Son Natesh and daughter-in-law Tina Makhan, Son Gavesh Singh Makhan, Sudhir Singh Makhan and wife Vimla Makhan and sons Samir Singh Makhan, Tanvir Singh Makhan, Satvir Singh Makhan; my sister Prabha Makhan and husband David Clairmonte, my sister Indira Padaruth, husband Vijay Padaruth and nieces Lakshi and Mitali and Son-in-law Ganesha Moorghen Murugan. To family members Mala Chummun Ramyead and Sadhna Ramlallah who are for ever by my side. It is in the family environment that the *Geet Gawai* sessions were given acceptability and the idea for their promotion germinated and nurtured.

At Belle Terre, my '*sasural*' I should like to make a particular mention for Bhowji; nephew Rajesh and daughter-in-law Brinda Boodhoo and grand-daughter Viveka Boodhoo for their love and affection, my mother-in-law Fooldie who introduced me to the *Geet Gawai* sessions of Mahadeo 'Bo' (Bahu) and Son Seenarain and sister Champa and their group in the village since my marriage in 1973.

Finally, a word of gratitude to all those whose names may have been missed in acknowledgement and in the book but who are very much remembered in this process of writing of *Geet Gawai–An Ode to Geetharines of Mauritius*.

I would also like to make a special mention of the leaders of the Socio Cultural Organisations and other Stakeholders who have supported the *Bhojpuri Andolan* in our endeavour to see that the Government re-introduces Bhojpuri language the vehicle of *Geet Gawai* as a teaching learning subject in the School Cursus and give it its much merited dignity in the comity of languages taught and spoken in Mauritius: Mr. Vinod Seegum President, Mr. Randheer Bundoo Treasurer at Government Teachers Union, Mr. Bhojraj Ghoorbin President, Mr. Gawtam Lalbeeharry Secretary General, Mr. Roshan Ramracheea Assistant Secretary at Mauritius Sanatan Dharma Temples Federation (MSDTF), Mrs. Luxshmee Ramdhun President and Mr. Hemandre Kumar Deepchand Secretary at Hindu House, Mr. Rajeshwar Auliar Executive Committee Member and Mr. Sarvan Kumar Bheenick Member at Gahlot Rajput Maha Sabha, Mr. Harrydev Ramdhony former President at Mauritius Arya Sabha, Dr. Kaviraj Sookon President at Mauritius Arya Ravi Ved Pracharini Sabha and Director of Open University of Mauritius, Mr. Premchand Boojhawon, MSK, CSK President at Human Service Trust, Mr. Suresh Ramburn President at Hindi Speaking Union, Mr. Rabindra Soobarah President at Brindaban Linguistic & Cultural Genocide, Mr. Jagdish Soobarah President of Brindaban Sarvajanik Mandir Samiti, Quatre Bornes, Mr. Bhagwansing

(Girish) Dabeesing President and Mr. Ghanshyam Seebundhun Vice President at Hindu Maha Sabha, Dr. Oudaye Narain Gangoo, Arya Neta, Arya Sabha Mauritius.

A special word of deep gratitude to Chachi Rajwant Lobin who cooked for me at moments when my head was deeply immersed in my documents and writings as well as to Smt. Kumari Lutchmun. A word for Professor Vinesh Hookoomsingh, linguist and former Pro Chancellor of the University of Mauritius, who has always believed in my mission. Mrs. Kiran Jankee Chuttoo, Researcher at AGTF and Dr. Arvind Bissesur Senior Lecturer and Head SMAS at the Mahatma Gandhi Institute for their constant companionship on the Bhojpuri trail. To the Chairman Mr. Rishiraj Kanhye and the Director Mr. Chand Ramgoolam of AGTF a great thank you.

Hearty thanks to my friends Jean Mark Poché, Senior Editor at *Le Mauricien*, Munawar Namderkhan freelance journalist, Vijay Shankar of Week End for support; Mrs. Aline Groeme Harmon, Culture Journalist at L'Express who always reminded me *"Mais quand ou pou ecrire ou livre Madame?"* (When will you write your book, Madam?) This must have given me a sharp jolt somewhere. Thank you Aline.

Corona

Corona has brought a great change in our lifestyle and activities. A first long lockdown announced by the Prime Minister on 18 March, 2020, gave me the opportunity to review my activities and attitude to life. I used to the maximum the time thus provided to me confined to home, as well as the second lockdown in 2021, to profuse writing. This work has been made possible thanks in a large way to the Sanitary Protocol thus imposed which has made me more home bound. Thus availing of this opportunity, I was able to complete the book, for I was running behind deadline!

Therefore, I think I owe it to the forced confinements to have been able to complete this work that needed much research work and reading.

—Dr. Sarita Boodhoo

□□□